Light for our path
2008

LIGHT FOR OUR PATH
2008
Bible readings with short notes

International Bible Reading Association

Cover photograph by Pamela Draycott
Editor – Kate Hughes

Published by:
The International Bible Reading Association
1020 Bristol Road
Selly Oak
Birmingham B29 6LB
Great Britain

Charity number 211542

ISBN 978-1-904024-89-7
ISSN 0140-8267

Designed and typeset by Christian Education
Printed and bound by 1010 Printing International Ltd

Contents

Foreword

Dear Friends

Welcome to this year's *Light for our Path*. As you will see, we have made some changes to the format which we hope will make the book easier to use. In response to requests from several readers, we have included photographs of many of our contributors; the few who did not want to be seen have a small map of where they come from in the allotted space instead.

We have also made some changes to the readings. In future years, we shall provide notes for six readings every week instead of seven. We feel that almost all our readers will read or hear other passages of scripture on Sundays and would be happy to forgo reading our notes as well. This year, meanwhile, we are in a state of transition and still have two readings for the Saturday and Sunday of each weekend. However, there is only one set of notes for the weekend; sometimes this covers both readings briefly, sometimes it focuses mainly, or entirely, on one of the readings; the writers have been left free to decide which they want to do. Whether you read these notes on Saturday or Sunday will depend on your personal circumstances.

The months of writing and editing these notes have been difficult for several of our contributors, with sickness and personal problems taking their toll. Yet very many of the biblical texts speak of the steadfast love of God and his care for us, and the joy of belonging to him. May you be reminded of this love and upheld by it as you journey through *Light for our Path* this year.

Kate

Kate Hughes (Editor)

Reading LIGHT FOR OUR PATH

- Before reading, be quiet and remember that God is with you. Ask for his Holy Spirit to guide your reading.

- If you do not have a Bible with you, you can work solely from *Light for our Path* by referring to the short Bible passage printed in bold type. (Only the editions printed in English have this.)

- You can begin by reading just the short extract from the daily Bible passage which appears in the notes. Or you may prefer to read the full text of the daily passage from your Bible. The weekly notes use a variety of Bible translations, which are named at the beginning of each week. You may like to see how the extract in bold type compares with the same passage in your own Bible. And if your Bible mentions parallel passages in other places, comparing these passages can widen your thinking.

- At the beginning of each week's notes there is a text for the week, which can be used as a focus for worship or reflection throughout the week.

- When you finish each day's reading, spend a little time reflecting on it. What does it say to you about God? About yourself? About others? About the world in which we live? Has it changed your thinking? Does it suggest something that you should do? Then use the final prayer (marked with a cross), or any prayer of your own you need to make.

- At the start of each week's notes, there are questions and suggestions for group discussion or personal thought. These are only suggestions – your own reading and prayer may have drawn your attention to other aspects which you would like to explore further. The important thing is that you should let God speak to you through his Word, so that as you read steadily through the year you will be able to look back and see that you have got to know him better and have grown spiritually.

Abbreviations and acknowledgements

We are grateful for permission to quote from the following Bible versions:

GNB   Scriptures quoted are from the *Good News Bible* ©1994 published by the Bible Societies/HarperCollins Publishers Ltd, *UK Good News Bible* ©American Bible Society 1966, 1971, 1976, 1992. Used with permission.

JB   From *The Jerusalem Bible*, Popular Edition, published by Darton, Longman & Todd, ©Darton, Longman & Todd Ltd and Doubleday & Company, Inc., 1974.

NEB   *New English Bible*, ©Oxford and Cambridge University Presses, 1970.

NIV   Scripture taken from the *Holy Bible, New International Version*®. Copyright ©1973, 1978, 1984 International Bible Society. Used by permission of Zondervan. All rights reserved.

NLT   Scripture quotations marked NLT are taken from the *Holy Bible, New Living Translation*, copyright 1996. Used by permission of Tyndale House Publishers, Inc., Wheaton, Illinois 60189. All rights reserved.

NJB   *The New Jerusalem Bible*, published by Darton, Longman & Todd, ©Darton, Longman & Todd Ltd and Doubleday & Company, Inc., 1985.

NKJV   Scripture taken from the *New King James Version*. Copyright ©1982 by Thomas Nelson, Inc. Used by permission. All rights reserved.

NRSV   Bible selections are from the *New Revised Standard Version of the Bible*, copyright 1989 by the Division of Christian Education of the National Council of the Churches of Christ in the USA. Used by permission. All rights reserved.

REB   *Revised English Bible*, ©Oxford and Cambridge University Presses, 1989.

RSV   *The Holy Bible, Revised Standard Version*, published by Thomas Nelson & Sons, ©Division of Christian Education of the National Council of the Churches of Christ in the United States of America, 1952.

The quotation in the notes for 4 March is from *The Basis of Union* and reproduced with permission. Copyright the Assembly of the Uniting Church of Australia.

* An asterisk beside the daily reading indicates that it appears in the Revised Common Lectionary during that week.

Refugees

1 The refugee experience

Notes by Kevin Ellis
based on the Good News Bible

Kevin Ellis is an Anglican vicar in the Diocese of
Carlisle, England. He lives with his wife Jennifer
and son Shaun and their menagerie of pets.

Introduction

The United Nations defines a refugee as a person who has 'a
well-founded fear of being persecuted for reasons of race,
religion, nationality, membership of a particular social group,
or political opinion'. From the Israelites under Pharaoh to Jesus
threatened by Herod there are many accounts in the Bible of
circumstances that force people to flee their homes. There are
also insights into the challenges faced by anyone who becomes
a refugee – the possible need to deceive others to preserve
one's own life, the agony of loneliness and despair, and the
uncertainty about whether or not to put down roots in a new
place.

Text for the week: Exodus 3:7-8   *3: 4-8*

*'I have seen how cruelly my people are being treated . . . I have
heard them cry out to be rescued . . . and so I have come down
to rescue them.'*

For group discussion and personal thought

• How many refugees are there in your town or
  neighbourhood? What is being done to help them? How
  can you get to know some of them, and help them to feel
  welcomed and supported?

Exodus 2.23 – 3.12   3: 1–12

Facing up to persecution and oppression

'I have seen . . . I have heard . . .' (*verse 7*). Seeing and hearing begin our response to the plight of others. Christians in the West often need to see and hear the injustices suffered by our brothers and sisters in order to take note, and then act. Indeed, writing in my comfortable vicarage, I struggle to appreciate what it must be like to be uprooted and forced to flee from home. Moses knows about being uprooted, although he was not made a refugee by other people. Moses' people know about being uprooted and alone, even in a land where many of them were born. God also knows:

> **'I have seen how cruelly my people are being treated . . .
> I have heard them cry out to be rescued . . . and so I have
> come down to rescue them.'**
>
> (part of verses 7 and 8)

Here God faces up to 'man's inhumanity to man', rolls up the divine sleeves and gets involved. God is not neutral on the issue of injustice and oppression. God is on the side of the downtrodden – both materially and spiritually. Think about those you know are oppressed in your own country, and pray for them. Then think of the oppressed in another country, and pray again. Then be willing to pray . . .

† *O God of the Exodus, change my heart that I may be on the side of the persecuted and the oppressed, no matter how costly this may be. Amen.*

young girls forced into prostitution –

1 Samuel 19:8–18

Moral challenges in being a refugee

Everyone is potentially a refugee. People would probably have thought it highly unlikely that the hero of Socoh (the place of Goliath's defeat) would be forced to flee by the very king whose champion he had become. Yet this is precisely what happens to David as a result of the jealousy of Saul. Refugees, by their very nature, have no earthly power. They are on the run, and therefore without a permanent place to lay their heads. Their need to flee can be because of big issues, like socio-economic changes, natural disasters, and so on, or, like David, because of deteriorating personal relationships. The choice then is what to do.

> **David escaped and went to Samuel in Ramah and told him everything that Saul had done to him. Then he and Samuel went to Naioth and stayed there.**
>
> *(verse 18)*

David demonstrates the rightness (righteousness) of his case by seeking help among his friends, the household of faith. At this stage – and in the future – he does not retaliate. Indeed, he has no power to do so. The refugee can, I imagine, be extraordinarily lonely, and, like David, need to seek friendship where it can be found. How many refugees live near you? What are their networks of friendships like? How willing would you be to put yourself out for them?

† *Loving God, you became powerless even though you are all-powerful. Help me, this day, to stand with those who have no power. Amen.*

3

On the run, alone, in despair

I must admit that this story of Elijah fleeing from Jezebel has always struck me as slightly humorous, not because I want to belittle his situation, but rather because I am intrigued that this prophet of God can take on 850† prophets of Baal and Asherah with relative ease – and run terrified from one person. But perhaps my attitude stems from my Western comfortableness rather than an engagement with the passage. Elijah is on the run from someone powerful. He is in despair and cries out to his God:

> **'LORD God Almighty, I have always served you – you alone. But the people of Israel have broken their covenant with you, torn down your altars, and killed all your prophets. I am the only one left – and they are trying to kill me!'**
>
> *(verse 10)*

But Elijah is not alone! God tells his prophet that there are several thousand who have not broken the covenant. Elijah is not alone because God is with him. The fact that God is there alongside those who are fearful and alone is the testimony of countless numbers of people of faith. Yesterday I asked how many refugees live near you and about their networks of friendship. How many of them do you think feel alone and in despair, even though, like Elijah, they trust in God? What can you do to support them today?

† *Loving God, help me today to help someone who is in despair. Amen.*

Whether or not to put down roots

The prophet Jeremiah was writing to exiles forced to live away from their homeland. Unlike the prophet Hananiah in chapter 28, Jeremiah tells the people to accept God's will for them:

> **'Build houses and settle down. Plant gardens and eat what you grow in them . . . Work for the good of the cities where I have made you go as prisoners.'**
> *(verse 5, and part of verse 7)*

I live in west Cumbria, which culturally is almost entirely white and Anglo-Saxon. Occasionally I encounter people with Polish surnames, because in the twentieth century Polish people came and settled in this part of the United Kingdom. They were migrants, not refugees, and had to choose whether to settle permanently or look forward to returning home eventually. Jeremiah's people also faced this choice. It is no easy choice, and the scriptures show both approaches: settling down and worshipping in a new context, or longing to go home. The key thing is to keep worshipping God and looking for his will. Where do the refugees around you come from? What do you know about their nations and their cultures? Why not take steps to find out more, by reading or by asking?

† *Loving God, be with all those, including refugees, who are uncertain about their futures. Help them to feel at home whilst living among us. Help me to remember that, as a Christian, I am a stranger but not friendless, because you are always with me. Amen.*

Epiphany

Jeremiah 40:7-16 / Matthew 2:13-23

Jesus the refugee

Joseph's obedience to the message of the angel kept Jesus safe, but not everyone in Bethlehem could escape, however much they wanted to. Being a refugee is not easy, but it is better than not being able to escape, or dying in the attempt, as happens to many people.

> **In this way what the prophet Jeremiah had said came true:**
> **'A sound is heard in Ramah,**
> **the sound of bitter weeping.**
> **Rachel is crying for her children;**
> **she refuses to be comforted,**
> **for they are dead.'**
> *(Matthew verses 17-18)*

This is a chilling lesson on this feast of Epiphany, when Christians celebrate Christ as the light to the nations. But perhaps on this day especially we need to recommit ourselves to praying that all people will be able to live freely and without fear.

After their time in Egypt, Jesus and his family returned to Nazareth, their home town. Joseph and Mary may have found the return difficult. In Saturday's reading from Jeremiah we see how the Israelites returning to Judea found that things – circumstances and people – change. Joseph had to re-establish his carpentry business, and they may no longer have had a house. Being a refugee, whether you stay or return, is never easy. Continue to bless and pray for them, and for those who cannot escape, and ask the light of the nations to shine upon them always.

† *Lord Jesus, may we and the whole of humankind receive your gifts of freedom and peace this day and always. Amen.*

Refugees

2 How can we respond to refugees? Insights from the Old Testament

Notes by Su Blanch
based on the New Revised Standard Version

Su Blanch has an active life juggling being a mother, work commitments and activities for the Church.

Introduction

We can all be refugees at some point in our lives: literally, as civil wars explode, or figuratively as major changes in our environment, at home or at work, make us aliens in our own situation. It's a frightening time: our life's foundations crumble. The places that we looked to for stability are ruined. The old meanings are lost, and new unfamiliar ones take their place. Everything is turned on its head and we no longer know where to put our trust. This should make us more understanding of the problems of those who are physical refugees in our country, and more willing to offer them the place of safety available to us – the security of God's love.

Text for the week: Numbers 15:15
You and the alien shall be alike before the LORD.

For group discussion and personal thought

- Have there been times when you have shouted out to God like the Moabite women?
- Who are the refugees that you come into contact with?
- Do you welcome strangers as if God has come into your presence?

Pleading with God

According to the prophecy, Moab will be laid to waste. The country that had been abundant and successful will suffer greatly: waters dry up, crops fail, there will be weeping from all sides. As a result the women will be sent to plead for their status as refugees:

> **'Give counsel,**
> **grant justice;**
> **make your shade like night**
> **at the height of noon;**
> **hide the outcasts,**
> **do not betray the fugitives . . .**
> **be a refuge to them**
> **from the destroyer.'**
> *(verses 3 and 4a)*

Shelter and safety is what they require: what have been described as the 'primary needs' of food, air, security and freedom. Once these are met, our human nature has more complex needs: affection, love, achievement, recognition and self-fulfilment. But at our lowest ebb, we require just the basics. The Moabites, who had been so full of pride and self-regard, had been brought down to wanting nothing more than the primary requirement of shelter. What God asks of the Israelites now is compassion.

When we are feeling comfortable in our lives, it is easy to ignore the need for God and feel we can cope without him. It is when we are shouting out to God, when we feel desperate and outcast like the Moabite women, that we can grow in faith. And the first sign of this growth may be in reaching out in compassion to others who need refuge.

† *Thank you, God, for helping me through the difficult times. May I grow secure enough in you to reach out to others in need.*

Caring for others

When you gather the grapes of your vineyard, do not glean what is left; it shall be for the alien, the orphan, and the widow.

(verse 21)

The laws shared by Moses are detailed and specific, and this one is no exception. It is described three times, relating to the wheat, olive and grape harvests. Those hearing this would then be in no doubt about the meaning: there must be enough for all in the community, regardless of their situation, and the farmers should not be so greedy that they take all their produce for their own needs.

Today, we have a wider knowledge about the world and the world's food production. There should still be enough for all in the community, although the community is much bigger: it's a global community. In terms of greed, big business and governments have the responsibility to check that their profit is not at the expense of those in need, whether they be refugees, orphans, widows, homeless people, AIDS victims, war victims, the elderly, or anyone else.

It seems that this world view is a long way off, but the statement we read in Deuteronomy could not be clearer. It is our responsibility to check how we live with regard to this: the products we buy, the decisions we make, and the prayers we offer up for change.

† Lord, help us to provide for those in need and not take more than our share.

Hospitality for strangers

> [H]e ran from the tent entrance to meet them, and bowed down to the ground.
>
> *(part of verse 2)*

Three strangers appear to Abraham, and Abraham looks to meet every need for the travellers in the desert: bringing them water, bread and meat, and providing them with shade and the means to wash their feet. Real hospitality for the travellers – you can feel Abraham's anxiety to get this right. The passage says at various times, 'he ran', 'he hastened' and again, 'he ran', all in the heat of the day, when surely he would have been happier resting. The passage does not explicitly state that the Lord is among the three men, although this could be inferred.

I think we can consider from this our own approach to unexpected visitors, both locally and nationally. Do I welcome all comers as if they were the Lord? I can easily bring to mind occasions when I have been busy and faintly cross that I have been interrupted when someone has phoned or called round. Instead of this, we should be welcoming strangers and meeting their needs as if it is Jesus approaching us.

† *Lord, as Abraham welcomed the strangers in the desert, let us welcome strangers too.*

Humble before the Lord

'May the LORD reward you for your deeds, and may you have a full reward from the LORD, the God of Israel, under whose wings you have come for refuge!'

(verse 12)

Ruth had given up a precarious life as a widow to accompany her mother-in-law to an unfamiliar land, where life was likely to be harder. In essence, her decision was entirely selfless. There was no need to be with Naomi, her mother-in-law; no laws or cultural norms required it and it would have been far more sensible to remain in Moab, where she was known and could possibly marry again. In Moab, she had some degree of status: in Bethlehem, she was a nobody, valueless.

Boaz had the insight to understand that, regardless of Ruth's race or background, the faithful values she aspired to should be recognised and praised. She had not considered the consequences of the move demeaning, but worked hard in the fields alongside the servants.

In order to receive her reward, Ruth had to be at her lowest ebb. She couldn't have got any lower. But because of her serious need for refuge and the generosity of Boaz she was given the greatest honour. Is this how we treat refugees? Are we as generous as Boaz?

† *Lord, when I am low and troubled, remind me that your generosity is vast and unchanging. I will find refuge under your wing. You are there for me. Help me also to be there for others.*

Numbers 15:14–16

Equality before God

You and the alien shall be alike before the LORD.
(part of verse 15)

Who is the alien to you? Possibly there are immigrants living with you or near you. Or there may be individuals who are aliens culturally, intellectually or in terms of religious beliefs. Those who are different to us in any way may make us feel suspicion or dislike − feelings we may be uncomfortable with, but that shouldn't be dismissed or submerged, but challenged and dealt with.

People with different backgrounds and different cultural experiences are not 'wrong' in how they approach God or how they worship. Because it is not what I am used to, it doesn't mean that I should find fault with it or worry about it. God doesn't see aliens or outsiders: we all have the ability and potential to come before God with equal and worthy offerings. We learn much from individuals who are not like us. We can be open to their differences and see similar patterns and dissimilar styles, and all of this is beneficial to share and increase God's kingdom.

† *Lord, we offer to you the wonder and diversity of human-kind. Help us to learn from each other and share your all-encompassing love.*

[T]hey have oppressed the poor and needy, and have extorted from the alien without redress.

(part of Ezekiel verse 29)

In Ezekiel's frightening list of wrongdoings, which includes profanity, devouring human lives and oppression, is the action of taking from immigrants without paying back. Israel had a strong identity in terms of who were its people (see Ezra) but the emphasis here is that aliens should be treated reasonably, and were protected by the law and by common decency.

Today, we should ask, who are the aliens in our society? Who are the outcasts and the undesirables? Even those we may judge to be beyond any redemption, who have committed horrific crimes and do not therefore deserve our sympathy – even these have the right to God's love. Refugees are aliens in our society, and many of them have suffered terribly at the hands of the wicked, But do we, as a society, treat them as unwanted, as outcasts and undesirables – or as those who, like us, have a right to God's love? It is easy to judge other people's lives, but it is God who judges. We should instead be focused on our own shortcomings so that we can become closer to God and more like Jesus.

† *Lord, remind me that whenever I judge others, I am displeasing you. Help me to save my energy for changing myself and bringing your love to all, especially the aliens in our society.*

Refugees

3 How can we respond to refugees? Insights from the New Testament and Psalms

Notes by Tim Brooke
based on the New Revised Standard Version

Tim Brooke has recently retired as an Anglican vicar, having previously worked as a teacher in a church school in southern Tanzania and as a social worker in London. He now works as a volunteer with refuges in Coventry.

Introduction

In the New Testament, just as in the ancient story of Abraham and Sarah and the three angels, strangers often turn out to have unexpected significance and it is in this light that we need to see refugees. In his parables Jesus challenges our prejudices – we are to remember that those whom some people would reject are still human beings like you and me, and may have more to contribute to society than those who are already part of it. The psalms teach us to understand the feelings of any people who have been forced to leave their homes.

Text for the week: Hebrews 13:2

Do not neglect to show hospitality to strangers, for by doing that some have entertained angels without knowing it.

For group discussion and personal thought

• The biblical message is clear: we are to welcome strangers. Does the same principle apply to other groups of people – including those we don't like?

• Does modern life make it more difficult to provide hospitality to the stranger? If so, what can Christians do about it?

• How has a stranger helped you in your life?

Welcoming the stranger

Commenting on this parable, Mother Teresa goes to the heart of what Jesus means: 'I am not sure exactly what heaven will be like, but I do know that when we die and it comes time for God to judge us, he will NOT ask, How many good things have you done in your life? Rather, he will ask, How much LOVE did you put into what you did?'

We are to welcome strangers not because it makes us feel good or because Jesus tells us to. We like it, of course, if someone else does make us feel good, and it can be pleasing to know that we are doing our Christian duty, but loving is about something different. Loving means beginning to try to see others as God sees them with all their lovable – and infuriating – characteristics.

> **I was a stranger and you welcomed me . . . Truly I tell you, just as you did it to one of the least of these who are members of my family, you did it to me.**
> *(part of verses 35 and 40)*

At that moment, loving God and loving our neighbour become one and the same thing.

† *Lord, give us the imagination to see other people, especially those we find different from ourselves, through your eyes. Help us to understand what there is in each one that makes you love them.*

Expect surprises!

Do not neglect to show hospitality to strangers, for by doing that some have entertained angels without knowing it.

(verse 2)

Offer food or drink to a stranger and who knows what sudden insight or wise words we may hear! The conversations I have over a meal with refugees can be more inspiring than those I have with family or friends. Most people could barely imagine the amazing examples I have heard both of human generosity and of human suffering resulting from torture, separation from family, and other causes. I get the impression of entertaining angels unawares – messengers from God bringing new insights into how human beings have so tragically distorted the world as God meant it to be, and yet how good can still overcome evil.

All too often we see refugees simply as people in need of help. But we may find that we receive more than we give. Angels come in many disguises and God can use the most unexpected messengers to speak to us.

† *Help us, Lord, not to miss the chance to entertain angels unawares.*

Hospitality to strangers

Rejoice in hope, be patient in suffering, persevere in prayer. Contribute to the needs of the saints, extend hospitality to strangers.

(part of verses 12 and 13)

Strangers can bring us closer to God. Most of the time I am self-centred, but then someone new turns up in my life. I can choose either to ignore them or to greet them and want the best for them.

It is easy loving the people I know and like. I take a risk if I reach out to someone I don't know – the sort of risk that God took when he created us, knowing that we could choose to come to him or to rebuff him ('He came to his own but his own received him not', *John 1:11*).

In this situation I become vulnerable but at the same time strangers take me out of myself. If I seek their good rather than mine I lose my self-centred focus (this is what St Paul means when he says 'Let love be genuine' in verse 9). In this way they bring me closer to God and to an understanding of his love. And if the strangers turn on me or ignore me, I catch just a glimpse of the vulnerability of God – and the cost of his love.

† *Lord, when we come across strangers, help us to dare to reach out to them.*

Recognising hurt

A film-maker asked to interview an asylum-seeker from West Africa whose application to stay in Britain had been turned down because he had not been able to prove that he would definitely be in serious danger if he went home. He spoke French and I was to interpret. It was only during the interview that it came out that he was contemplating suicide.

Most people that I meet seeking refuge in Britain are suffering from depression. So too were the Jews who had been forced to leave their homes and move to a strange land. 'Cheer up! Why don't you sing us one of your songs?' is not a helpful response. The memory of painful experiences is too raw. A more loving response is to follow the example of the Samaritan in tomorrow's reading (*Luke 10:33*) and come out of our comfort-zones to be alongside people where they are, and to listen and love, even if all we hear is despair and thirst for vengeance. The healing of depression begins not with advice or criticism from others but with knowing that your desperation has been understood.

> **By the rivers of Babylon –
> there we sat down and there we wept
> when we remembered Zion . . .
> Happy shall they be who pay you back
> what you have done to us!**
> *(verse 1 and part of verse 8)*

† Teach us, Lord, to resist the temptation to speak when we should listen, and give us the courage to let ourselves feel others' pain.

Why not 'the good Jew'?

'A man was going down from Jerusalem to Jericho and fell into the hands of robbers . . . a Samaritan while travelling . . . went to him and bandaged his wounds . . . [and] brought him to an inn.'

(parts of verses 30, 33 and 34)

Jesus must have enjoyed watching his hearers' faces when he told the story of the Good Samaritan. For them the priest and the Levite should be the heroes. The hated enemy of the Jews, the Samaritan, should be the villain. Instead, the Samaritan becomes the hero. The parable is not ultimately about showing kindness but about turning people's view of the world upside down. Who is your neighbour? The least likely person you can imagine.

Jesus asks us to go one step beyond loving the stranger in need and to admit that we have our own needs and that the stranger, and not a friend, may be the best person to meet them.

A refugee couple from Africa were homeless and stayed with us for ten weeks. We developed a huge respect for their fortitude in the face of setbacks. They brought a lot of laughter into our lives. It was an unexpected privilege to have them with us. They were just what our family needed.

† *Lord, help us to see who are 'Good Samaritans' where we live.*

Luke 16:19-31 / Luke 24.13-32

Even the destitute have names

There was a rich man who was dressed in purple and fine linen and who feasted sumptuously every day. And at his gate lay a poor man named Lazarus, covered with sores.

(Luke 16, verses 19-20)

The rich man in this parable doesn't actually do anything to hurt Lazarus; he just accepts a destitute man as part of the landscape. When I am on duty at our local night-shelter for destitute asylum-seekers, the first thing I say to anyone who arrives is 'I am Tim. What is your name?' I and the other volunteers then welcome them and share a meal. There are a lot of things we don't say. We don't ask about people's families. They may have been murdered in front of their eyes. We don't ask what job they used to do. That can just emphasise the humiliation of being destitute. But we always share names. Interestingly, in this story Jesus gives Lazarus – but not the rich man – a name. Knowing someone's name means we recognise them as a person, a unique child of God. Once we know them, other things about them become familiar – like the action of breaking bread which showed the disciples at Emmaus who it was they had invited to supper (*Luke 24:31*). Recognising the individual and offering them hospitality – this is the least we can offer to God's children, including refugees.

† *Help us, O Lord, when we see someone destitute, not to be indifferent. May we remember that they too have a name and are your children.*

Readings in Deuteronomy

1 God's faithfulness to his people

Notes by Marcel V. Macelaru
based on the New Revised Standard Version

Marcel V. Macelaru is a Romanian preacher and teacher of the Bible. At the time of writing he is living in Osijek, Croatia, where he teaches the Old Testament at the Evangelical Theological Seminary.

Introduction

The book of Deuteronomy is deemed by many to be the theological centre of the Old Testament. Although conceived as Moses' addresses to the Israelites as they prepare to enter the Promised Land, its message transcends time, space and cultures. It offers vital guidelines for living a thriving, blessed life. In this regard, Deuteronomy teaches us three important things: it emphasises the importance of obeying God's commandments, for obedience brings God's blessing upon our lives; it encourages us to remember God's mighty acts of deliverance, for such reminiscence is central to understanding who we are; it brings uniquely into focus God's love for his people, for it is loving that motivates him to enter into a covenant with, and redeem, sinful people.

Text for the week: Deuteronomy 6:4-5
Hear, O Israel: The LORD is our God, the LORD alone. You shall love the LORD your God with all your heart, and with all your soul, and with all your might.

For group discussion and personal thought

- What is your contribution towards building a society where justice is done fairly for all regardless of who they are? Do you have such a concern? What about your church?
- When and with whom did you last speak about God?
- Does your love for God have emotional, intellectual and practical aspects?

God's alternative to social favouritism

'Give the members of your community a fair hearing, and judge rightly between one person and another, whether citizen or resident alien. You must not be partial in judging: hear out the small and the great alike; you shall not be intimidated by anyone, for the judgement is God's.'

(part of verses 16-17)

Deuteronomy teaches that comprehensive wellbeing for all people is God's ultimate intention for humanity. The reading for today addresses one aspect of this intent. It emphasises that God expects his people to manage their community in a way that will ensure that justice is done fairly to everyone. Whether powerful or weak, wealthy or poor, resident or alien, the Israelites are on an equal footing before God and his judgement. Consequently, proper procedures need be in place to ensure that all members of this community are treated equally by human judges as well.

This understanding of the unity of all people before God, portrayed here as a perfect brotherhood of all the members of the community, is a pervasive idea that occurs frequently in Moses' teachings in Deuteronomy. Its message for us is clear: we need to promote within our communities a justice system which provides protection for the individual from the acts of injustice and oppression that inevitably occur within hierarchical social arrangements.

† Lord, we have failed to build communities where justice is done fairly to everyone. Give us the wisdom to correct this shortcoming.

The danger of amnesia

So be careful not to forget the covenant that the LORD your God made with you . . . For the LORD your God is a devouring fire, a jealous God.

(part of verse 23, and verse 24)

Forgetfulness is a common human experience. As such, it may seem surprising that in the reading for today this is not an acceptable alternative for the Israelites. Rather, a conscious activity of retelling on their part is required in order to ensure that the memory of the covenant God made with them at Sinai remains preserved within their national consciousness (*verse 9*).

Anthropologists have observed that by retelling significant events from their past people define who they are in the present. That is why amnesia is here perceived as a threat – their very identity as a group is at stake. The metaphors of 'fire' and 'jealousy' reflect the severity of God's reaction to such a possibility. There is, of course, a lesson here for all of us as well. The threat of losing sight of the one true God is as real as ever. We need constantly to remind ourselves of what the Bible teaches us about him – that he is the only God, Creator and Sustainer of everything, and that he will not share our allegiance with anyone or anything else.

† *Lord God, reveal yourself to us once again and cure the forgetfulness that has afflicted our lives. You are the one and only true God!*

God's commandments here and now

Hear, O Israel, the statutes and ordinances that I am
addressing to you today; you shall learn them and
observe them diligently. The LORD our God made a
covenant with us at Horeb. Not with our ancestors did
the LORD make this covenant, but with us, who are all of
us here alive today.

(part of verse 1, and verses 2-3)

Most readers will recognise the list of principles at the heart
of today's reading as the so-called 'Ten Commandments'.
Given by God to the Israelites, these rules of behaviour
were a constituent part of the covenant he made with them
after freeing them from Egyptian oppression. As such, the
commandments functioned as identity markers, which led to
the transformation of the Israelites from a group of liberated
slaves into a 'holy nation' (*Exodus 19–20*). Nevertheless, the
reading for today insists that this covenant still applies here
and now, therefore making the commandments themselves
universally valid and true. Thus we may say that they transcend
time, for they apply to all generations, and that they transcend
space, for they apply to all peoples on earth. Observing these
commandments today is as mandatory as it was for the
Israelites on the plains of Moab, and their role to transform us
into a holy people of God remains equally true.

† *Lord God, thank you for making a covenant with us and for
your commandments. Give us the will and understanding to
observe them diligently.*

The greatest commandment of all

The reading for today contains a phrase which many interpreters have recognised as the greatest theological affirmation of the Old Testament:

Hear, O Israel: The LORD is our God, the LORD alone.

(verse 4)

This is both a firm declaration of faith in one God and a statement about the uniqueness of this God in whom we believe. And being set in a context of lawgiving, the phrase is also an imperative, a command. It conveys a demand for a full loyalty and unreserved commitment to God which is expressed in terms of loving him totally and completely:

You shall love the LORD your God with all your heart, and with all your soul, and with all your might.

(verse 5)

The three spheres in which such devotion is revealed include the affective (heart), the intellectual (soul), and the practical (might); and their effect should not be taken separately, but rather cumulatively. Only when shown together do they express the depth of one's commitment. Thus, emotional input should be accompanied by a diligent intellectual effort to learn about God, and both are complementary to practical gestures of care for the needy, for Jesus has made clear that loving God with all our might includes loving our neighbour as we love ourselves (*Mark 12:30-31*).

† Lord God, you are the one and only God, eternally unique. I love you with all my heart, all my soul, and all my might.

To live a successful life

Do what is right and good in the sight of the LORD, so
that it may go well with you, and so that you may go in
and occupy the good land that the LORD swore to your
ancestors to give you, thrusting out all your enemies
from before you, as the LORD has promised.

(verses 18-19)

These verses carry the implication that living a successful life is
simply the result of close observance of God's commandments.
The setting of the commandment to obey and its implications
for cause and effect in life is a particular feature of the book
of Deuteronomy. Thus, although the covenant relationship
between God and his people is described in Deuteronomy
as 'divine love' and 'divine choice', enjoying the promised
blessings is not a given. We have seen earlier in the week that
the threat for the believer is not a conscious choice to disobey
God, but the possibility of forgetfulness. Here we see that the
very prosperity promised and given by God may result in such
amnesia.

Nevertheless, a solution is also offered. Such amnesia can
only be counteracted by a conscious choice to embrace
God as well as his commandments. In a context where
prosperity and wellbeing are promised, this means a conscious
acknowledgement of the blessing and of the one who blesses
at every point in life.

† *Thank you, Lord, for all your blessings and provision, for all
good things in my life come from you.*

No middle way

Know therefore that the LORD your God is God, the faithful God who maintains covenant loyalty with those who love him and keep his commandments, to a thousand generations, and who repays in their own person those who reject him.

(chapter 7, verse 9 and part of verse 10)

The contrast evident in these verses characterises the readings for the weekend. Having recounted the Sinai covenant and the commandments that accompany it, Moses presents the Israelites with two choices: either keep God's commandments and be blessed, or reject God and be doomed! This contrast develops further the cause-and-effect relation that we observed yesterday. There is no middle way offered here, no possibility of neutrality; not keeping God's commandments implies an automatic rejection of God himself.

Today, the idea that God's choice to be faithful *must* be answered with obedience from our side may seem logically problematic, for it appears to oppose contemporary conceptions of freedom of choice. Nevertheless, Deuteronomy stresses that the relationship in question is a covenant relationship. As such, it operates according to equal expectations for both covenant partners. God's free act of love in making a covenant with human beings is matched by an equal urge to obedience addressed to the believer.

† *Lord God, we have failed you and have not kept your commandments. Thank you for your love and faithfulness, to which we will respond by keeping your commandments.*

Readings in Deuteronomy

2 God's demands on his people

Notes by John Holder
based on the Revised Standard Version

John Holder was born in Barbados and for several years was Deputy Principal of Codrington College, the Anglican theological college for the province of the West Indies. He is now Anglican Bishop of Barbados, and is married with one son.

Introduction

The book of Deuteronomy is like a conversation between God's agent Moses and Israel. In this conversation, Moses highlights the great demands that God has placed upon his people. These demands are articulated in terms of law, or as a reminder of all the good things God has done for his people, which demand a response from them. The dominant theme of Deuteronomy is the land. In our readings we find two important ideas about the land: it is God's greatest gift to Israel, but it is also a gift that Israel, given her history, does not deserve.

Text for the week: Deuteronomy 10:12

'And now, Israel, what does the LORD your God require of you, but to fear the LORD your God, to walk in all his ways, to love him, to serve the LORD your God with all your heart and with all your soul.'

For group discussion and personal thought

• What second chances have you had in your life, and what did you make of them?

• How do you express what you believe about God in the ordinary things of your everyday life?

God's great gift and Israel's stubbornness

> [T]he LORD your God is not giving you this good land
> to possess because of your righteousness; for you are a
> stubborn people.
>
> *(part of verse 6)*

This survey of Israel's history paints a very dismal picture: not
appreciating the sacrificial work of Moses, creating the golden
calf as a substitute for God (*verses 12, 21*), making God very
angry (*verse 8*). But Israel's shortcomings are highlighted only
to emphasise the goodness of God, above all his gift of the
land, and his patience and love in the face of sin and rebellion.

Like the Israelites, each of us has something in our lives for
which to be thankful. It may be a land, a country, to call our
own. How do we respond to the goodness of God? And do we
acknowledge that, like the Israelites, whatever we achieve in
life is achieved through the mercies of God? God is portrayed
in this passage as a God who never abandons his people in
spite of all their wrongdoing. Here is a powerful message
of solidarity, compassion and forgiveness for people today.
In a world where many people experience vengeance and
destruction, we, like Moses, are called to be God's instrument
of compassion and forgiveness.

† *O God, heal our stubborn hearts and minds and make us
instruments of your compassion.*

Second chances

'Hew two tables of stone like the first and come up to me on the mountain.'

(part of verse 1)

Obedience to the law occupies a large part of the book of Deuteronomy and is central to the message being sent to the community to which Deuteronomy was addressed, which was probably tempted to leave the traditional religion of Israel and follow other religions. Deuteronomy is uncompromising: there can be no variations to the inherited laws and traditions.

Our passage emphasises this by retelling for a later generation the old story of Moses receiving the law on the mountain, to remind them that the laws that they were tempted to replace were none other than those given to Moses by God. Here, the laws are written for a second time, since Moses in his anger had destroyed the first edition (9:17). God was giving his people a second chance, a central theme in the book of Deuteronomy, which was written some 600 years after the Exodus but is set in the wilderness, with Moses again leading the people to their land. They have a second chance, with the help of the law, to put right what went wrong.

As Christians, we too believe that God often gives us a second chance to put right what has gone wrong. Have you experienced this? And when did you last share this particular gift and give someone else a second chance?

† Thank you, O God, for all our second chances.

God's greatness and Israel's responsibility

[T]he LORD your God is God of gods and LORD of lords,
the great, the mighty and the terrible God.

(part of verse 17)

This passage clearly tells a community tempted to follow other
religions what it must do: resist! Yesterday's reading showed
God and Moses working to give the people a fresh start, in
spite of many setbacks. Now it is up to the people:

What does the LORD your God require of you, but to fear
the LORD your God, to walk in all his ways [and] to love
him.

(verse 12)

The call is for total commitment; there is no room for allegiance
to any other god. And God is not only the Creator, he also
provides for and sustains the poor and the disadvantaged
(*verse 18*), and his people must do the same. We too must
apply all we say we believe about God, all our teachings about
God, to the everyday practical things of life that are important
for people's existence, including justice. The God who has
made the universe is concerned that each and every one of his
children should have adequate clothing, food and the other
basics of life.

† *O God, help us to live up to the great responsibility you have
entrusted to us.*

A good and gracious land

[T]he land which you are going over to possess is . . . a
land which the LORD your God cares for.

(part of verses 11 and 12)

The great gift of God, the land, is portrayed as the best place
on earth, 'flowing with milk and honey' (*verse 9*), a well-
watered land of hills and valleys 'that the LORD your God looks
after' (*verse 11*). Some scholars believe that Deuteronomy
was written at a time when the land was controlled by the
Assyrians, the superpower of the day, and the community then
might not have seen their land as the best place on earth.

But Deuteronomy represents the land as a place where the
community will very soon experience (once more) God's
goodness and blessings. In spite of present experience, the land
is still good, still God's greatest gift. Deuteronomy is above all
a powerful message of hope. God who liberated his people
from Egypt will continue to care for them. But the message has
two sides: the community must follow a given path to reap the
blessings in store for it. God is good and gracious, he reaches
out and embraces us, but there still needs to be a response
from us. For Deuteronomy this response was to follow the
path of the law, a path of obedience but also of justice and
compassion, respecting the rights of all.

† *We thank you, O God, for all your good and gracious gifts
to us.*

Israel's focal point

[Y]ou shall seek the place which the LORD you God will choose out of all your tribes.

(part of verse 5)

Life in a community, if it is to be lived with a sense of purpose and meaning, needs a focal point. The writers of Deuteronomy understood this. In a time of political and religious turmoil, their community desperately needed a religious focus, which for Deuteronomy was only the temple in Jerusalem. The rejection of other places of worship emphasised that the religion of Israel and those of other peoples were totally incompatible. Other religions, especially those of the Canaanites, were threatening Israel's traditions and beliefs about God (see *verses 2-3*). The writers of Deuteronomy, a group of faithful people dedicated to their inherited religious beliefs, strongly believed that the God who had brought the community thus far would continue to support them. But he demanded total allegiance as symbolised by the one place of worship.

The Church in every age has had to make the choices that the writers of Deuteronomy asked their community to make, between holding on to the faith, or trading it for something else that may be little more than the latest fad of life. This is still a choice that every Christian is called to make.

† *Help us, O God, to keep our focus on you.*

February

Food and holiness

> [Y]ou are a people holy to the LORD your God.
> *(verse 2)*

The laws about which animals are unclean were not a matter of health but of religion – perhaps because they were animals with ritual significance for other religions. The command not to eat any abominable thing (*verse 3*) is not simply about diet; it is an instruction to the community: stay clear of any food associated with the worship of gods other than Yahweh. Total allegiance expressed in holiness of life. Deuteronomy links holiness to election, being chosen by God.

In the face of Assyrian occupation, Israel maintained its identity through its special relationship with God, expressed through (amongst other laws and rituals) that most everyday and ordinary act, eating. A meal, and what is eaten, become a symbol and reminder of election and so a symbol of hope. To follow the ritual laws relating to food is to acknowledge the breadth of the community's allegiance to God. The ordinary and the everyday become an important element in this allegiance. And eating can also express our thankfulness and our concern for the poor: gratitude for God's gifts in eating as part of worship in the temple, and concern in sharing what God has given us with those who are powerless and hungry. Simple, everyday actions which, both for the Israelites and for us, can express our sense of election, our gratitude, and God's compassion.

† *Grant us, O God, your grace to express your holiness, generosity and compassion in every detail of our lives.*

3 The people serving God

Notes by Catherine Williams
based on the New Revised Standard Version

Catherine Williams is an Anglican priest working as Vocations Officer for the Diocese of Gloucester, England. Her role is to help individuals and churches discern God's call on their lives. Catherine is married to the Vicar of Tewkesbury Abbey and they have two daughters.

Introduction

When the Israelites settled down as a community they required guidance on how to follow God in a new land and how to live together successfully. The book of Deuteronomy is filled with ways to go about both these enterprises. The laws and decrees enrich and enhance community life, and remind the people of their first calling to belong totally to God. This is the code for living used by Jesus, who deepened and broadened what was required, so that life might be lived in all its fullness.

Text for the week: Deuteronomy 30:16
If you obey the commandments of the LORD your God . . . then you shall become numerous, and the LORD your God will bless you in the land that you are entering to possess.

For group discussion and personal thought

• In which areas of your life do you struggle to obey God?

• During this season of Lent, how might you serve God better in your local community?

Open hands and open hearts

In the book of Exodus, God commanded that the land be left fallow every seventh year so that the soil might rest and be restored. This decree is expanded in the book of Deuteronomy so that a rest year – a sabbatical – is laid down for debtors. Every seventh year the slate is to be wiped clean and all Israelite people released from their debts to one another, ensuring that no member of the family will enter into extreme poverty. On a daily basis generosity is called forth from God's people:

> [D]o not be hard-hearted or tight-fisted toward your needy neighbour. You should rather open your hand, willingly lending enough to meet the need, whatever it may be.
>
> *(part of verse 7, and verse 8)*

We are reminded that there will always be need in our world, a sobering thought echoed by Jesus (*Matthew 26:11*). But we have the power within ourselves to make a difference to the needy amongst us. This requires a generosity of spirit and an openness of hand and heart. Such generosity comes from the realisation that all we have is from God, and given to us to use wisely and well. In addition, Jesus on the cross released us from all our debts for eternity. Such overwhelming love and generosity lavished on us by the Lord should temper all our dealings with one another.

† *Lord, may all my acts and words reflect your love and generosity.*

Let's celebrate

For the Israelites, the rhythm of the seasons was marked by a series of pilgrimage festivals during which the people gathered together, presented offerings to God and celebrated. Passover reminded the people of their deliverance from Egypt by the power of God. The Festivals of Weeks and Booths (or Tabernacles) celebrated the beginning and end of the harvest. Such festivals served to remind the people of their reliance on God both for ultimate rescue and salvation and for the day-to-day business of living. The festivals were inclusive celebrations where all were welcome:

> **Rejoice before the LORD your God – you and your sons and your daughters, your male and female slaves, the Levites resident in your towns, as well as the strangers, the orphans, and the widows who are among you.**
> *(part of verse 11)*

During the celebratory time of the Passover, Jesus gave this memorial festival new meaning. The Last Supper inaugurated for us a new celebration, holding together past, present and future in the giving and receiving of Christ's body and blood, and in the remembering of our salvation story made possible through the death and resurrection of Jesus.

Our Christian festivals help to shape our worship of God, and our pilgrimage through life. And none more so than the Eucharist, which we should attend frequently and faithfully – celebrating with joy and thanksgiving Christ's eternal gift of himself for the world.

† *Lord, thank you for the gift of Holy Communion.*

God alone

Cultures since the dawn of time have used superstitious practices in an attempt to please the gods, tame natural forces and predict the future. The Israelites entered a land where such practices were rife. The chosen people are reminded that they are not to practise divination, sacrifice their children, cast spells, consult ghosts or seek oracles. These are inappropriate ways in which to seek God, who chooses to be made known to the Israelites through the prophets – and Moses in particular. The scriptures are firm here:

You must remain completely loyal to the LORD your God.
(verse 13)

We too, as the people of God today, are to be clear about where our loyalty lies. God loves us, and will never let us go. Through the power of the Holy Spirit, Christ is at work in us today and has redeemed us for eternity. We need have no fear of the future and no time for superstitious practices or the 'quick fixes' peddled by our societies.

Today is Ash Wednesday – the beginning of the forty days of Lent, which lead into the great celebration of Easter. This period is a time for repenting of our sins and coming back into a right relationship with God. It's a time for renewing our faith, growing in our spirituality and leaving behind those things that separate us from complete loyalty to God.

† *Examine my life, O God, and show me where changes need to be made.*

Everybody needs good neighbours

You shall not watch your neighbour's ox or sheep straying away and ignore them; you shall take them back to their owner ... you shall do the same with a neighbour's garment; and you shall do the same with anything else that your neighbour loses and you find. You may not withhold your help.

(verse 1 and part of verse 3)

Whether it is returning stray sheep, helping overburdened donkeys regain their footing, recovering lost property, respecting creation, or adhering to safety regulations in buildings, every successful community needs its people to be good neighbours to one another. Neighbourliness is part and parcel of the smooth running of everyday life. Communities run best when everyone is looking after each other, and all are considerate and helpful. In this way disputes and hardship are avoided and peace and harmony encouraged.

Jesus was to take these commonsense stipulations a step further by challenging his disciples to go the extra mile in all their dealings with people. In Luke 6 we are commanded to love our enemies, pray for those who hate us, give our shirt away as well as our coat, give to all who beg from us and not ask for our things back when they are taken.

Are we good neighbours to all we meet? Are we walking on the path of sacrificial love prescribed by Jesus?

† *Lord Jesus, teach me to be a good neighbour.*

'Thank you'

When we're given a gift, it is the usual practice to say 'thank you'. We do this not just because we're polite, but because we're pleased and excited, sometimes overwhelmed, and sometimes very grateful. Our natural response is to thank the giver. The Israelites were encouraged to thank God for the gift of the Promised Land by dedicating to God the 'first fruits', or choicest parts of the harvest:

> **When you have come into the land that the LORD your God is giving to you as an inheritance to possess, and you possess it, and settle in it, you shall take some of the first of all the fruit of the ground, which you harvest from the land that the LORD is giving you, and you shall put it in a basket and go to the place that the LORD your God will choose as a dwelling for his name.**
>
> *(verses 1-2)*

As these gifts were given back to God, the Israelites remembered the story of their deliverance from Egypt and the wandering in the wilderness. They told again the good news of God's saving acts and gave thanks for the land.

As Christians we too have been liberated into the freedom of God's kingdom, not through any effort of our own, but by the gift of grace given to us through God's saving act in Jesus Christ. This gift, which is beyond price, should be honoured with a generous and wholehearted response.

† *Lord, thank you for all you have given me.*

Choose life

What is really exciting about faith in God is that it's for everyone. Keeping the commandments of love and faithfulness are not reserved for a select group. You don't have to travel a long way to love God, or climb mountains to get faith right. God comes to the people, firstly through the prophets like Moses and ultimately in the person of Jesus Christ – God with us. God takes the initiative and comes to where we are with the good news of love, forgiveness and freedom.

> **[T]he word is very near to you; it is in your mouth and in your heart for you to observe.**
>
> *(chapter 30, part of verse 14)*

The Israelites had a clear choice set before them. They could follow God, obey his commandments and walk in his paths. This choice meant life in the land they were entering and the promise of many descendants. Turning away from God and pursuing other gods would lead to a dead end. God's people chose life and, led by Joshua, entered the land. Our passages from Deuteronomy conclude with a looking back to the time when Moses surveyed the land to which he had led his people, and then died to this life. He is remembered as the greatest of prophets.

† *Lord, thank you that your people chose life. Help me to remain faithful to their choice.*

The Seven Deadly Sins vs What is Good

1 Pride versus true humility

Notes by Paula Fairlie OSB
based on the New Jerusalem Bible

Paula is a Benedictine Nun and lives in Chester, England.

Introduction

The idea of Seven Deadly Sins developed in the Middle Ages, rather than from the Bible, but they are certainly all there in the Bible! Our readings for this theme link together stories from the Old and New Testaments with the teaching of Jesus in the Sermon on the Mount and each week ends with Christ, who exemplifies the opposite virtue.

We will only find God in spiritual poverty: God resists the proud. As nuns we commit ourselves to God and monastic life with an underlying commitment to poverty, chastity and obedience. The later prophets spoke of a spiritual 'remnant' in society after wars and social disruption. These were poor, oppressed people, bowed down by the burden of life. They were called 'the poor of Yahweh' (*anawim*). They were the seed of the kingdom of God. As nuns we are called to become *anawim*, spiritually poor and dependent. That is the call to all who follow Christ in the teaching of the Beatitudes.

Text for the week: Isaiah 2:11
Human pride will lower its eyes, human arrogance will be humbled, and Yahweh alone will be exalted.

For group discussion and personal thought

- What exactly is pride?
- Why does pride impede love?
- What is true humility?
- Does actual physical need impair spiritual life?

Don't be a show-off!

Be careful not to parade your uprightness in public to attract attention; otherwise you will lose all reward from your Father in heaven.

(verse 1)

Those of us who are familiar with the prayer of Saint Ignatius of Loyola, in which he prays that all his service and toil should be done purely for the love of God, are slightly shocked when we realise that we are to *expect* a reward from our Father in heaven for our 'uprightness'. The good we do will be rewarded but if our motive is wrong, our good deeds are valueless. In a monastery the individual nuns can only 'give alms' of service, kindness or a listening ear. Charitable donations are the concern of the Abbess and Bursar. The same must be true in families. So kindly service becomes our alms, done without 'parading' our good works.

In my community we all pray the Liturgy together, and are also required to pray for an hour privately. This is not being 'ostentatious' but obedient. Good example can be strengthening, and this quiet fidelity can stir us to greater fervour. The quality of our prayer, in the inner 'chamber' of our heart, is known to God alone. Only an aura of quietness around us may indicate a heart at rest. Our prayer would be valueless if we boasted about our spiritual experiences!

† *Lord, help us to serve one another in the gentleness of love, knowing that this is your will.*

February

Flee to your mountain

'Flee To Your Mountain' advised the 'enemy' in Psalm 11 (verse 1), and here Jesus withdraws to the hills of the Judean wilderness to be tested in his understanding of God and his mission. As the Israelites were led by God through the desert, so was Jesus led by the Spirit. His testing was really a testing of God. Can he do it or can't he?

> **Do not put the Lord your God to the test.**
> *(part of verse 7)*

Jesus was taken to the holy city, to the pinnacle of power, and told to jump: God would save him. People would either see him carried on angels' wings, or plunging to his certain death. But how many of them would really notice him, and his proud temerity? It would be a momentary marvel either way, and achieve nothing. The supreme temptation of any public figure is to be centre stage. Jesus continued to put God first, not himself.

'Flying with eagles' wings' has haunted our unconscious and spiritual lives. Some children dream that they can run so fast that they launch into flight. Some spiritual states, described by the prophets, seem to raise us to a higher level of perception. Fasting and prayer may also heighten our awareness, or drag us down through physical misery.

There are no shortcuts to holiness or glory, and we do well to pray:

† *Lead us not into temptation but deliver us from evil.*

The day of the Lord

As Christians we expect the coming of God. There is a three-fold coming for all of us: in grace and sacraments, in liturgy and prayer, and at the hour of our death. Beyond that is the definitive Day of the Lord, described as a day of darkness and terror, a great and terrible day when

> **Human pride will lower its eyes**
> **human arrogance will be humbled,**
> **and Yahweh alone will be exalted.**
> *(verse 11)*

It is a day of judgement, of cringing terror, when God overturns everything which we see as strong, enduring and secure. Our worldly values are unworthy of trust: our possessions will not save us. Escaping from this cataclysm of wrath, humankind will seek refuge in holes in the ground – in storage-pits, cisterns and natural cavities. We shall go empty-handed into the dark, having thrown away all that we previously valued...

As nuns, we are called by God into a restricted area so that we can concentrate on essentials: seeking God and learning to love. The virtue most emphasised in the Benedictine Rule is humility, the knowledge that without God we are nothing, and that any good we do is entirely his gift. Yet even this is not enough to make us one of the 'poor of Yahweh', totally dependent upon him. We are provided with spiritual tools to use, only to discover that we shall always be beginners.

† *May our prayer always be: Thy kingdom come. . .*

Humble remnants

We, and all our society, are called to conversion. Repentance is essential even for the afflicted, the oppressed poor, the *anawim* for whom the prophets demand justice:

> Seek Yahweh,
> all you humble of the earth [*anawim*]
> who obey his commands.
> Seek uprightness,
> seek humility:
> you may perhaps find shelter
> on the Day of Yahweh's anger.
> *(verse 3)*

Why was God so angry with the whole of creation? Because the people were worshipping alien gods and following alien practices. Those of us who enter monasteries make a promise of *conversion of life:* we will turn away from 'worldly conduct' and live a simple life based on the teaching of the gospel. Every time Christians renew their baptismal promises during the Easter Vigil they affirm the same intent: we reject Satan and choose God.

Yet however much we try to follow the precepts of the gospel, at the end of each day we sing the verse: 'O Father bring us back again, who on this day have strayed from you...'

Zephaniah speaks of a remnant saved by Yahweh, who will graze their sheep where proud towns once flourished. This remnant of people would be the seed of a holy nation. This idyll of a peaceful life was never realised, as it will never be fully realised in a monastery. So live as the repentant poor of Yahweh, every one of us, and look to God for compassion and love.

† *May the good seed bear fruit for the kingdom of God.*

Seed dispersal

In Genesis there are two accounts of how God 'filled' the earth with humankind. One was peaceful, as human beings migrated in search of land (*Genesis 10*). The other, today's reading, was a drastic reversal of human aspiration. The proud thoughts and actions of united mankind were against the will of God. To stop human beings misusing their gifts for selfish purposes, God spread confusion and fear by taking away the gift of mutual comprehension. All fled from Babel into the unknown, no longer trusting each other. We can only be truly at one when God is the focal point.

'The whole world' had been at peace, held together by mutual understanding. The people wanted to make themselves both renowned and powerful, determining their own way of life and religious practices. The tall tower was to reach heaven, so that God would be there on demand.

Let us make a name for ourselves, so that we do not get scattered all over the world.

(part of verse 4)

Their punishment was dispersal, what they had feared most. It was God's plan to unite heaven and earth, but in his own way – the way of Jacob's ladder (*Genesis 28:12*). In the end, it was the tree of the cross which became the only effective ladder uniting heaven and earth. In life it is through 'climbing down' that we becoming pleasing to God.

† *To thy name be the glory.*

My soul proclaims the greatness of God

These readings reach their climax in the Prayer of the Poor, the song of the Daughter of Zion put on the lips of Mary, the mother of Jesus. This canticle is rooted in the Hebrew Scriptures. Many Christians sing this canticle at Vespers or Evening Prayer, just before sunset. We leave the chapel awaiting a new birth of Christ within ourselves. This is a song of reversal: God does not come to the rich and self-sufficient but to those who know their need and are poor in the eyes of the world. Those who wait upon God are the spiritual remnant with whom God will do great things.

> **Make your own the mind of Christ . . .**
> **he emptied himself . . .**
> **becoming as human beings are . . .**
> **he was humbler yet,**
> **even to accepting death,**
> **death on a cross.**
>> *(Philippians, verse 5,*
>> *part of verse 7, and verse 8)*

We shall never 'be' the loving Christ, who rejected all arrogance, force and pride, and gave himself up in humble love. We believe that when he was raised up on the cross he raised up the whole fallen world with him, as was foreshadowed at his baptism. We do not need man-made ladders to reach heaven. Now we have the immortal tree, the cross of Christ, which unites heaven and earth. Together with Christ, we can reach out to God and the whole world in prayer.

† *Lord, may we become like you.*

2. Wrath versus perfect love

Notes by Philip Wetherell
based on the New English Bible and Jerusalem Bible

Philip Wetherell is the Director of Christians Abroad, an ecumenical advice and information agency that helps Christians and others to explore vocations to work in mission and world development. He has also worked as desk officer for a mission agency (at different times covering Southern Africa and Latin America).

Introduction

Any newspaper, radio or TV news today will be full of stories of violence – from local street robbery through to international incidents. The stories of personal violence will centre on murder – the worst crime in every society, the deepest example of human wrath, provoking the most anger and calls for retaliation. Jesus' forefathers were no different – 'a murderer must be brought to justice' (*Matthew 5:21*).

But Jesus goes much deeper. While he reinforces God's given law, he shows he has come to complete it – a teaching he proves in his own life. Love will only overcome our wrath when God guides our inner selves, our motives and our emotions. Then we move closer to the perfection Jesus demonstrated in his own life.

Text for the week: Matthew 5:48
There must be no limit to your goodness, as your heavenly Father's goodness knows no bounds.

For group discussion and personal thought

Each day ask yourselves:
• What in the news today has provoked anger?
• What were your feelings?
• How did you want to respond to that?
• What would Jesus have said or done?
• Which words of Jesus are a guide?

Matthew 5:21-26, 43-48

Respond in love

Love, whether of a partner, a parent or a child, is the emotion that brings the most joy in our lives. Perhaps the love given by a small child is closest to the picture Jesus paints here: uncritical and open, accepting and unquestioning. A child can see a parent or grandparent as perfect, regardless of their actual behaviour. Sadly, that can change as children grow and begin to see that their love is not always returned – as I witnessed on a train, where a drunken mother was not returning the concern of her sad and tearful child. It is not surprising that Jesus gives these famous words as the climax of this part of his Sermon on the Mount.

> **'You have learned what they were told, "Love your neighbour, hate your enemy." But what I tell you is this: Love your enemies and pray for your persecutors; only so can you be children of your heavenly Father.'**
>
> *(verses 43-45a)*

The difference of course is that here the 'parent' has the perfection that children dream of, and deserves all that childlike trust and confidence from us. We show we are God's children by responding in love. The hardest and ultimate love is for those who might take advantage, who do not love in return – but this is exactly what the Father did in giving his beloved Son.

† *Lord, help me today to show love to just one person I would normally ignore.*

Inadvertent sin

In ancient Jewish tradition 'sin offerings' were made by community leaders or 'men of standing' who had done wrong things without knowing it. Ordinary people also made offerings but with different animals:

> **If any person among the common people sins inadvertently and does what is forbidden in any commandment of the LORD . . . and the sin he has committed is made known to him, he shall bring as his offering . . . a she goat without blemish.**
> *(part of verses 27 and 28)*

We can easily be technically guilty of a crime we did not know we had committed – driving at night unaware that one of our lights is not working, for example. We can sometimes offend other cultures by breaking traditional rules. Visiting a small village in east Africa I ate all of a meal I didn't much like in order not to offend my host — but discovered later that I had offended because the custom was to leave some to show they had provided plenty.

We may upset local custom, break laws or, in the biblical example, be technically guilty of 'sin'. Sacrificed goats are no longer expected, but we have to give something of ourselves, offer recompense, apologise, pay penalties and seek forgiveness for our ignorance and lack of thought. We also have to pray that those we offend will react with love and not wrath.

† *Lord, help me to live my life attentively so as not to offend unwittingly.*

51

God laughs

We see so many examples of how people who do not care for God's law seem to prosper – whether internationally at the level of business or politics, or locally in our own communities. Sadly it happens too in some churches, where the leader's prosperity implies that those who are poor must have done wrong. We are sometimes angry and want action – tempted to imitate their methods.

Psalm 37 puts us right, describing the contrasting fates of the virtuous and the wicked, and telling us to be different.

> **Do not strive to outdo the evildoers**
> **or emulate those who do wrong . . .**
> **Be angry no more, have done with wrath;**
> **strive not to outdo in evildoing.**
> *(verses 1 and 8)*

The righteous anger that we feel about those who exploit the poor in the world must not become wrath, mimicking those we oppose. We will not change the world that way. Later in the psalm we are told of the Lord who is a lover of justice, that the law of God is in the hearts of the righteous, and they will possess the land and live at peace (*verses 28, 31, 29*). And then, God laughs. God laughs only three times in the Old Testament, each time in a psalm, laughing at those whose time is coming – we hope that is because he knows they will see the error of their ways.

† *Father, may I love justice and hold your righteousness in my heart.*

Cause and effect

These two sections of Proverbs 30 share a common theme – certain actions produce certain results. The trouble starts in the family setting, with a defamed father and unblessed mother (*verse 11*) but ends with abuse of the poor. Family values that include love and mutual respect are spurned by the 'sort of people' who in selfishness deny their inherited values. While they impress each other (*verse 12*), their teeth are like swords (*verse 14*) and their wrath results in the vulnerable suffering the most.

Little, it seems, has changed and it is easy to see parallels with the way the powerful today often abuse rather than love the poor – politicians and those who have power in business as well as those whose selfishness is more personal.

The final verses remind us how easy it is to go down that path:

> **If you have been foolish enough to fly into a passion**
> **and now have second thoughts, lay your hand on your lips.**
> **For by churning the milk you produce butter,**
> **by wringing the nose you produce blood,**
> **and by whipping up anger you produce strife.**
>
> *(verses 32-33, JB)*

Whether as a group (*verses 10-14*) or on our own (*verses 32-33*), if we make a start in wrongdoing (especially venting our anger against others) we must check ourselves immediately because continuing will lead to strife, as we smother our love and angrily abuse others.

† *Father, help my anger to diminish and my love to grow.*

February

God's forgiveness

Four chapters into the story of God's created world, Adam and Eve have left Eden and the first murder is committed – alarmingly by brother against brother. Cain's envy and bitterness in response to God's preference for his brother's gift gave birth to wrath (*verse 5*). Bitterness destroys the love that every culture expects to see as the basis of family life.

We can only guess at the sin Cain is supposed to have committed to make God choose Abel's gift, but he is warned that this, rather than love, will overwhelm him.

> If you do well, you are accepted;
> if not, sin is a demon crouching at the door.
> It shall be eager for you, and you will be mastered by it.
> *(verse 7)*

Yet despite this murder of God's preferred gift giver, one of the only two children of God's created 'mother of all who live' (*Genesis 3:20*), Cain is forgiven. God's love, shown here in forgiveness, is deeper than any human could ask of another at any point in history. Whether in the family, in wider society, between communities or nations, we do well to remember the extent of this forgiveness. How does it relate to our views on capital punishment when a crime is committed in our own community, or to the way our nation works to resolve current international disputes?

† *Loving God, may I always be ready to forgive, as you have forgiven me.*

Love brings joy

The community to be built around Jesus is to be based on love – the same love given by Jesus himself, which itself reflects the Father's love for his Son. This love is unselfish:

'There is no greater love than this, that a man should lay down his life for his friends. You are my friends.'
(verse 13 and part of verse 14)

The contrast with much of what we encounter every day is suggested in Ephesians: wrath or anger can eat away at the soul, and is particularly damaging if it stays with us too long (*verses 26-27*). It can seem as if humanity has not progressed at all since yesterday's story of the first recorded murder . Change in individual lives and in the world will only come when we truly follow the loving example of Christ. The amazing result of this is not miserable obedience to strict laws removing all enjoyment from life, but total joy. If we dwell in Jesus' love then joy and not anger will stay with us:

'Dwell in my love. If you heed my commands you will dwell in my love as I have heeded my Father's command and dwell in his love. I have spoken this to you so that my joy may be in you and your joy complete.
(John, verses 10-11)

† *Father, may the love of Jesus permeate me through and through.*

The Seven Deadly Sins vs What is Good

3 Envy and avarice versus true poverty of spirit

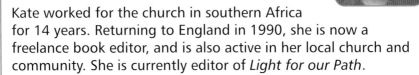

Notes by Kate Hughes
based on the New Revised Standard Version

Kate worked for the church in southern Africa for 14 years. Returning to England in 1990, she is now a freelance book editor, and is also active in her local church and community. She is currently editor of *Light for our Path*.

Introduction

Having grown up in England immediately after the Second World War, with shortages of many things from butter to building bricks, my view of what is necessary for a comfortable life is rather different to that of younger people born after the electronics revolution of the 1960s. I am constantly amazed at how much money people in Britain can earn and spend – and very aware of how much poverty there is as well. But poverty is not simply about not having material things or money in the bank; at bottom, it is about where we put our trust and confidence – in iPods or God.

Text for the week: Matthew 6:21:
Where your treasure is, there your heart will be also.

For group discussion and personal thought

• Where is your treasure?

• How much do you worry about the safety of your possessions or about loss of income? What do you think is the right Christian approach to money and material possessions?

• In the light of this week's notes, think about, and pray about, your aims, wants and priorities in life.

Needed: a health warning

None of our readings this week says that money and possessions are necessarily wrong *in themselves*. It is what we do with them, and the way that having them or trying to get them affects our behaviour, that causes deep concern to Jesus and a number of New Testament writers. We shall be looking at their views throughout this week. Money and possessions need a health warning: This product can seriously endanger your spiritual health! But Jesus tells us to get our priorities right, focus on God and his will for us, and God will provide all that he knows we need (which may not be the same as what we think we need, even less what we want and envy others having).

> **'Strive first for the kingdom of God and his righteousness, and all these things will be given to you as well.'**
>
> *(verse 33)*

One of the worst dangers in having money and possessions is that we immediately start worrying about keeping them safe. We get involved in bolts and bars, insurance, burglar alarms, we walk the streets afraid of being mugged for our mobile phone or our Rolex watch. Do we really need that jacket which costs enough to feed a poor family for a year? Our bodies need water – they don't actually need tea, coffee, Coke or wine. God will give us what we need if we are faithful to him.

† *God, help us to put your kingdom values first in our lives.*

Priorities

We all have times when we are so absorbed in what we are doing that we forget to eat. We miss a meal and discover, perhaps to our surprise, that it does us no harm at all. On the other hand, if we are just sitting around doing nothing, and dinner doesn't arrive, we immediately start feeling more and more hungry, and the state of our stomach becomes more and more important. But when we are focused on what is important to us, it becomes easier to keep food and work and the other necessities of life in their proper place. Jesus focused on God as he prepared for his life's ministry – and was able to go without food for forty days. Peter and Andrew, James and John focused on Jesus – and were able to walk away from their work and their family business to take up the new work to which Jesus called them.

Immediately they left their nets and followed him.
(verse 20)

As we concentrate on God and try to live according to his will, we may be surprised to discover how little we need, how many things become unimportant. And how much freedom this gives us to get up and go after Jesus when he calls us.

† Lord, help us to leave behind our excess baggage and concentrate on following you.

Save your energy

Working all hours to get more money than we need, collecting things which are so precious that they need to be kept in a safe and never seen or used, fretting because someone else has more than us, or something that we want – it's all such a waste of energy. Energy that could be used for other, more worthwhile things: making sure our employees are properly treated, that any extra money is used to help those in need, that we have time to pray and work for God. And there is no guarantee that we will even still be alive tomorrow.

> **[Y]ou do not even know what tomorrow will bring.**
> *(part of verse 14)*

If we feel the need to make and keep more and more money and collect more and more things, we are effectively saying that we don't trust God to look after us. We need our own security, because God may not be able to keep us safe. But millionaires also suffer and die, and God's love extends to all his children and cannot be bribed to favour the rich. So save your energy for what is really important – sharing the love of God with everyone.

† *God, help us to use our energy in your service, not waste it on vain attempts to provide our own security.*

Contentment

(Note that in other translations the second half of verse 5 begins a new sentence – for example, in GNB: 'They think that religion is a way to become rich'.)

Making money becomes an addiction: the more you have, the more you want. Of course, we would all like to earn enough money to feed and educate our families, keep a roof over our heads and pay the bills. But the money we have over and above that needs to be handled with care. It is the *love* of money which leads us into sin (*verse 10*), when it absorbs our thoughts, time and energy, makes us neglect our family and community, and when we give it the love and worship that we should give to God.

> [I]f we have food and clothing, we will be content with these.
>
> *(verse 8)*

Having enough money for our basic needs should bring us contentment, gratitude to God, and time and energy to help those less fortunate. The word 'content' is related to the word 'contain': both come from the Latin verb 'to hold'. Contentment is being happy to remain within the boundaries of your life – the boundaries of time and place, family and community, what you have and the people you love. Discontent drives us out from where we are contained, endlessly seeking what will not bring us contentment. Contentment is to rest peacefully within God's hands, secure in his love and care.

† *Hold me in your hands, Lord, that I may know the contentment of being loved by you.*

Honesty

It is recorded that the early Christians impressed their non-Christian neighbours by their care for each other: 'See how these Christians love one another!' They used their wealth in the right way – to care for those in need. But this was a willing and voluntary giving. God leaves us free to choose what we do with our money, to choose the way of envy and avarice or the way of poverty of spirit. No one would have criticised Ananias for selling his property and keeping some of the proceeds to supply his own needs. But he pretended that he was bringing the whole amount to the apostles, to be used for the poor. His wrong love of money led him into the sin of dishonesty.

> **'You did not lie to us but to God!'**
> *(part of verse 4)*

As always, it is not money itself that is evil but the sin which unnecessary love of money can lead us into. Honesty in matters of money is highly prized in the business world, but even in our personal finances, where we may be dealing with a few hundred pounds instead of millions, we need to be open and honest, to refer back constantly to God and his standards, to check that we are not becoming too absorbed in making money that we do not need, and that we are truly giving all we can afford to help others.

† *Lord, help me not to be led into sin by money and possessions.*

61

March

Riches and poverty

Psalm 112 gives a lovely portrait of a rich man who uses his wealth in the right way, so that it becomes a blessing to himself and others. But being rich is not simply a matter of having money and material possessions. We can be wealthy in many ways: in our intellectual achievements, in our creative gifts, in our enjoyment of life and the world around us, in our family and friends. Part of the spiritual danger in having a lot of money is that it gives us power over other people. We also have power because we are well educated, or speak with the 'right' accent, or can manipulate others with our personality, or belong to a particular group or family – these things are also part of our wealth and can be used in good or bad ways. Jesus had all the wealth of God: his power as creator and sustainer of the universe, his command of legions of angels, his ability to be present everywhere and in all times. Yet he gave up all this wealth and accepted the limitations and powerlessness of a human being.

> **Though he was rich, yet for your sakes he became poor, so that by his poverty you might become rich.**
>
> *(2 Corinthians part of verse 9)*

And through the poverty of Jesus, we become immensely wealthy, possessing all the love of God and the power of his Spirit. What is money compared to that?

† God, help us to use wisely all our power and wealth, of whatever kind.

4 Lust and gluttony versus purity of heart

Notes by Joan Stott
based on the New Living Translation and the New International Version

Joan Stott is a Lay Preacher in the Uniting Church in Australia, has served in a variety of leadership roles in Australia, and extensively in the World Federation of Methodist and Uniting Church Women.

Introduction

Jesus introduced a new understanding of humanity and its true value to God, by becoming one of us – God embodied in human flesh. Thus, humanity was exalted to new heights of honour, and because of this honour the Apostle Paul sought to encourage the new believers to develop more Christ-like behaviour and relationships. 'Lust' and 'gluttony' can be defined as an 'excessive obsession with self-indulgence' and relates to food, drink, sex, power, career or acquiring materialistic things. Anything that obstructs our relationship with God has the potential to become sinful; but God's love, made known to us in Jesus Christ, is more powerful than any sin, and that love can help us overcome our sinfulness. What is good is that, through Jesus' example, pure-hearted people will encourage Christian hope and prayerfully seek the best for all people as their faith develops

Text for the week: 1 Corinthians 13:7 (NIV)
[Love] always protects, always trusts, always hopes, always perseveres.

For group discussion and personal thought

- If true love protects, trusts, hopes and perseveres, will we ever learn from our mistakes or failures?
- The 'Seven Deadly Sins' seem to be part of everyday life, so what is so 'deadly' about them?

Filling life's emptiness?

Originally, fasting was a way of mourning the death of a loved person. In Old Testament times, this gradually changed to include remorse for past actions. The only official Jewish fasting time was on the Day of Atonement, but soon people chose to initiate additional fasts, as they thought this brought them greater spiritual rewards.

Eventually fasting publicly became 'fashionable' as a sign of piety or self-discipline, rather than an outward sign of inward penitence. In Jesus' time, the days for fasting were Monday and Thursday, which coincided with market days, so anyone fasting publicly would have a large 'audience'.

> 'And when you fast, don't make it obvious, as the hypocrites do, . . . so people will admire them for their fasting. I assure you, that is the only reward they will ever get.'
>
> *(part of verse 16, NLT)*

Responsible fasting can be healthy, but it depends on the motivation. Drawing attention to oneself often demonstrates an unfulfilled personal need, and exceeds the usual reasons for fasting. What is good is that Jesus said: 'My purpose is to give life in all its fullness' (*John 10:10b*). Jesus came amongst us to share the power of his love, giving of himself to all who would receive him, and he offered to people a sense of hope and fulfilment that is wholesome and lasting.

† *May the power of Christ's indwelling presence and its fulfilment grow in me. Amen*

DIY – do it yourself?

'Do-it-yourself' (DIY) is a popular concept, which challenges house owners to maintain their house and garden at minimal expense. Such self-care of our responsibilities helps to develop a strong sense of pride in achieving results. Jesus was tempted to 'DIY' when he was hungry after his long fast, and the small stones nearby could easily be mistaken for traditional bread shapes.

'If you are the Son of God, change these stones into loaves of bread.' But Jesus told him, 'No!'
(part of verses 3 and 4, NLT)

Jesus' wilderness temptation, to set his own pace and style for ministry rather than obediently follow God's pace and plan, is a familiar temptation to all Jesus' disciples. The desire for control over our life, our relationships, our career, our future, and even our faith, is a very powerful temptation, especially when serving one's own desires is recognised as self-sufficiency. Our self-indulgent attitude of 'doing it my way' can lead to personal isolation and destruction, and we need to declare Christ's convincing 'No' to this temptation.

What is good is that 'Christ reaches out to command people's attention and awaken their faith; he calls people into the fellowship of his sufferings, to be the disciples of a crucified Lord' (Assembly of the Uniting Church in Australia, *The Basis of Union*, 1992).

† *May the power of Christ's commitment grow in me Amen*

March

The pretenders

Did you play 'dressing-up' as a child? Do you remember dancing around in adult clothes, walking around in too-big shoes, and miming exaggerated gestures and actions? However, no matter how hard we tried, we never succeeded in convincing anyone we were adults! The game of 'pretending' is not limited to children. Many adults experience the need to deliberately act in childlike ways; and people can so easily convince themselves that they are mature, responsible and honest people, even spiritually inclined people – but they cannot deceive God. In today's text, the prophet struggled to pass on that message to his listeners:

> **'you are living only for yourself.'**
> *(part of verse 3, NLT)*

Whilst they pretended to be pious people of faith, in reality they were wrongfully imprisoning people, oppressing and depriving workers of their wages, denying people hospitality and bodily needs, spreading vicious lies, and not accepting responsibility for needy relatives. Jesus experienced the same double standards, and godless humanity still has not changed its ways! Self-indulgence at the expense of another's welfare is not God's way. What is good is that these words were not the prophet's final message. God gives the promise of hope if people cease their pretensions and worship God in reality.

> **'If you do these things, your salvation will come like the dawn. Yes, your healing will come quickly.'**
> *(part of verse 8, NLT)*

† May the power of God's hope and promises grow in me. Amen

My security light

Security lights are well named! Whenever I step into the range of the sensor beam, the security light comes on immediately and the darkness is destroyed. The light surrounds me wherever I move within the range of that sensor beam. I also remain visible to other people, and they can see my actions and judge whether I am any threat. I become part of that light and it becomes part of me. This means that I can confidently carry out my tasks, even in the night-time. I am also secure in the knowledge that any personal danger will be illuminated.

> **For though your hearts were once full of darkness, now you are full of light from the Lord, and your behaviour should show it! For this light within you produces only what is good and right and true.**
>
> *(verses 8-9, NLT)*

Stepping beyond the range of the sensor beam plunges me immediately into darkness, with an even greater loss of sight. My eyes must readjust to living again in the darkness, with all its potential dangers. What is good is that when we come within the sensor range of Christ's light, we absorb the Christ-light into the depths of our beings and become children of the light. The power generated by that Christ-light of love transforms our inner being and all our actions, even our 'secret sins'!

† May the power of Christ's light shine through me. Amen

The birds and bees

It's springtime now, and my garden is alive with birds, butterflies and bees hovering over flowers. The power of colour, shape and perfume is easily seen as nature's reproductive processes continue, with the help of God's creatures. When a person is gifted with physical attractiveness, a pleasant personality, and is popular because they excel in their career choice, they have considerable power. When the advantages of royalty are added to these other gifts, the temptation to use these powers is very great.

> **One evening David got up from his bed and walked around on the roof of the palace. From the roof he saw a woman bathing. The woman was very beautiful, and David sent someone to find out about her.**
> *(verse 2 and part of verse 3, NIV)*

Human sexuality is one of God's gifts and, wisely used, its power brings great blessing. However, both men and women are often victims of lust-induced sexual abuse. What is good is that Paul's epistles record 'self control' as one of the Holy Spirit's most powerful gifts to us. King David is remembered for his commitment to God, and his psalms bring blessing and comfort to people, especially Psalm 51, reputedly written out of David's sense of deep remorse over his actions towards Bathsheba and her husband. Misuse of the gift of power is always a betrayal of that gift.

† *May the power of the Holy Spirit's gifts grow in me. Amen*

Claiming the perfect gold

Gold has always been recognised as valuable and fascinating, because of the power it gives and its flexibility of use. I grew up in the region called the 'Golden Triangle', where some of the world's greatest discoveries of gold were made in the 1850s, and great 'nuggets' of gold were found along local creek and river beds, as water had carried the gold along until it became a nugget. The 'Gold Rushes' brought thousands of adventurers to Australia, with miners buying or sharing in a 'claim' of land. Successes were varied, but some actually did 'strike' gold, with the ultimate prize being to find a nugget of gold. Most miners only found specks of the precious metal, however, and many more people found only 'fool's gold', a look-alike metal of little value.

Love is the 'gold' of all emotions, and it reaches the full power of its expression between people when it is given and received in trust. In Jesus Christ, we experience the fullness of God's love in human form, as he lived out God's message with the ultimate act of self-giving love.

[W]hen perfection comes, the imperfect disappears.
(1 Corinthians, verse 10, NIV)

What is good is that God's love in and through Christ is the 'purest gold', and the perfection of love is found only in Christ, which is never ever 'fool's gold'!

† *May the power of Christ's love grow in me. Amen.*

The Seven Deadly Sins vs What is Good?

5 Sloth versus single-minded faithfulness

Notes by Elina Templin
based on the Revised Standard Version

Elina Templin lived in South Africa for many years, raising a family and performing and teaching music. In the 1990s she was ordained in the Presbyterian Church of South Africa and spent six years in full-time ministry. Returning to her Canadian roots in 1998, she lives in Toronto, where she teaches music and, now an Anglican, sings in the choir and occasionally preaches in her local church.

Introduction

Historically, sloth has been interpreted as laziness, sadness, depression and apathy; the term used for it was *accidie*. In modern times, it signifies simply being lazy, unwilling to act or to care. Perhaps the Italian poet Dante defined it best: 'Failure to love God with our whole heart, mind and soul'.

Text for the week: John 4:34
'My food is to do the will of him who sent me, and to accomplish his work.'

For group discussion and personal thought

• In your own Christian life, where do you encounter sloth – laziness, boredom, lack of interest, depression? What causes it, and what can you do about it?

Beyond the law

It would be hard to imagine a world without laws. They are there to protect innocent people from the activities of criminals, from those who drive too fast, from the taking of a life. But the law has its limits. Can we legislate love? Jesus taught us that the greatest commandment is to love God with our whole heart, soul, mind and strength. For this there are no limits. The love of a mother (or father) for their child motivates them to go to any lengths, even beyond the law, to sacrifice even their own lives. Could God do less?

> **'For I tell you, unless your righteousness exceeds that of the scribes and Pharisees, you will never enter the kingdom of heaven.'**
>
> *(verse 20, RSV)*

It has been said of the Sermon on the Mount (*Matthew 5–7*) that Jesus gives us a pattern of living that is not only impractical but impossible! But God knows what he is doing. As the Father sends the Son, so Jesus sends us (*John 4:34*). We are a sent people. We do not make the Christian journey according to our own wishes and desires but are sent to be salt and light in the name and spirit of Christ. Every Sunday I hear the words 'Go forth in the name of Christ', and our congregation goes forth as the rays of the sun go forth, rays of unconditional love, beyond all law.

† Lord, help me to love as Jesus loved.

March

Driven or called?

It is rare today to find someone who lives and works effectively within their limits. An elderly character in a television comedy is surrounded by a busy family and a busy world. In self-defence he says, 'I am content to do very little – slowly.' Is this laziness? Or a wise use of time?

> **Go to the ant, O sluggard;**
> **Consider her ways, and be wise.**
> *(verse 6, RSV)*

Today's reading holds up the ant as a model of industry. But the busy life of the ant is not a model for how we use our time. The great psychiatrist, C J Jung, wrote that hurry is not of the devil – it *is* the devil. Our model is rather the way the ant uses its energy and resources. We need to be true to who we are and the gifts we have been given. We are to put our lives, and those gifts, at God's service and disposal, and to trust God to use them in his way and his time.

† *Lord, help me to wait in quiet confidence for the guidance of your Word.*

Today if you hear his voice...

Christians have a vision. We live by that vision of a new heaven and a new earth when God will be over all. No more tears, no more death or pain. Former things have passed away, and all things will be made new. This vision of new life has begun in Jesus. It is still to be fulfilled. But time is not empty while we wait.

'Therefore keep watch . . . be ready, because the Son of Man will come at an hour when you do not expect him.'
(part of verses 42 and 44)

Jesus sends us his Spirit, our helper. The Spirit helps us to hear God's voice and recognise God's word to us in our daily lives. In his book on the rosary, *Five for Sorrow, Ten for Joy*, J Neville Ward writes that every experience is a kind of annunciation, or announcement, that God wants us to receive something, do something, endure something, and if we are willing to say 'Yes', our receiving, our doing, our enduring will be a kind of listening and readiness to respond, like Mary's 'Let it be to me according to your word' (*Luke 1:38*).

† *Spirit of God, open our hearts to your guidance, free us from our fears and fill us with your light.*

The armour of God

Paul wrote this letter to the Church from prison. As a prisoner he is under constant guard by soldiers. He compares the armour of the soldiers to the armour of the Christian. As the soldier is protected by outer armour, so the Christian has the armour of the Spirit. We do not follow Christ without resources. God gives us more than enough to withstand all trials and troubles.

> **Finally, be strong in the Lord, and in the strength of his might. Put on the whole armour of God, that you may be able to stand against the wiles of the devil.**
>
> *(verses 10-11)*

In 1987 Terry Waite was sent to Lebanon as a hostage negotiator but became a hostage himself. For almost four years he was in solitary confinement. The words of the Anglican *Book of Common Prayer*, memorised over many years, acted as armour against despair and loss of hope as he prayed them and kept them in his heart.

† *Lord, grant that we may never take our Christian resources for granted, but use them faithfully and well – and often.*

Nevertheless . . .

When we are tempted to think that it was easy for Jesus to do the will of God and accomplish his work, we need to look again at the beginning and end of his ministry. The twin struggles in the wilderness at the beginning and Gethsemane at the end frame his ministry – and we can be sure that there were many others between these two experiences of inner conflict. Jesus warns the disciples of severe trials to come. Their faith will be shaken. Is he really the Messiah?

> **'Father, if thou art willing, remove this cup from me. Nevertheless, not my will, but thine, be done.'**
> *(verse 42)*

How easy – how tempting – it would have been for Jesus to take the comfortable way out! Give the Romans – the power of the time – what they wanted and just go away. Which would mean denying who he was, going into hiding and starting a political movement against the Roman Empire. Nevertheless . . . thy will be done. God comes to us, and leaves us, in vulnerability. This pattern of Christian behaviour that we have been given calls us to be open to our lives and the experience of life, day by day, hour by hour.

† *Lord, may we be given the grace to pray with our whole hearts. 'Nevertheless...'*

Food for the journey

Jesus' meeting with the Samaritan woman at the well in John 4 sums up this week's theme. As he leads her to faith, he speaks of nourishment for the soul:

> **'My food is to do the will of him who sent me, and to accomplish his work.'**
>
> *(John 4, verse 34)*

Food occurs in the earlier encounter of Jesus with Satan in the wilderness. Resisting Satan's temptation to turn stones into bread, Jesus replies: 'Man shall not live by bread alone, but by every word that proceeds from the mouth of God' (*Matthew 4:4*). All that Jesus is, does and says is rooted in his communication with the Father. We can only give what we have been given. Yet our life with God does not end there. As we grow closer to God, doing his will and work, we carry back into the world more and more of what we have received, as gifts to others. God calls us here, now, moment by moment, drawing us by his love. All we have is the present. The past is gone, the future is in God's hands. When we listen faithfully to God's voice and watch for his way, there will be no room left for the worry or anxiety about 'the day of the Lord' described in 1 Thesssalonians 5. We are equipped for the journey. It is enough.

† O God, our strength and our hope, free us from all that keeps us from loving you with our whole heart, mind and soul.

1 Passion

Notes by Philip G O'B Robinson
based on the New Revised Standard Version

Philip Robinson is a former President of the
Jamaica District of the Methodist Church in the
Caribbean and the Americas (MCCA) and of the Jamaica Council of
Churches. He is also a former Chairman of the National Religious
Media Commission. He is Methodist Chaplain to the University of
the West Indies (Mona Campus) and the University of Technology,
both in Jamaica. He is also chaplain to the Excelsior Education
Centre, the largest educational institution of the MCCA.

Introduction

The readings for this week represent the climax of Jesus'
ministry and the fulfilment of the purpose of his coming. In this
most dramatic portion of the gospel we can see a marvellous
unfolding of the revelation of the Jesus of history as the Christ
of the Christian faith. The readings touch the core of the gospel
message and some of the main pillars of Christianity.

Text for the week: Matthew 28: 5-7
*The angel said to the women, 'Do not be afraid; I know that
you are looking for Jesus who was crucified. He is not here, for
he has been raised, as he said.'*

For group discussion and personal thought

• What is the significance of 'the cry for deliverance' for the
  world of the twenty first century?
• In light of the Resurrection, what do you make of the
  numerous emerging theories that question this fact?

The cry for deliverance

'Hosanna to the Son of David!
Blessed is the one who comes in the name of the Lord!'
(part of verse 9)

Living under Roman oppression, the Jews believed that God was going to intervene and establish the kingdom promised through Abraham. The dramatic display of Jesus fulfilled the prophecy of Zechariah 9: 9-10. No wonder they felt that this had to be 'the man with the plan'. The greeting 'Hosanna' means 'Save now'. It was essentially the cry of a people for deliverance. However mistaken they might have been about how God was going to deliver them, they yearned for help in the midst of their suffering.

On a larger scale, the cry of the people was the cry of humanity. This was why Jesus had to come in the first place, to 'save his people from their sins' (*Matthew 1:21*) – the Jews, the Romans, the world of the twenty-first century. The world today echoes this cry as we face the visible expressions of oppression, abuse of power, corruption, untold suffering and the more subtle and wicked forces of evil. Sin had to be overcome before the total human situation could be changed for eternal good. So Jesus 'set his face to go to Jerusalem' (*Luke 9:51*).

† *Saviour and Lord, we remember before you the suffering peoples of the world (especially. . .). Amidst the echoes of their personal and collective cries, hear and deliver them as only you can, and give us all victorious hope. Amen.*

What is the value of your service?

'Why do you trouble the woman? She has performed a good service for me.'

(part of verse 10)

God sees the real value of our actions and the motive behind them. When the woman anointed Jesus with very costly perfume, the disciples saw extravagant waste. Jesus saw in it preparation for his burial, commended the act and valued it as 'a good service'. In Genesis 4, God saw the real value and the purer motive of Abel's sacrifice over that of Cain, his brother; 'through [which] he received approval as righteous, God himself giving approval to his gifts' (*Hebrews 11:4*).

The true value of our service is not so much its monetary value as its quality and the purity of the motive behind it. What is the real value of your service to Christ? What is the cost of your discipleship? How well will your motive for serving stand the scrutiny of the Lord? As Jesus predicted, this woman's worshipful and priceless service is remembered today and stands as an example for us all. As in her case, no price tag should be placed on our service, for no cost can be too high when we are serving the Lord. We cannot quantify the price that he has paid for our redemption.

† *Lord Jesus, we thank you that on the cross you paid the ultimate price for our redemption. May we, too, be prepared to serve with pure motives and without counting the cost. Amen.*

Thirty pieces of silver

'What will you give me if I betray him to you?' They paid him thirty pieces of silver.

(verse 15)

What drove Judas to betray the Lord? Was it inordinate love of money and because he was a thief (*John 12:6*)? Was he hoping to force Jesus to assert his messianic authority and set up an earthly kingdom? Luke 22:3 tells us that Judas came under the influence of Satan, who took advantage of whatever flaws there might have been in his character, be it greed, selfishness, ambition or something else.

We can learn from the story of Judas that we must watch our motives for doing things. It is possible to attend church and even work in the church and yet not be loyal to Christ, who is Lord of the church, especially when personal interests are at stake. It is possible to preach the kingdom of God and God's righteousness and not be committed to the ideals of that kingdom or seek that righteousness for our own selves. Judas' life-story should make us examine ourselves more carefully and more often lest we also betray Jesus for the proverbial thirty pieces of silver – or less. Paul's warning against naïve self-confidence, lest we fall (*1 Corinthians 10:12*) is timely advice for us as well.

† *Lord, make me aware of my sinful nature. Strengthen me, that I may loyally and joyfully seek and pursue your will and purpose for my life.*

Paid in full

'Take, eat; this is my body . . . This is my blood of
the covenant which is poured out for many for the
forgiveness of sins.'

(parts of verses 26 and 28)

The solemn declarations of Jesus, as he instituted what we
know today as the Lord's Supper, point to two distinctive ideas:
sacrifice and covenant.

Under a former covenant (agreement) that God, in an act
of grace, made with his people, he accepted a sacrifice, an
offering of the blood or flesh of an animal, as substitute
compensation for their sins, instead of having them pay with
their lives. This ritual offering was made repeatedly. In offering
his body for all humanity, Jesus, as God's sacrificial lamb, has
made full payment for the sins of all humanity, once for all.

In John 6:35,48 he refers to himself as 'the bread of life'. As
food satisfies physical hunger, so Christ satisfies, completely
and for ever, the deep spiritual hunger of humanity. It is this
that we remember in our observance of the Lord's Supper.

Under the Old Covenant the blood of animals was poured out
as satisfaction for people's sins, thereby obtaining forgiveness;
in the pouring out of Jesus' blood on the cross a New Covenant
is established, with better conditions (*Hebrews 9:13, 14*).

† *Lamb of God, thank you for the symbols of your undying
love and for the hope they hold for our salvation. May our
observance of them be a pledge of our allegiance to you.*

Mission accomplished

Then Jesus cried again with a loud voice and breathed his last.

(verse 50)

Matthew (*27:50*), Mark (*15:37*) and Luke (*23:46*) record that Jesus cried with a loud voice and breathed his last, but John (*19:30*) records that Jesus said, 'It is finished' (in Greek, *tetelestai*). The word indicates a goal attained, a tremendous task accomplished and a debt paid in full, once for all. It is like a runner winning the prize at the end of a gruelling race: pain is imprinted on his face but the spirit of triumphant joy is unmistakable; or the end of a hard-fought, costly and bloody battle for a just cause, which demanded every ounce of courage and determination, but the victory is incomparably sweet.

Jesus on the cross is a picture and a story of heart-rending physical and emotional suffering, but it ends with an irrepressible shout of triumph. Our Saviour had made full payment for our sins. It only remains for us to accept the offered grace by accepting him as Saviour and Lord of our lives. Philip Bliss (1838–1876) sums up the reaction of the human spirit to what God has done through Christ:

> Guilty, vile and helpless we;
> Spotless Son of God was He:
> Full atonement— can it be?
> Hallelujah! What a Saviour!

† *Jesus, Saviour, the salvation you offer is free but not cheap. Help us to appreciate the cost to you, to acknowledge your love for us, and to show our gratitude in our living.*

Truth undefeated

Pilate said to them, 'You have a guard of soldiers; go, make it as secure as you can.'

(Matthew 27, verse 65)

Truth attracts resentment and opposition because it exposes the true character of people and things. The truth of Jesus' life and ministry challenged the religious leaders and the status quo of his day. So they sought to eliminate him. Having got him out of the way, they endeavoured to keep him there, sealing into the tomb not just a body but all that Jesus represented. All they did, in fact, was make the truth of the resurrection watertight, because no one could have removed the body. Jesus stands alone in history as the only person who has made the claims he did and substantiated them by infallible proofs. The Resurrection is the acid test that proved beyond doubt that the Jesus of history is the Anointed One of God and it is the fundamental reason why he is the Christ of the Christian faith.

The angel in Matthew 28:5-6 not only told the women that Jesus had been raised; he invited them to see for themselves the evidence of the empty tomb. Jesus knew that, like Thomas (*John 20:19-29*), most of us want to see and touch for ourselves, so the message through the angel was 'He is going ahead of you to Galilee; there you will see him.'

† *Risen Lord, may we be renewed in the promise that, because you live, we who believe in you shall live also.*

2 Resurrection and the end

Notes by Emmanuel Borlabi Bortey
based on the New International Version

Emmanuel Borlabi Bortey is a minister of the Methodist Church in Ghana. For 23 years he served Asempa Publishers (the publishing house of the Christian Council of Ghana) and the International Bible Reading Association, Ghana office, first as an editor and later as General Manager. Since 2004 he has been the Superintendent Minister in charge of the Akosombo Circuit in the Eastern Region of Ghana.

Introduction

This week's readings begin with the evidence for the resurrection of Jesus and then focus our minds on various aspects of the end of the age, what theologians call eschatology: a study of the end times. What kind of life shall we lead at the end? What kind of reward shall we receive? What criteria will be used to determine who enters the kingdom of God? Clearly, Jesus does teach about an end-time, but his main concern is with what we do in the here and now. If we endeavour to live responsibly before God, we need never worry about our fate at the end of time.

Text for the week: Matthew 16:25
Whoever wants to save his life will lose it, but whoever loses his life for me will find it.

For group discussion and personal thought

• Do you believe our world is heading towards an end-time of final judgement, punishments and rewards? What makes you accept or reject this idea?

• How does Jesus' teaching about the end impact upon our lives in the present world?

The evidence of the empty tomb

Some people may have difficulty accepting the disciples' declaration that God raised Jesus from the dead. However, one aspect of the evidence seems conclusive: the body of Jesus was no longer in the tomb where he had been buried. So the chief priests had to help the military guard to find an explanation:

'You are to say, "His disciples came during the night and stole him away while we were asleep." If this report gets to the governor, we will satisfy him and keep you out of trouble.'

(verses 13 and 14)

Everyone is entitled to draw their own conclusions about the undisputable fact that the tomb of Jesus was empty. The speculation that Jesus' disciples stole his body, however, cannot stand any strict scrutiny. These people were declaring openly everywhere that their master had risen from the dead. Surely the authorities would not have allowed this to continue if they had evidence to the contrary? From a Christian perspective, nothing is more convincing than the assertion that 'Jesus is alive!' He has overcome death to assure us that death does not have the final say: one day our last enemy, death, will be eliminated and human beings will live for evermore. 'I believe in . . . the resurrection of the body and life everlasting.' Do you?

† *Lord, let us live in the now in the full assurance that this life is a preparation for the life that knows no ending. Amen.*

March

Who deserves to be at God's wedding feast?

How will people gain access to the kingdom of God? Today's parable suggests that God's kingdom is open to all who want to enter: the king's servants 'gathered all the people they could find, both good and bad' (verse 10).

> '[The king] noticed a man there who was not wearing wedding clothes. "Friend," he asked, "how did you get in here without wedding clothes?" The man was speechless. Then the king told the attendants, "Tie him hand and foot, and throw him outside, into the darkness."'
> *(part of verse 11, verse 12, and part of verse 13)*

If all are invited, 'both good and bad', how can some be thrown out? The guests had come off the streets, yet had to wear suitable wedding clothes and become worthy guests. So entry into God's kingdom is not really unconditional: *all* are invited, but they need to respond in an acceptable way. We must get rid of our filthy garments and put on appropriate clothes. It is not a question of one person deserving to be accepted and another not deserving. No one is qualified; but God accepts everyone who is willing to put off their old ways and put on the wedding clothes of righteousness and so become a worthy guest. Some risk rejection and missing out on God's wonderful feast. Don't be a drop-out!

† *Father, grant us grace to bear fruit worthy of repentance and to be found acceptable, at the last, into your kingdom. Amen.*

March

What will our resurrection life be like?

The Sadducees tried to argue that because some acts which God permits in this life cannot be replicated in an afterlife, therefore the notion of an after-life must be a fallacy. For instance, who, in the afterlife, will be the husband of a woman who is the widow of seven men?

> **Jesus replied, 'You are in error because you do not know the Scriptures or the power of God. At the resurrection people will neither marry nor be given in marriage; they will be like the angels in heaven. But about the resurrection of the dead – have you not read what God said to you, "I am the God of Abraham, the God of Isaac, and the God of Jacob"? He is not the God of the dead but of the living.'**

(verses 29-32)

Jesus' reply suggests that the resurrection life will not be an exact replica of life in this world. We cannot tell what it will be like, and this need not bother us. What concerned Jesus more was that the Bible speaks of Abraham, Isaac and Jacob as if they continue to live. So we too shall live beyond the grave. What we should be concerned about is the need to conduct ourselves in this world in a way that identifies us as the heirs of the faith of Abraham, Isaac and Jacob.

† *Lord, make us fit to be identified with your saints in your heavenly kingdom. Amen.*

The value of human life

[W]hoever wants to save his life will lose it, but whoever loses his life for me will find it. What good will it be for a man if he gains the whole world, yet forfeits his soul? Or what can a man give in exchange for his soul?

(verses 25-26)

True life does not consist in the things we possess. The more we place ourselves at the service of others, the more fulfilling we are likely to find our daily lives. Jesus gives an eternal dimension to all this: there is an end-time yet to come when people will be rewarded on the basis of how much they have given to others rather than how much they have accumulated for themselves. Indeed, we are likely to miss Jesus' ultimate reward for humankind if we concentrate on making ourselves happy in the here-and-now, especially if we do this at the expense of others.

Jesus' words could imply that any single human life is more valuable than all the riches of our world put together. No wonder Jesus was willing to lay down his life for the salvation of humankind. He calls us to do likewise: to accord the utmost dignity to every human person we encounter in this world.

† *Dear Lord Jesus, grant us grace to so conduct ourselves in the here and now that we may be found worthy of receiving an eternal commendation at your hands in the hereafter. Amen.*

Fairness and generosity

At the last, when the Judge of the world asks humankind to reckon for our lives in this world, there are likely to be some pleasant surprises. This is illustrated in Jesus' parable of the landowner and the hired labourers.

> '"Friend, I am not being unfair to you. Didn't you agree to work for a denarius? Take your pay and go. I want to give the man who was hired last the same as I give you. Don't I have the right to do what I want with my own money? Or are you envious because I am generous?"'
>
> *(verses 12-15)*

Only God knows who deserves to be rewarded for a faithful work done. However, in the end, will it even be a matter of merit? Is God going to reward human beings for faithfully discharging their responsibilities in his world because they *deserve* to be rewarded? The Judge of all the earth can never be unfair but, to our great delight, he is more than willing to be generous with the 'compensation packages' he has prepared for us. No one person has a better claim than anyone else to being rewarded by God. On judgement day we shall all be surprised (some pleasantly, some shockingly) at *who* receives *what*. For now, we all need to go about our duties conscientiously with a deep sense of humility.

† *Merciful God, we can only count on your generosity and fairness when we appear before your judgement throne at the end of our sojourn in this world. Amen.*

Called to serve

These two gospel readings both focus our attention on the need to concentrate on the work to be done. Jesus urged his disciples to stop wrangling about who will be the top officer (*Matthew 20:24-28*). What matters is to get the job done: to serve. What is the content of this service?

'Therefore go and make disciples of all nations, baptizing them in the name of the Father and of the Son and of the Holy Spirit, and teaching them to obey everything I have commanded you. And surely I will be with you always, to the very end of the age.'

(chapter 28, verses 19 and 20)

Jesus gave his disciples the task of going to 'make disciples'. As he had taught them, so they should also go and teach people to be obedient to Jesus. The Son of Man came for this purpose: to make his life impact positively on the lives of others, 'to give his life'. We are called to do likewise: to serve, to make our lives contribute positively to enhancing the quality of life in our world; to make our lives count for others; to be a means of rescuing others who might otherwise make a shipwreck of their lives.

† Lord, grant me grace to think more of what I can contribute to make life more meaningful for others than of what benefits I can derive from others serving me. Amen.

Children in the Bible

1   Children in the Old Testament

Notes by Elizabeth Bruce Whitehorn
based on the New International Version

Elizabeth Bruce Whitehorn grew up in
Edinburgh. After many years spent working as a
teacher and adult educator, she became Senior Editor for NCEC
(now Christian Education) and IBRA. She is a member of the
United Reformed Church and now lives in Cambridge. She has
four nieces and nine step-grandchildren.

March

Introduction

In the Old Testament, children are often mentioned as a sign
of God's blessing (see Psalm 128:3-6, for example). There are
not many stories of individual children, however. The biblical
writers tended not to be concerned with details that might seem
important to us, such as name or age.

News bulletins frequently feature stories of children as victims
(of poverty, ignorance, exploitation or abuse, for example), and
occasionally as heroes. Children are both extremely vulnerable and
remarkably resilient. Whether you have children of your own or
not, you once were a child. This week's notes encourage you to
reflect prayerfully on some of your own childhood experiences and
to use them as a stimulus to pray for children today – whether in
your family or church, in your neighbourhood or in the news.

Text for the week: 1 Samuel 3:10
'Speak, for your servant is listening.'

For group discussion and personal thought

• What new insights do you gain from reflecting on your own
  childhood experiences?
• Do you know any children who are going through similar
  experiences, What can you do to support them?

91

Belonging

Most children cause their parents heartache as well as joy; no doubt many children would say the same of their parents! Abraham's family was no exception. In his desperation to have a child, Abraham fathered Ishmael by Hagar, his wife's Egyptian maidservant. In today's passage we see Abraham torn apart by his love for Ishmael in the face of opposition from his wife, Sarah:

> **But God said to him, 'Do not be so distressed about the boy and your maidservant . . . it is through Isaac that your offspring will be reckoned. I will make the son of the maidservant into a nation also, because he is your offspring.'**
>
> *(part of verse 12, and verse 13)*

Whether Ishmael was a small child at the time of this incident, as the writer implies, or whether he was a teenager (compare Genesis 16:16 with 17:17), it must have been traumatic for him to be sent away from the family group where he belonged by the father who loved him so much. The UN Convention on the Rights of the Child describes the family as 'the fundamental group of society and the natural environment for the growth and well-being of all its members and particularly children'.

Prayerfully consider your own childhood experience of belonging.

† Welcoming God, we pray for children who have been forced from their homes and now live on the streets or in refugee camps. Turn our concern into action that will make a difference.

Trusting

This is not an easy passage to read. God seems to be asking Abraham to give up all his hopes for the future. Having already sent Ishmael away, he now prepares to kill Isaac, the son for whom he and Sarah had longed for so many years.

> **Then [Abraham] reached out his hand and took the knife to slay his son. But the angel of the LORD called out to him . . . 'Do not lay a hand on the boy.'**
> *(verse 10 and parts of verses 11-12)*

Now it is Isaac's turn to be shocked. Would he ever be able to trust his father again?

All too often today we hear of children who suffer at the hands of adults they have loved and/or respected. Some are killed but many are abused or exploited in one way or another. Children are turned into soldiers, slaves or sources of sexual gratification; all of these are robbed of their childhood. Will they ever be able to trust anyone again? What kind of adults and parents will they become?

As the Declaration of the Rights of the Child states, 'the child, by reason of his physical and mental immaturity, needs special safeguards and care, including appropriate legal protection, before as well as after birth'.

Prayerfully consider your own childhood experience of trusting adults.

† *Healing God, we pray for children who suffer as a result of adults' behaviour. Turn our concern into action that will make a difference.*

Chosen

In patriarchal societies it is expected that the eldest son will inherit. Yet in Genesis we read of the inheritance passing from Abraham to Isaac to Jacob, in each case the younger son. Now Jacob elevates two of his grandsons (the sons of Joseph, his favourite, though not eldest, son) to the same status as his sons. In their presence, he says to Joseph:

> '[Y]our two sons born to you in Egypt before I came to you here will be reckoned as mine; Ephraim and Manasseh will be mine, just as Reuben and Simeon are mine. Any children born to you after them will be yours; in the territory they inherit they will be reckoned under the names of their brothers.'

(verses 5-6)

What is more, when Jacob blessed the two boys, he went on to put Ephraim, the younger one, ahead of his older brother (verses 12-20). We are not told how the two boys reacted to this, but we can imagine it would not be easy for either of them, particularly for Manasseh who would have expected to take precedence. How would their uncles, Joseph's brothers, have reacted when they heard about Jacob's action?

Prayerfully consider your own childhood experience of being chosen unexpectedly or of not being chosen.

† *God of all, we pray for children who are trying to come to terms with others' choices and decisions. May they know they are special to you. Turn our concern into action that will make a difference.*

Responsible

We don't know how old Moses' sister was, but it is likely that her name was Miriam (see Exodus 15:20). Even allowing for the possibility that she had been carefully prepared by her parents, she still shows considerable presence of mind in a potentially dangerous situation:

Then [Moses'] sister asked Pharaoh's daughter, 'Shall I go and get one of the Hebrew women to nurse the baby for you?'

(verse 7)

Only a child could have succeeded in interceding for the baby Moses like this; an adult would presumably have risked punishment or death for disobeying the Pharaoh's order.

'You're not old enough' can be a natural adult response to a child's request. Yet all over the world there are children who take on responsibility beyond their years, either from choice or necessity. Some care for a sick or disabled parent. Some have to become the head of their family when their parents die of AIDS. Many have to do essential household chores, including fetching water, before going to school each day. Others have to do hard and unpleasant work such as sorting through mounds of rotting rubbish on the town's refuse tip instead of attending school, so that their family can have something to eat that day.

Prayerfully consider your own childhood experience of taking responsibility.

† *Caring God, we pray for children who take on responsibility beyond their years. May they themselves receive care and support day by day. Turn our concern into action that will make a difference.*

Promising

After many trials and tribulations, Ruth marries Boaz and gives birth to a son. At last Naomi has a grandson.

> **The women said to Naomi: 'Praise be to the LORD, who this day has not left you without a kinsman-redeemer. May he become famous throughout Israel! He will renew your life and sustain you in your old age.'**
>
> *(verse 14 and part of verse 15)*

What a weight of expectation was put on this new baby! The Bible does not tell us anything about Obed as a person. However, we do know that he was the father of Jesse, the father of David who became king of Judah, so it is likely that Obed turned out well.

It is natural to have hopes and dreams for one's children and grandchildren, but it is also important to give them freedom to make their own life choices if possible. Grandparents are often uniquely placed to support children as they wrestle with life's big questions. Time, a listening ear and an open mind can be exactly what children need when they are finding life difficult. Children who are accepted as they are, rather than for what they can become, find it easier to accept themselves.

Prayerfully consider your own childhood experience of trying to live up to others' expectations.

† *Accepting God, we pray for children who find it hard to live up to others' expectations. May they learn to accept themselves. Turn our concern into action that will make a difference.*

Prompted by God

'Speak, for your servant is listening.'
(part of 1 Samuel 3, verse 10)

In both passages, we read of God using a child to communicate with an adult. Young Samuel learns to recognise God's voice and has to pass on a difficult message to Eli, the priest who was responsible for training him. A servant girl, captured and taken away from home and family, sees her master's need and makes a helpful suggestion.

It can be difficult for adults to accept that children can have 'real' faith in God. Perhaps we put too much emphasis on intellectual understanding. Nurturing children's faith means more than teaching them to recite the Lord's Prayer or allowing them to hand out the hymn books or even take up the offering, important as these things are. Sometimes a child's question or insight can be the catalyst for an adult's search for faith. Do we in the church really believe that children are worth listening to? Do we allow them to speak and do we listen for God's voice speaking through them? Do we believe that God can speak to us and through us, whatever our age and experience?

Prayerfully consider your own childhood experience of God. How was it different from your current experience of God?

† Ever-present God, we pray for children who are learning to recognise your presence in their lives. May they be supported and nurtured on their faith journey. Turn our concern into action that will make a difference.

2   Children in the New Testament

Notes by Gillian Kingston
based on the New International Version

Gillian Kingston is a Methodist Local Preacher, living in Shinrone, Co. Offaly, Ireland. For many years, she has been involved in inter-church activity in Ireland, Britain and further afield. She is President of the Irish Council of Churches and co-Chair of the Irish Inter-Church Meeting and a member of the Council of the Glenstal Ecumenical Conference, based at Glenstal Abbey, Co. Limerick. She and Tom have three sons and a daughter.

Introduction

In our Sunday School room in Bandon there hung a picture of Jesus. He had flowing blonde hair and a beard and wore a white robe and blue cloak. His gentle blue eyes gazed pensively into the middle distance, while at his knee stood a group of children, about seven or eight years old, one dark, one Oriental, one Caucasian and maybe one or two others. Sentimental – yes; Victorian – probably; politically incorrect – undoubtedly; historically anachronistic – certainly. But it taught us very important things – Jesus loves us all, regardless of who we are or from where we come; Jesus loves the little ones, whoever those little ones are.

Text for the week: Luke 2:49
'Didn't you know I had to be in my Father's house?'

For group discussion and personal thought

- What new things have you seen in these readings?

- Can you remember what you thought about Jesus and 'faith things' when you were little? Have your beliefs changed greatly in the meantime? Be honest!

Where on earth is he now?

That gut-wrenching moment when you realise that your little darling is not with you and neither is s/he with your other half . . . Where is he? Has she gone off with someone? Is he safe? When and where exactly *did* either of you see her last? And the utter relief (and anger!) when s/he is found!

> **Son, why have you treated us like this? Your father and I have been anxiously searching for you.**
>
> *(part of verse 48)*

Mary asks the obvious question, but she does not get the obvious answer. No doubt she wanted an explanation, an apology, some recognition of her anguish and anxiety, but no. Her son responds in a way which seems heartless and arrogant; he responds, indeed, with his own questions: Why . . . ? Didn't you know . . . ? With enviable hindsight, of course, we understand, we would have known better – but would we?

Perhaps one of the lessons that gets lost because this is an all-too-familiar story is that we need to ask, expect, the right things of children. We become hurt, anxious, because we are unable to see things from their perspective. God has something in mind for each of them too and it may not be what we expect.

† Loving God, give us the grace to let our children be themselves and the sense to ask the right questions.

Take care . . . she's only small!

A little girl wanders into a room full of grown-ups, most of them men. Sucking her thumb pensively, she looks at them; one or two make to shoo her out, but one puts out his hand and gently pulls her to him. He smiles, she smiles and suddenly things are different. He speaks, they listen and suddenly they are all nodding and smiling – and she feels included.

> **Whoever welcomes this little child in my name welcomes me . . . he who is least among you all – he is the greatest.**
> *(part of verse 48)*

This story is about a little boy, but it could just as well have been about a little girl, couldn't it? The important thing is that the unexpected focus of attention is a child, a little one, the least of the least. The disciples have been arguing about rank and status. Maybe Jesus wasn't intended to hear them, but he is aware of what they are thinking. Sometimes words aren't enough, it takes a gesture, an object lesson – they can see him, standing there beside Jesus, next to him, recognised and loved. Now who is in the most important place? Who is next to the Master? That's what it is all about – being close to Jesus.

† Welcoming God, teach us that being close to you is true greatness.

Anything is worth a try!

When someone you love is critically ill, you'll do anything, even if it seems ridiculous; even if it's contrary to customs where you come from – who cares? If there's even a glimmer of hope, you'll go for it! And, anyway, this man had turned water into wine, so why not ask him? So what if he is of another faith and nation? It's my child who matters.

The man took Jesus at his word and departed. While he was still on the way, his servants met him with the news that his boy was living.

(part of verse 50, and verse 51)

Can you imagine the stir it must have caused? A Roman official coming all the way from Capernaum, making his way to Jesus to beg for healing for his son! Didn't he have better things to do with his time? It was only a child, after all. But here is a loving, caring father, coming on behalf of his son to the Son of a loving, caring Father. Love and faith overcome all obstacles – custom, culture, nationality, politics. And Jesus uses this approach to show those around him that his love *is* for all: the stranger, the child, the distant. None is beyond his compassionate touch, all are included.

† *Compassionate God, help us to reach out to those we usually dismiss as outsiders.*

What does that child want here?

You really can't have children getting in the way, wandering in and out when there are things to be organised, especially when there's a crisis. Anyway, what can they possibly have to offer?

> **Here is a boy with five small barley loaves and two small fish, but how far will they go among so many?**
>
> *(verse 9)*

Matthew, Mark and Luke report that the five loaves and two fishes were produced by the disciples when Jesus asked. Only John tells us about the little boy bringing his meal to Jesus. Perhaps the child just wanted the teacher to have something to eat, but Jesus takes the impossibly small and uses it to feed an enormous crowd – five thousand men, women and children. It is truly amazing what God is able to do if we give him what we can, even if it is small.

And another thing – notice that it is Andrew who brings the boy to Jesus. Clearly an approachable sort of person, he also brings Peter and, later, some Greeks to him. Are you, am I, a person a child would come to when he or she wants to help? Might we be stopping a little one from coming to Jesus? A worrying question.

† Giving God, enable us to give our all to you and to enable others to as well.

What? Them too?

When they are older, they'll understand what all this is about, but for the moment . . . well, it might be better if they stayed quiet and out of the way; stayed at home, even. Anyway, they might get frightened and that would put them off for life, wouldn't it?

> **'The promise is for you and for your children and for all who are far off – for all whom the Lord our God will call.'**
>
> *(verse 39)*

The disciples and their companions had waited so long for the promised Holy Spirit and now it had happened! And Peter, at the end of his rousing speech to the astonished crowd, says it is for children too! Now that's a surprise – are you quite sure?

Sometimes we suppose that the deeper things of the faith are not really suitable for children, they won't understand (well, do *you* understand everything?), they may be frightened (well, aren't *you* frightened sometimes by the magnitude of God's working?), they might ask too many questions (well, aren't there things *you* would like explained?), they might cry (well, don't *you* want to cry sometimes too?). Perhaps we are more concerned about the child in each of us than about the children around us in the church – worth a thought.

† *Father God, we are all your children, teach us to include each other.*

April

Families!

'Friends are the family we choose for ourselves'! That's what the fridge magnet says, and there is something to it, isn't there? 'Blood is thicker than water', they say, and there's something to that too. We call ourselves the family of God and that means our own families *are* special, even when that takes a bit of effort!

> **[D]o not exasperate your children. Instead, bring them up in the training and instruction of the Lord.**
>
> *(Ephesians 6, verse 4)*

> **[C]ontinue in what you have learned . . . because you know those from whom you have learned it.**
>
> *(2 Timothy 3, part of verse 14)*

Living in relationship is something we have to work at, whether it is with God, with a partner, or with children. It is not just fathers who get exasperated, mothers and children do too, believe me! But we have responsibilities to each other – of obedience and respect, tolerance and forgiveness. The best way of passing on the faith is in the atmosphere of love and trust thus created and through modelling in our lives the generosity and forgiveness of God. Paul points to this happening through three generations – Lois, Eunice and Timothy. It's not easy, but it is worth the effort, even if we sometimes fall short of the ideal.

† *Generous God, enable us to give ourselves to each other and so to point the way to you.*

The Hidden God

1 Hidden by pain, revealed by grace

Notes by Deborah Dunn
based on the New King James Version

Deborah Dunn is a licensed marital and family therapist in private practice near Raleigh, North Carolina, USA. She specialises in marital, family and community crisis and is also the author of a recent book for women about romance addiction entitled *Trapped in the Magic Mirror* (Cook Communications, 2006). You can visit her website at www.deborahdunn.com.

Introduction

We live in an earthly world that continually tells us that if we are doing all the right things then we will be happy and prosperous. But for Christians, the path to holiness is through suffering, and we have an enemy who desires to destroy our witness. Sometimes the journey becomes so difficult and lonely, we wonder if God has forsaken us, and if our trials are worth the pain we are experiencing.

However, just when we are about to lose hope, God reveals himself to us in the darkness. The treasures we discover when we find him there are often so wonderful we are compelled to rise, pick up our crosses, and follow him, wherever the path may lead.

Text for the week: Isaiah 45:3
I will give you the treasures of darkness and hidden riches of secret places.

For group discussion and personal thought

- Share with others those times when God revealed himself to you in your darkness and gave you 'hidden treasures in secret places'.

God will prevail

My husband of 37 years had a very serious heart attack a few weeks ago and almost died. Fortunately, he had skilled surgeons and so we are praising God for his life and restored health. However, the experience frightened me badly. For weeks now, I wake up every morning with an impending sense of dread and fear, in spite of my prayers. I daily cry out to the Lord for peace, rest and protection. But our trials have continued. Medical bills, car troubles and family crises have plagued us. It is easy to fall into self-pity or anger. It was tempting to blame God for abandoning me. But we know he will prevail.

> **Our fathers trusted in You;**
> **They trusted, and You delivered them.**
> *(verse 4)*

We just have to remember that we have an enemy, Satan, who is bitter because my husband is praising God for his life.

† Please Lord, help me to realise that because Jesus took my sin on the cross, you have a covenant with me that you will never forsake me, even when my days are dark and difficult. Help me to cling to the cross, while I wait for this season of trial to pass.

Turn, O Lord, save my life

In the Psalms, David cried out over and over for the Lord to save him. It is clear David was sick of his own weakness and failures. There is no doubt David knew he was his own worst enemy in this world, even when he was being chased by those who would slay him. How often do we think God is punishing us, or that Satan is attacking us, when in truth we know that in our shame and guilt we are simply sabotaging ourselves? How can we feel the love of God, when we have no love for ourselves?

> **O LORD, do not rebuke me in Your anger,**
> **Nor chasten me in Your hot displeasure.**
> **Have mercy on me, O LORD, for I am weak;**
> **O LORD, heal me, for my bones are troubled.**
>
> *(verses 1-2)*

It is difficult unless we stay in the Word, especially in the Psalms. It is there that we are told that God loves us in spite of the things we have done. In truth, it is our failures that bring us to our knees, and it is on our knees that we are closer to him.

† *Father, I know you love me in spite of my failures. Your tender mercies prove this over and over again. Thank you for loving the flawed, weak creatures that we are. Help us to love others in their weakness as well.*

April

Confession and healing

As a marriage and family therapist, I hear a lot of stories about the deep wounds of the spirit brought about by sinful choices. I see first-hand the consequences of divorce, infidelity, substance abuse and immorality. The destruction wrought by sin is enormous – the price we pay for our fleeting pleasures is way too high. But I chose this profession because I know about the power there is in Christ for healing. I am honoured to be in the presence of the Holy Spirit when I see marriages restored, betrayals forgiven and love renewed. Remember that we all have a counsellor. We can go to him, confess our sins, and be healed. We can approach his throne boldly, and he is always ready to open his arms.

> You are my hiding place;
> You shall preserve me from trouble;
> You shall surround me with songs of deliverance.
> *(verse 7)*

† *Mighty Counsellor, please forgive us for not being faithful to confess our sins to you so that you can heal our hearts, restore our relationships, and set us free.*

God sees our trouble

Does God really see our trouble? And if he does, why doesn't he do something about it? That is the question everyone asks at some point in their life, especially when we see children being hurt, good people suffering from terminal illness, and what seems to be such unnecessary pain and suffering in the world. It is easy to believe that God is some remote being who turns a blind eye to the troubles of his children, while letting the wicked rule the earth.

In my lifetime I've seen many undeserving people flourish, while good servants of the Lord struggle just to survive. But one of the pleasures of growing old is watching many situations come around full circle. Eventually it all comes out right, even if it takes a while. The wicked self-destruct, while the good die in peace with the assurance of heaven in their hearts. This is the promise of salvation, and the wonderful message of the gospel.

> **But You have seen, for You observe trouble and grief,**
> **To repay it by Your hand.**
> **The helpless commits himself to You;**
> **You are the helper of the fatherless.**
>
> *(verse 14)*

† *Father, help us not to fall prey to discouragement when we see the wicked enjoying life, while your servants suffer.*

How long must I bear pain in my soul?

For three very long, agonising years we never saw and rarely heard from our beautiful, very gifted and beloved daughter. I remember taking a walk in the woods, sobbing my heart out and begging the Lord to send my daughter back home. But I heard nothing in return except a few birds singing and the wind whispering in the trees.

> **How long shall I take counsel in my soul.**
> **Having sorrow in my heart daily?**
> *(part of verse 2)*

But, thankfully, he eventually did bring his child back home and we are restored in our relationship now. She is happily married and expecting a baby, and we are thrilled to be grandparents. Looking back, I realise now that the long three years forced me to find creative ways such as writing to deal with all the energy created by my anger and pain. That writing led to the publication of a book that is helping thousands of women everywhere, and has changed my life for ever. My winter of suffering has harvested great fruit which tastes very, very sweet.

† *Father, I pray for those waiting for a sweet release from suffering: the wives of soldiers, the parents of missing children, those longing for the return of prodigals, and those who have lost hope during the long, dark night of their souls. Use this time to plant seeds for a great harvest and sweet fruit in the spring.*

Darkness is as light to the Lord

Writing my first book, finding a publisher and being discovered by readers took about five years in all. But the process helped to produce a better book. Our lives are like this. Jesus, the Great Author, edits what we write, changes our sad endings, and turns our mediocre stories into great epic tales of grand adventure. As Psalm 27 says, it is worth waiting for him.

And waiting can turn darkness into light. Sometimes the full moon is so big, white and bright in the Carolinas that you can walk around in the middle of the night as if it were daytime. The shadows cast by trees and buildings are very dark indeed, but somehow this only accentuates the beauty of the light. The shadows of our lives form a backdrop for Christ to illuminate himself in us as well. Without the dark nights in our lives, our Lord would not be seen for who he is. He would not be revealed to the world as the one who can lead us into the dawn of a new morning.

The darkness and the light are both alike to You.
(Psalm 139, part of verse 12)

† *Father, speak to us in the darkness. Give us eyes to see in the dark – eyes to see all the beauty that surrounds us –- how you are illuminating the forest, even when we cannot see beyond the circles of our own tiny fires.*

2 Hidden by enmity, revealed by encouragement

Notes by Kate Hughes
based on the New Revised Standard Version

For Kate's biography, see p.56.

Introduction

'Truly, you are a God who hides himself' says Isaiah (*Isaiah 45:15*), but he adds 'O God of Israel, the Saviour.' God seeming to hide himself does not interfere with his role as our Saviour, the one in whom we can always put our trust – the ultimate encouragement in our spiritual journey. But we can hide ourselves from God by setting up a barrier of sin between us – meeting the violence of our enemies by a violent desire for revenge, for example – which puts us in danger of sharing the fate of the wicked. In this week's readings we explore the psalmist's progression from noisy demands for vengeance to a peaceful sharing of God's silence and finding his only hope in him.

Text for the week: Psalm 62:5
For God alone my soul waits in silence, for my hope is from him.

For group discussion and personal thought

• In what ways do our sins create a barrier between ourselves and God, so that he seems hidden from us?

• Have you experienced sharing God's silence? What was it like?

April

Forsaken among the dead

To the Israelites, death was the end, the moment when the human person was finally cut off from God. To be at odds with God, either through circumstance or through sin, was like being plunged into Sheol, the place of the dead. God seemed so distant, withdrawn behind the curtain of his anger. And not just God – the psalmist feels forsaken by his friends as well, isolated in utter aloneness.

> **Your wrath lies heavy upon me,**
> **And you overwhelm me with all your waves.**
> *(verse 7)*

Most if not all of us have experienced this withdrawal of God in the face of our sin, or at times when life is being difficult. When my youngest nephew was small, he used to have tantrums when he thought life – or Aunt Kate – was being unfair to him, or he had to face up to his own naughtiness. It was useless trying to talk to him when he was so angry or upset. I simply had to stand by, let the tantrum take its course, and then sit down with him and talk things through. Perhaps this is why God seems to be leaving the psalmist alone – the time for talking has not yet come, and until he is calmer about the situation and more willing to hear God, there is nothing that God can do or say. So he seems to be hidden.

† *Father, help us to remember that when you seem hidden in our time of need, you may simply be waiting for the right moment to speak or intervene.*

Desire for justice or lust for vengeance?

Isaiah wisely said that 'your iniquities have been barriers between you and your God. And your sins have hidden his face from you' (*Isaiah 59:2*). Sometimes God hides himself from us, but often we exclude him by our sin.

> **O God, break the teeth in their mouths;**
> **Tear out the fangs of the young lions, O LORD!**
> *(verse 6)*

No doubt the psalmist would like to feel that he is expressing righteous indignation and a desire for justice. But in truth he is so busy demanding vengeance on those he considers 'the wicked' that he has pushed God out of the situation. God has not hidden himself – he has been shut out. Human anger alone achieves nothing; only by aligning ourselves with God's anger will we be able to change what is wrong. When we recognise injustice, we do not need to prompt God to act by wasting our energy shouting; he recognises it more quickly than we do. We need to make ourselves available to him, to be used as his instruments for change when the time is right.

† *Lord, help us to recognise injustice and wrong when we see it, and to be willing to become part of your plan for dealing with it.*

Do not drag me away with the wicked

The temptation when we meet wickedness with anger and
the desire for vengeance is that we commit the very sins we
complain about in others, and are therefore in danger of
sharing their fate. The fifteenth-century writer Machiavelli first
expounded the principle that 'The end justifies the means' in
his book *The Prince*. But this is not a Christian principle; we
cannot overcome evil by evil means. This may mean that we
have to be patient and not rush in with instant action; the
alternative is to risk sharing the fate of the wicked. Our only
way forward, our only hope, is to let ourselves be carried by
God.

> **O save your people, and bless your heritage;**
> **be their shepherd and carry them forever.**
>
> *(verse 9)*

When God seems hidden, we must believe that he is still
holding us. If a butterfly comes through the open window and
seems unable to find its way out, I gently cup it in my hands,
carry it to the window and let it free. While it is cupped in my
hands, it must seem to the butterfly as if the world has gone
dark and it is trapped; in fact it is held safe and on its way to
freedom. So are we carried by God.

† *Lord, help us to recognise that in our times of darkness we
are held safely in your hands and on our way to release.*

My times are in your hand

Our readings this week are a progression. No longer is the psalmist getting so angry that he shuts God out, or ends up committing the very sins for which he was demanding vengeance. Psalm 31 is a psalm of trust, a handing over to God of all that disturbs and hurts the psalmist.

> **Let your face shine upon your servant;**
> **Save me in your steadfast love.**
>
> *(verse 16)*

It no longer matters that God seems hidden. In the words of another psalm, 'the darkness is not dark to you; the night is as bright as the day, for darkness is as light to you' (*Psalm 139:1*). Because we cannot see God, because he seems to be shrouded in darkness, does not mean that he is not there. He can work in darkness just as effectively as in the light.

Thirty years ago, when I first went to Africa, a friend who paints icons made me a little picture of a round, dark circle like a womb, with a flower sprouting from the top – a prayer for me to blossom in Africa after a time of great darkness. Ever since, whenever I move house, my little icon is the first thing I put on my new walls, to remind me that the darkness of God is where we grow the most.

† *Lord, help me to rest peacefully in your darkness, like a baby in the womb or a seed in the earth, waiting to emerge into your light.*

This I know, that God is for me

In God, whose word I praise,
In God I trust; I am not afraid;
What can flesh do to me?
(verse 4)

The comparative serenity of this psalm contrasts vividly with the almost incoherent rage and ranting of Tuesday's Psalm 58. The psalmist's troubles have not gone away; he still recognises injustice and is ill-treated by enemies. But he also recognises that human beings have no ultimate power over him, because God is greater. If retribution is required, God will see to it. Rescue by God is not something for the future, something that will happen one day. He has already delivered the psalmist's soul from death and his feet from falling (*verse 13*); his response is obedience and thankfulness (*verse 12*) and a commitment to continue walking in the light (*verse 13*). Yet God remains hidden, in the sense that we human beings can never fully understand the extent of his power, the depth of his love, the Godness of God. We have to take him on trust, believing that he is for me; perhaps an awed silence is the only adequate response to this incredible fact.

† *Lord, many people ask, when trouble and suffering strike, 'Why me?' I ask 'Why me?' when I am able to believe and trust in you and know you are for me, when so many people in the world are ignorant of you. There is no answer to my question except that you are love. Thank you.*

April

Silent with God

**For God alone my soul waits in silence,
for my hope is from him.**

(Psalm 62, verse 5)

We started this week with God seeming to withdraw into aloof silence while the psalmist accused, shouted and demanded vengeance. We end the week with the psalmist not only accepting that God's hiddenness does not mean that God is not active on his behalf, but actually joining God in his silence.

St Therese of Lisieux, that tough young nineteenth-century Carmelite nun, said something on the lines of 'We are not called to overcome temptation but to undergo it.' Often what God asks of us in our times of testing is not heroic struggle to overcome, but peaceful endurance; a patient, quiet waiting in the darkness, knowing that God is keeping us company even if we cannot see or hear him, knowing that he is working on our behalf. Paul says that God 'will not let you be tested beyond your strength, but with the testing he will also provide the way out so that you may be able to endure it' (*1 Corinthians 10:13*). This is the basis of our hope.

God's silence is not necessarily the silence of not being there. Often it is the silence between old friends, or a long-married couple, who trust each other and do not need words.

† O God, our gracious silence, help us to discover the peace and joy of resting safely in your love, where words are not needed.

The Hidden God

3 Hidden by mystery, revealed by action

Notes by David Huggett
based on the New Revised Standard Version

David Huggett is a Baptist minister. After pastoral experience in the north of England and London, he worked with the Bible Society, the Leprosy Mission and in adult Christian education. Now retired, he lives in Somerset and remains involved in preaching, writing and local church life.

April

Introduction

Modern technology can distance us from other people. I hate those automatic telephone systems when a recorded voice instructs me to press first one button, then another, and another. If I have a problem or a query I prefer to talk to a person – preferably face to face. Communication with God also needs to be personal, although, as C S Lewis remarks in his book *A Grief Observed*, written after his wife's death, just at those moments in life when we most need God he is silent, and 'the longer you wait, the more emphatic the silence'. This week's readings look at some of those mysterious moments in our experience but may also give us clues about the way God acts in and through them.

Text for the week: Psalm 66:12
We went through fire and through water; yet you have brought us out to a spacious place.

For group discussion and personal thought

• How would you describe your experience of becoming a Christian? How much of that experience is unique to you?

• What advice would you give to someone struggling with a 'significant pause' in their life? Would any of your experiences be of help to them?

Suffering in silence

Job's suffering was extreme – the loss of his wife, family, possessions, even his health. But he still had four friends who tried to explain why he suffered. Their logic was flawless. God is just, so must punish sin. Job is suffering, therefore he must have sinned. Job cannot accept that. Not only does he plead innocence, but he makes the valid point that if God really *is* just, he ought to allow Job to state his case.

At the end of the book it becomes clear that God has been listening all the time. He gives Job the opportunity to speak, although he gives no clear answer to Job's questioning, any more than Jesus got an answer to his anguished cry, 'My God, my God, why have you forsaken me?' (*Matthew 27:46*) But while he waits for that answer – not even sure that it will come – Job shows great maturity of faith. In spite of the mystery of God's silence Job reminds himself that God is at work.

[He] does great things beyond understanding, and marvellous things without number.

(verse 10)

To that the Christian can add, in the light of Christ's suffering for us, the knowledge that God loves us.

† God of love, help me to be a true friend to those who suffer. Prevent me from giving glib answers to their real questions.

April

April

When the silence is broken

During the years Zechariah had been faithfully carrying out his priestly duties, nothing much happened. The last prophet had preached nearly 500 years earlier, and God seemed silent. Maybe Zechariah had learned not to expect anything else. Then it all changed. Zechariah was chosen by lot to enter the Holy Place to offer incense – a privilege few priests ever enjoyed. While there he had this amazing experience. Bearing in mind that Zechariah did not know the end of the story, as we do, it is little wonder that

he was terrified; and fear overwhelmed him.
(part of verse 12)

When God suddenly and unexpectedly comes into a person's life it can be a frightening experience. It challenges us. It upsets the status quo. Maybe Zechariah asked questions like, 'Why me?' It must have seemed unreal. Was he dreaming the whole experience? Was it just wishful thinking? Was it simply part of an exciting spiritual high that he was enjoying on this very special day? Then the irony – God had been silent, and now his servant was literally dumbfounded.

† *God of mercy, help me to hear your voice even when I do not expect it, and when you are silent help me to remain faithful in my service for you.*

An incomplete answer

It's another red-letter day for the elderly priest – he can speak again. That in itself seems to be a parable. God's silence had now been broken, not just for Zechariah and Elizabeth, but for all prepared to listen. Everything about this baby was deeply attractive to the devout Jews of his day. The remarkable birth to elderly parents would remind them of Abraham and Sarah (*Genesis 18*), and Elkanah and Hannah (*1 Samuel 1*). His mysterious childhood spent in the desert (*verse 80*) and dramatic lifestyle would confirm that here was someone special. Little wonder the proud father burst out in a song of praise. Yet, although he understood something of the significance of his baby son, the revelation he received was only partial:

> **And you, child, will be called the prophet of the Most High; for you will go before the Lord to prepare his ways.**
> *(verse 76)*

Much more was to come. God does not hide things from us for the fun of keeping us in the dark. He revealed enough to enable Zechariah to play his part in the unfolding drama. God was about to speak in the greatest event of all – the birth of Jesus.

† *God of wisdom, you show me enough to enable me to take the next step. Help me to have the courage to take that step, and at the same time to be ready and waiting for your further unfolding purposes.*

Life's mysterious pauses

I like the humour in this scene – the disciples standing there open-mouthed, and two men in white politely asking,

> **'Men of Galilee, why do you stand looking up toward heaven?'**
>
> *(part of verse 11)*

The disciples thought everything had been resolved. They had lost him once and then found him again. They had listened with delight to his further teaching about his kingdom (*verse 3*). Then suddenly he's gone. They are left in a kind of limbo – what Karl Barth described as a 'significant pause'.

Such pauses are not uncommon in the Christian's life, and they are not always easy to handle. Perhaps a strained relationship, a change of career, or some other critical point in life demands a careful decision. And just at that moment God seems to go away and leave us to it with no other instruction than 'Wait' (*Luke 24:49*). So Ascension Day is important in the Christian calendar because it reminds us that the Christ who was crucified is now risen and enthroned. Whatever our circumstances may seem to say to the contrary, *he* is in control. That gives us the proper perspective on our 'significant pauses'.

† *God of glory, forgive us that we become so engrossed with our immediate and temporary needs that we fail to see your eternal glory. Help us to get things in perspective.*

When we are defeated

Patients suffering from loss of memory often have difficulty in understanding who they are. Memory is so important that our very identity as individuals is bound up with it. Maybe that is why, as we get older, we become so frustrated when we forget someone's name, or lose the thread of a conversation.

The early Christians developed the calendar we still use, especially the regular celebration of the Eucharist, to help us remember who we are and where we have come from, as well as reminding us of the great facts of our faith. The Psalmist, too, understood how memory can help us deal with the demands of our spiritual life. He had some bad memories of defeat when God seemed very far away (*verses 10-12a*). He vividly describes their enslavement (*verse 11*) and how, when defeated in battle, the enemy charioteers literally mowed them down (*verse 12a*). But he does not dwell on defeat. He majors on the memory of God's deliverance:

**we went through fire and through water;
yet you brought us out to a spacious place.**
(part of verse 12)

† *God of faithfulness, thank you for the gift of memory.
Remind me of the wonderful things you have done for me.
Help me to encourage those whose bad memories blight their
lives.*

Encountering mysteries

Nicodemus was a man of learning, which may have been why he found it difficult to cope with things he could not understand, like Jesus' words about being born 'from above' (*John 3, verse 3*). Mystery can make us feel uncomfortable. The security of knowledge is important, but so is grappling with things that are hard to understand. Christianity is not about getting everything right, or understanding it all: it is about putting our trust in the person of Jesus and learning bit by bit to relate to him:

that whoever believes in him may have eternal life.
(John 3, verse 15)

A first reading of Saul's dramatic conversion may seem to imply that it was sudden. Often it has been used as a pattern of what becoming a Christian should always be like. Some Christians feel inadequate or even guilty if they have not had such a 'Damascus Road' experience. But a more careful reading of Paul's life shows that God had been dealing with him for a long time. Even the events of Acts 9 took place over several days. God deals with each of us as individuals. Each is unique, so our experience of God will differ from Saul's or anyone else's. But like Saul we need to be open to God's initiative, however it comes.

† *God of insight, choosing unlikely people as your followers, thank you for intervening in my life. Help me always to see your light and to hear your voice.*

May

125

The Hidden God

4   You will see . . .

Notes by Jember Teferra
based on the New International Version

Jember Teferra and her team attempt to alleviate
poverty in some of the worst slums in Addis
Ababa, Ethiopia, focusing their ministry on the poorest of the
poor whom she is called to serve. Her ministry is known as 'The
Integrated Holistic Approach Urban Development Project'.

Introduction

Our readings this week show God reaching out to a patriarch
(Jacob), a prophet (Elisha), and an ordinary man (Nathanael),
despite their shortcomings as human beings. We also learn
the greatness of God: his supremacy, his rightful place above
everything in heaven or in earth; he suffered like any human being,
but overcame all difficulties to continue to rule the entire universe
– he, being Alpha and Omega, will rule for ever . . . infinitely.

Text for the week: Revelation 1:8
*'I am the Alpha and the Omega,' says the Lord God, 'who is,
and who was, and who is to come, the Almighty.'*

For group discussion and personal thought

- Compare and contrast how God reached out to Jacob the
  Patriarch, Elisha the Prophet and Nathanael an ordinary man.

- If God calls us in different ways, how do we recognise his
  call, and how do we respond?

- What difficulties have you encountered in answering your
  call to follow Jesus?

The gate of heaven

'I will not leave you until I have done what I promised you.'
(part of verse 15)

I am neither a patriarch like Jacob nor a prophet, but I can understand God's call, encouragement and instructions and how he spoke in a dream to Jacob. At the age of 10, during the last week of Lent, which in the Ethiopian Orthodox Church we call 'Hemamat' (the painful week for Jesus), our school chaplain gave us a most moving scripture lesson and afterwards I had a very vivid dream clearly instructing me to minister to the poor. Of course, it was the joke of the school for many weeks when the chaplain encouraged me to tell my story in front of some 1000 students during morning devotion.

I am not a great dreamer, but I had another vivid dream at the age of 38, immediately after my release from political imprisonment – this time calling me to work in the slums. I look upon Jacob as a role model, because he accepted his dream and his responsibility without question. I am still mystified that an insignificant child and ex-political prisoner could get a clear call and instructions to do what the Good Lord had assigned to her. But oh, it is possible: he calls and enables – it is a package deal.

† Dear Lord, you call people of different races and backgrounds, individuals who are regarded as insignificant. Help all those who find it difficult to accept your challenge to go ahead and obey – increase our faith!

2 Kings 2:9-14

God honours good intentions

Elisha reminds me a bit of the Apostle Peter: both of them so badly wanted to be faithful and special, and yet were weak and lacked confidence. I see this typical human shortcoming both in many Christian colleagues and in myself – the good intention is there, but only God can build up the courage and confidence.

> **'Where now is the LORD, the God of Elisha?'**
> *(part of verse 14)*

Elisha wanted Elijah to remain with him and did not really believe that God had allowed Elijah's spirit to pass to him. Despite Elisha's lack of confidence, others trusted in him and were watching him closely. At last, he got his proof – when he struck the River Jordan with Elijah's cloak, the waters divided so that he could cross over. It always surprises me how patient God is with our doubt and fears. Like many others, I have repeatedly seen incredible miracles both in my personal life and my ministry, and yet, when faced with today's difficulties, I forget what happened yesterday. I have seen God doing the impossible, so why can't he do it again today? Of course he will, and continues to do so without fail. Fortunately, he forgives us when we are like 'doubting Thomas'!

† *My Father, my Lord, my King – King of Kings and God of the impossible – help me to remember each time I am faced with a new challenge that you can also deal with every new difficulty – nothing is impossible to you!*

Greater than we can know

'You shall see greater things than that.'
(part of verse 50)

When I was a political prisoner I was sent *Born Again*, a book written by Charles Colson, Nixon's 'hatchet man' in the Watergate scandal. Despite his vivid experience of being born again and the complete change in his political views and values, I still condemned him. In prison, his whole personal life went wrong. His son was in trouble with the law, requiring his presence. His two Christian mentors, American senators, offered to bail him out and, so strong had his faith grown, Colson was sure that God would use this difficult time to have him released. From being so judgemental, I ended up being influenced by Charles Colson's release. I had to ask God's forgiveness for my negative picture of him, because I realised that I lacked faith about my own release.

I began to push my brother, who was helping my mother care for my children, to appeal for my release because my sister, who had been supporting me, had died and they were having difficulty making ends meet. Three months after the appeal God brought about the release of myself and six fellow-prisoners. In 1983 I was able to tell this to Mr Colson personally. Nathanael did not believe that anything good could come from Nazareth – but ended up following Jesus, the Israelite Son of God.

† *Jesus, help us to acknowledge that you are bigger than our limited knowledge of you, so that we may recognise you as the Son of God, King of Kings and Lord of Lords.*

129

Look to Jesus

Consider him who endured such opposition from sinful men, so that you will not grow weary and lose heart.

(verse 3)

The urban ministry to which God has called me is a real challenge. So many obstacles hinder our work. How often I have said, 'If God had not called me to work with the poor, I would have given up long ago.' His package deal enables us not only to fundraise successfully, but also to have thick skins and thick skulls! The call to follow Jesus does not guarantee a smooth ride: Jesus had three years of fierce opposition, hindrances and hardship – why shouldn't his followers experience the same?

**God has not promised,
Skies always blue,
Flower-strewn pathways
All our lives thro' . . .**

**God has not promised
We shall not know
Toil and temptation,
Trouble and woe;
He has not told us
We shall not bear
Many a burden,
Many a care.**

**But God has promised
Strength for the day
Rest for the laborer
Light for the way,
Grace for the trials,
Help from above,
Unfailing sympathy
Undying love.**

Annie Johnson Flint

These verses were a comfort to me in prison and still are today; may they comfort you also, especially if you have to deal with difficulties.

† Lord Jesus, help all those who follow you not to give up when given a ministry and facing difficulty. Help us to keep looking up to you for courage and persistence.

The cost of following a persecuted Lord

Suffering is not a matter of reward or punishment. It is a privilege that rightly understood enables us to learn, to be strengthened, to grow, to deepen our faith by depending on God to give us victory. Sometimes we suffer because of our mistakes; if we follow him he will teach us a lesson, forgive us in his mercy and ultimately help us to grow stronger.

> **Dear friends, do not be surprised at the painful trial you are suffering, as though something strange were happening to you.**
>
> *(verse 12)*

When I was imprisoned with my husband throughout the Marxist revolution, I frequently asked, 'Why me?' When, after a short period of happiness, I lost my husband and son on the same day, I again asked 'Why me?' and 'Where is God?' Soon after my bereavement I myself nearly died.

Even now, my ministry encounters many obstacles and problems, but I have stopped asking 'Why me?' Since I chose, with the help of the Holy Spirit, to follow Jesus he has given me special grace which is 'sufficient', and enabled me to grow spiritually. I have much to be thankful for: my remaining children are settled and I have two grandchildren. God has also blessed our work with a dedicated team and sufficient funds. Praise God!

† *Our mighty God, only you know why you allow suffering, and only you can enable us to overcome suffering while we wait to see you in full glory.*

The Almighty

In these two readings, God reveals himself as the Almighty, the Controller of the world he has created. When we were children we used to watch the famous film *Tarzan*, in which the hero beats all his enemies. But I also knew that God was bigger and stronger – though the infinite was difficult to imagine; for those who know him it is still mind-boggling! But what a privilege to have such a supreme being to love, worship, know and follow till we meet him face to face. We are so often let down and disappointed by leaders, politicians and even role models; it is good to know that there is one great and mighty God who is always there, never changes and never lets us down.

When I was a political prisoner, and during the 'Red Terror' when thousands who were seen as anti-revolutionary were killed in the city streets, we all expected to be executed; if I was never to see my family again, I was so comforted by the thought that I would see the Good Lord face to face. What a joy – and how sad for those who do not know and follow him and have nothing to look forward to.

'I am the Alpha and the Omega,' says the Lord God, 'who is, and who was, and who is to come, the Almighty.'

(verse 8)

† *Lord, thank you for the privilege of knowing you. When things go wrong, always remind us that you are the beginning and the end.*

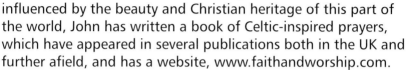

1 Making all things new

Notes by John Birch
based on the New International Version

John is a Methodist lay preacher and worship leader living in south-west Wales. Very much influenced by the beauty and Christian heritage of this part of the world, John has written a book of Celtic-inspired prayers, which have appeared in several publications both in the UK and further afield, and has a website, www.faithandworship.com.

May

Introduction

As we approach Trinity Sunday, it is appropriate to remind ourselves of God's interaction with his creation and people throughout history. God breathes life into this world and individuals through his Spirit, bringing hope and purpose to a world that is sadly lacking in both. God's love, demonstrated through Jesus Christ, restores lives that are broken and empowers hearts that are open.

Text for the week: Titus 3: 5-7
He saved us through the washing of rebirth and renewal by the Holy Spirit, whom he poured out on us generously through Jesus Christ our Saviour, so that, having been justified by his grace, we might become heirs having the hope of eternal life.

For group discussion and personal thought

Do you see evidence of God's Spirit working
• in your own lives?
• in your church and fellowship?

A new beginning

In the beginning God created the heavens and the earth.
(verse 1)

And unfortunately for many Christians it ends there: God's creativity is given full rein for the duration of the creation story, but once God has a day off and declares that he is well pleased, it is assumed that the process is complete! Yet the truth of God's creativity is that it is ongoing. The world in which we live is not a static lump of rock: it is constantly shifting and changing. Mountains are being raised up by huge underground forces, valleys carved by rivers, landscapes transformed by earthquake, wind and sea. Look more closely and the wind carries seeds to germinate and grow in distant places; and insects and wild animals spread out to colonise ground abandoned by man. This is God's creation in action!

But the real joy of God's creativity is that he has passed on this gift to us. God's creative Spirit is breathed into lives and manifests itself not in big bangs and the construction of universes, but in the beauty of art, song, fashion, poetry and all those areas of our lives that give us pleasure. We are made in the image of a beautiful God, and we carry within us the desire and the Spirit to make this world a more beautiful place.

† Lord, release within me the gift of creativity that I may make a difference to the world you have created for me.

A new purpose

> 'Therefore say: "This is what the Sovereign LORD says:
> I will gather you from the nations and bring you back
> from the countries where you have been scattered, and I
> will give you back the land of Israel again."
>
> *(verse 17)*

Restoration is at the heart of the Bible. God restores his
scattered people to the place where he would have them
be, despite the knowledge that they are a fickle bunch – one
minute worshipping him, another sacrificing to foreign gods.
God also restores individuals to the place where he would
have them be, in a right and loving relationship with him. We
don't deserve such love, but this is the very nature of God and
beyond our understanding.

In the UK there is a TV programme called *Restoration*, where
viewers get the chance to vote for worthy but neglected
buildings that sometimes are almost beyond repair. The
winning building is brought back to life and made useful again;
the others are presumably left to decay and die. Fortunately it is
not like that with God! His gracious love extends to all, and his
restoration is available to all, through his son Jesus Christ. But
restoration doesn't end there: such love demands a response,
of gratitude and service, and gives a new purpose to lives that
were lost.

† *Thank you, gracious God, that you considered me worthy of
restoration! Help me never to lose sight of my worth in your
eyes, and always to be grateful.*

May

A new strength

> He asked me, 'Son of man, can these bones live?' I said, 'O Sovereign LORD, you alone know.'
>
> *(verse 3)*

We all go through periods of spiritual dryness at some point in our lives. For some it comes at times of stress or bereavement, for others it is a crisis of faith when they find it difficult to believe, when hope fades. For most of us this barrenness lasts only a short while, but for others it can linger for many years and the struggle to reconnect with God can seem almost as daunting as breathing life into dry bones. 'Son of man, can these bones live?' asks God. 'You alone know. . .' is the sigh of one who understands that they can do nothing in their own strength. And it is at that point of total dependence upon God that the wind starts to blow, breathing life into the parched bones of a fragile faith.

> 'I will bring you back . . . I will put my Spirit in you and you will live.'
>
> *(part of verses 12 and 14)*

'And then you will know that I am God!' (*see verse 13*). When we are spiritually dry, there is nothing that we can do by our own efforts, but everything that God can and will do, if we will open ourselves to the wind of his Spirit.

† Sovereign Lord, let your wind blow and bring these dry bones to life, that I may find new strength in you.

A new power

> 'Even on my servants, both men and women,
> I will pour out my Spirit in those days.'
> *(verse 29)*

God is no respecter of position or power; in his eyes all are equally deserving of his love and blessing. Common sense should tell us this, because God created humankind in the image of himself, and gave stewardship of this world not to a select few who are better educated or of a particular skin colour, age or ethnic origin, but to Adam and Eve equally, as representatives of the human race. So it is within our churches and homes. These are the last places in which we should find prejudice of any kind, and whether it is the 90-year-old or the 20-year-old who stands up and proclaims God's word to us, we should give each their opportunity, and thank God for his blessing.

God's gifts are sadly underused in our churches today. Where, within the structures we impose, is time for healing, for prophesy, for the word of knowledge? Where, within our own spiritual lives, is the opportunity for God to do what he foretold through his prophet – to empower individuals?

It wasn't a promise, it was a certainty: 'I will', says the Lord, not 'I might'. But God's will depends on our willingness to accept his blessing.

† *Gracious Lord, grant me the willingness to open my heart to your Spirit, that I may be a blessing to others.*

May

A new family

For you did not receive a spirit that makes you a slave again to fear, but you received the Spirit of sonship. And by him we cry, 'Abba, Father.'

(verse 15)

God's spirit is all about freedom. We are set free from the fear of death, set free from the guilt of sin and set free to be the sons and daughters that God always intended us to be. When the temple curtain was torn in two at the point of Jesus' death, the barrier that kept humankind apart from God was also destroyed. God always wanted us as a part of his family. God grieves when we go our own way, as the prodigal's father grieved over the loss of his son, and rejoices when we turn around and walk back into his loving arms.

Is that how you feel about your relationship with God? Do you feel welcomed, wanted, part of God's family? If not, then maybe you have some turning back to do. If that is the case, then now is the time to act, not tomorrow. God's spirit frees us from slavery, and empowers us to make that choice, says Paul. Your heavenly Father wants to see his prodigals growing up in a way that delights him.

† *Help me, Lord, to breathe in the freedom that you have given me, to feel it in my soul, and know it in my heart.*

A new hope

He saved us through the washing of rebirth and renewal by the Holy Spirit . . . so that, having been justified by his grace, we might become heirs having the hope of eternal life.

(Titus 3, part of verse 5, and verse 7)

One great truth about Christianity is that everyone starts on a level playing field – we are just as much sinners and in need of God's saving grace as anyone else (good or bad). 'There but for the grace of God, go I,' said George Whitefield as he saw a man headed for the gallows.

When someone converted to Judaism, he was treated like a little child. It was as if he had been reborn and life had begun again. And that's a lovely picture of what happens when we accept Christ as Saviour – life begins again. We are reborn to a new life that has little to do with our previous existence because at its centre is not self, but Christ.

Set your hearts on things above, where Christ is seated at the right hand of God.

(Colossians 3, part of verse 1)

Furthermore, we are renewed day by day through the power of the Holy Spirit so that, reborn, we might live the life of those who have God's promise of eternal life.

† There but for your Grace, Lord, I would indeed be lost. Thank you for the change you have made to my life, and the hope that you have given.

The Renewing Spirit

2   The Spirit at work

Notes by Joy Pegg
based on the New International Version

Joy has been living and working with her
husband in the north of the Philippines since
2003, helping train young ethnic minority students in a
small Pentecostal bible school. There are also opportunities
to encourage rural pastors who work in the great mountain
ranges of this area.

Introduction

Unless we know the working of the Holy Spirit in our lives and
the churches we belong to, all will be in vain, for our text for
the week is quite adamant. This is no suggestion for how you
could polish your performance, or increase your power. This is
most definitely not a gem of 'self-help' wisdom. We will do well
to take heed of this great proclamation.

Text for the week: Zechariah 4:6
*'Not by might, nor by power, but by my Spirit,' says the LORD
Almighty.*

For group discussion and personal thought

• What do you have, either in time, talents or gifts, that you
  can share freely with others?

• Have you received freely of the Holy Spirit?

• What examples of real encouragement have you seen in the
  life of your church?

• What specific ways can you think of to bring glory to Jesus
  this week?

Awesome

On the Day of Pentecost the promised Holy Spirit had come upon the disciples as they were 'all together in one place' (*verse 1*). With a mighty rushing wind and with tongues of fire the Spirit came and they were 'all filled with the Holy Spirit and began to speak in other tongues as the Spirit enabled them' (*verse 4*). A crowd soon gathered and responded to Peter's preaching. Their numbers grew from 120 to over 3000 that day. How did this brand-new church cope?

Everyone was filled with awe, and many wonders and miraculous signs were done by the apostles. All the believers were together and had everything in common. Selling their possessions and goods, they gave to anyone as he had need . . . and ate together with glad and sincere hearts, praising God and enjoying the favour of all the people.

(verses 43-45, and part of verses 46 and 47)

The Spirit is working here in the infant church in Jerusalem. Given to them as a gift, the people are awed to see a united, sharing and worshipping community. You can see that the practical and the spiritual aspects of their life together were closely entwined. Great joy was one of the hallmarks of this time. How is it in your community? Are you allowing the Holy Spirit to work generously and gloriously through you?

† *Lord, I ask that you will show me any way that I may be blocking the work of the Holy Spirit*

May

The free gift

The unity in Jerusalem was shattered by persecution – but there was a positive outcome: 'Those who had been scattered preached the word wherever they went' (*verse 4*) and soon Philip had preached Christ to a group in Samaria, where those baptised included Simon, a sorcerer.

> **When the apostles in Jerusalem heard that Samaria had accepted the word of God, they sent Peter and John to them. When they arrived, they prayed for them that they might receive the Holy Spirit, because the Holy Spirit had not yet come upon any of them.**
> *(verses 14-15, and part of verse 16)*

We are not told exactly what happened but something caught Simon's attention.

> **When Simon saw that the Spirit was given at the laying on of the apostles' hands, he offered them money and said, 'Give me also this ability so that everyone on whom I lay my hands may receive the Holy Spirit.'**
> *(verses 18-19)*

What an error! First, Simon coveted the ministry of another, and then he thought he could buy what he considered to be their power. He did not recognise that the Holy Spirit is a gift, freely given; he thought only of furthering his own career and power base. As you serve the Lord, check your heart that nothing more 'spectacular' catches your eye and produces discontent or greed in your heart.

† *Lord, I praise and thank you for the wonder of the free gift that you have poured out in your Holy Spirit.*

An encourager!

Do you know someone who encourages you? Or perhaps you are an encourager yourself. Today we see the Holy Spirit at work in the life of Barnabas, and the results that followed. Barnabas had been sent to investigate the church in Antioch, at about the same time as Peter and John's visit to Samaria that we looked at yesterday (*verse 22, cf. Acts 8:14*). Jesus had commissioned his disciples to be his witnesses 'to the ends of the earth' (*Acts 1:8*). Antioch was to be the jumping-off point for the great expansion that would occur through Barnabas and Saul. But first the church itself needed strengthening.

> **[A] great number of people believed and turned to the Lord. News of this reached the ears of the church at Jerusalem, and they sent Barnabas to Antioch. When he arrived and saw the evidence of the grace of God, he was glad and encouraged them all to remain true to the Lord with all their hearts. He was a good man, full of the Holy Spirit and faith, and a great number of people were brought to the Lord.**
>
> *(part of verse 21, and verses 22-24)*

Since the Holy Spirit is the great Comforter, we see Barnabas full of encouragement as he teaches, trains, observes and spurs on the new Christians to know the Lord.

† *Lord, give me eyes to see the evidence of your life in the Body and in individuals. Then grant me the grace to encourage them fully.*

143

Glory

Do you have a favourite walk, or a book that you love reading, or a view that you can't get enough of? The most natural thing is for us to talk about how beautiful, touching, or exhilarating we find these things, so that others can delight in them too. But we are completely outdone by the Holy Spirit!

> **'He will bring glory to me by taking from what is mine and making it known to you.'**
>
> *(verse 14)*

What a rave review! Jesus was talking to his disciples in the last hours he had with them before his arrest, and he wanted to tell them about the work of the Holy Spirit.

> **'I have much more to say to you . . . But when he, the Spirit of truth, comes, he will guide you into all truth. He will not speak on his own; he will speak only what he hears . . . All that belongs to the Father is mine. That is why I said the Spirit will take from what is mine and make it known to you.'**
>
> *(part of verses 12 and 13, and verse 15)*

We've seen how the Holy Spirit moves through people in the church, bringing conviction and encouragement. How much more should we all follow our guide and seek to bring glory to Jesus!

† Dear Jesus, may my life be so full of your Holy Spirit that I bring glory to you in all I do and say today.

Preservation

At the age of 8, Josiah was made king of Judah. At 16, 'while he was still young, he began to seek . . . God' (*verse 3*). At 20 he began to clear the land of idolatry. Then at 26 he ordered the repair of the temple. Quite an extraordinary start to his reign. Fifty years earlier the seer had told King Asa, 'the eyes of the Lord range throughout the earth to strengthen those whose hearts are fully committed to him' (*2 Chronicles 16:9*). The one who does this strengthening is the Holy Spirit (*cf. Revelation 5:6*) and, although not specifically mentioned in today's passage, you detect the Spirit working. Hilkiah the priest found the Book of the Law and gave it to Shaphan, who

> **took the book to the king . . . [and] read from it. When the king heard the words of the Law, he tore his robes. He gave these orders . . . 'Go and enquire of the LORD . . . about what is written in this book that has been found.'**
> *(parts of verses 16-21)*

The response was immediate, humble and appropriate. The result was a renewing of the Covenant, a magnificent celebration of the Passover and the preservation of part of the scriptures. Even today the Spirit directs us to the Word and to potentially life-changing possibilities.

† *Thank you, Lord, that you always see into my heart and come and take me so much further than I could ever imagine.*

May

The source

Have you ever had a good idea and tried to bring it about in your own strength? This is a question we all need to consider. Let's ponder these two passages.

> **'Not by might, nor by power, but by my Spirit,' says the LORD Almighty.**
>
> *(Zechariah 4, verse 6)*

> **'[Y]ou have abandoned the love you had at first.'**
> *(Revelation 2, part of verse 4)*

In a vision Zechariah saw a bowl on top of a gold candlestick, with channels that continually fed seven lamps. While they were connected, oil flowed and the light shone. Oil speaks of the Holy Spirit, and all our human efforts will not achieve what he alone can do. The lampstand may look beautiful, but there will be no light.

The church at Ephesus, like the other churches in Asia Minor, was patiently enduring persecution. But over the years since their conversion, the heart had gone out of the Ephesian Christians; they had lost their first love for their Lord – perhaps everything had become a bit automatic and rather boring. We all know the feeling. And that's the time for a spiritual checkup! We need the Spirit's help.

† Lord, speak to me this weekend about my own life and its source, and that of my church.

3   God in action

Notes by Chris Duffett
based on the New International Version

Chris Duffett is a Baptist minister, evangelist, and founder of The Light Project, a charity which demonstrates the Christian message in active and relevant ways and trains others in evangelism. He and his wife Ruth have three children.

Introduction

As Christians we serve an active God, intimately involved in every facet of our lives and able to attend to all his children at once! The popular idea of God seated on his throne observing us from a distance is strange. God remains the high king of heaven, but he is also the incarnate God, the theologian Søren Kierkegaard's 'messy God'. Like the dad of the Prodigal Son, God waits and watches on the driveway for his children's homecomings, and when he sees them in the distance, he scoops up his robes and runs to embrace them, mess and all.

Text for the week: Isaiah 61:1
He saved us through the washing of rebirth and renewal by the Holy Spirit, whom he poured out on us generously through Jesus Christ our Saviour, so that, having been justified by his grace, we might become heirs having the hope of eternal life.

For group discussion and personal thought

- How can you demonstrate to others that the Spirit is upon you?
- Whom do you know who needs a miracle in their lives? Spend time praying for them and ask God how you can bring hope to their situation.
- In a quiet place, ask God to reveal the song of rejoicing that he sings over you.

Help!

We serve a big God who is ever attentive to each individual within populations, and each population within his world. Jeremiah reminds us that it is God alone who is able to care for and transform entire nations:

> 'Hear the word of the LORD, O nations;
> proclaim it in distant coastlands:
> "He who scattered Israel will gather them
> and will watch over his flock like a shepherd.". . .
> I will turn their mourning into gladness;
> I will give them comfort and joy instead of sorrow.'
> *(verse 10 and part of verse 13)*

Even in the tough, hopeless times of exile, God reveals that it was he who scattered his people and he is now able to turn their lives upside down. Even though today's verses are for a group of people, I also believe they are for us too. Do you need help? Are you mourning? Are you in sorrow? Through this word we are reminded that God is able to bring comfort and joy and gladness to us. Allow the good shepherd to change your hopelessness today.

† *Where I am in pain, I welcome you to care for me.*
Where I am in sorrow, I welcome you to pour afresh your love into me...
Where I am in mourning, I receive your gift of joy.
Where I need the knowledge of your care for me, I welcome you, right now, right here.

The God who sings a love song

The hands of our God, which sculpt mountains and valleys and hold the oceans like a drop in a bucket, are also tender loving hands that gently cradle us:

> 'The LORD your God is with you,
> he is mighty to save.
> He will take great delight in you,
> he will quiet you with his love,
> he will rejoice over you with singing.'
> *(verse 17)*

At breakfast this morning my three young children seemed to gang up to make as much noise as possible! Our baby was crying, our son was shouting for his juice, and our daughter joined in by screaming loudly that she didn't like her toast! My reaction to the crescendo of noise was to shout for quiet. God uses a different method to quieten us! In all our needs, turmoil, uncertainty, busyness and self-importance, he quietens us not with a booming heavenly voice but with a gentle song declaring his love, a song full of his delight in us, with a calming melody that reminds us of his presence: he is with us. Take time to appreciate this declaration of his love for you; listen quietly, not expecting to be shouted at, but wooed with love and affection.

† *I would love to hear that song of love sung over me today,*
  I would love to catch some of those words that speak of your delight,
  I would love to really experience today what you think of me.

149

The God who always turns up

How close do you feel to God today? Despite how we feel or our experience of God, one thing is for sure: God is always coming to reveal more of himself to you:

> 'Let us acknowledge the LORD;
> let us press on to acknowledge him.
> As surely as the sun rises,
> he will appear;
> he will come to us like the winter rains,
> like the spring rains that water the earth.'
> *(verse 3)*

These verses in Hosea give me hope. As an evangelist I have the joy of leading a big team of people, but it's not always a pleasure working with others! I have recently emerged from a difficult personal time that has lasted 18 months, caused by work relationships breaking down and people leaving the church. It was a dark time of feeling lost and uncertain, a time of pressure and having no confidence, a time when I felt very distant from God. Perhaps you too have experienced or are going through this kind of remote time. Let these words from Hosea remind you of the constant nature of God. Like the sun rising, he will appear.

† Heavenly Father, in the name of Jesus, come to meet with me now. Where I am parched and thirsty, pour out your Spirit and water me, deep within, every dry part of my being that cries out for you; come and refresh and fill me again with the closeness of you. Amen.

God's plan for you

Once we receive Jesus into our hearts by his Spirit, the process of sanctification starts. We become more and more like him every day:

Though outwardly we are wasting away, yet inwardly we are being renewed day by day.

(part of verse 16)

If we believe what this verse says, we can lose the pressure and guilt that accompanies trying to be as holy and perfect as God (*Matthew 5:48*). This is because Paul places the responsibility on God, at work in our very being, and not on our striving. God's plan for each one of us is unstoppable, inevitable as a new day; so we are certainly being renewed inside day by day.

However, there are some practical points that can help this process of being renewed; they may not be fashionable, but they are vital for us day by day. Firstly, John says that if we let God know about our sins, he is faithful and just and will forgive us our sins and purify us (*1 John 1:9*). Secondly, we can tell others about our sins and ask for prayer. If we do this we will be healed from the sin that binds us (*James 5:16*). Thirdly, we can meditate on the truth that we are not under any condemnation (*Romans 8:1*) but wonderfully renewed and made alive in Christ (*Ephesians 2:4*).

† *Create a clean heart within me, O God, so that I may become your chosen shelter and the resting place of the Holy Spirit. Amen.*

(Taken from Northumbria Community, Celtic Daily Prayer: Prayers and Readings from the Northumbria Community, Collins: 2005)

Not in vain

Recently I met three people who independently thanked me for my prayers and words, yet who months or years previously had all responded negatively to what I had to say! Eight years ago Betty used to swear at me in the streets and tell me that God couldn't help her. Last week she thanked me for praying for her and the words I had shared, because her helpless situation had been remedied.

Last summer I asked a couple I met on the streets if I could pray for them; they reluctantly agreed and mentioned that their baby niece was unwell, but also said that they were sceptical about prayer. Yesterday I bumped into them and with great joy they told me how God had answered my prayer.

And two years ago Susan was a hopeless heroin addict, living in a car, away from her 10-year-old daughter. I told her I was asking God to help her. Recently we have been exchanging emails and she wrote from her new home to say thank you: she is living with her daughter, holding down a job and has stopped taking drugs.

> '[S]o is my word that goes out from my mouth:
> It will not return to me empty,
> but will accomplish what I desire
> and achieve the purpose for which I sent it.'
>
> *(verse 11)*

† Despite how difficult it can be, help me to let others know what I passionately believe, help me to share the powerful words of the gospel. Amen.

The Spirit of the Lord is on me

Just as the Spirit rested on Christ so the Spirit rests on us – though not primarily for our benefit. Jesus' vision statement at the beginning of his ministry can also be true for us, because even though God is actively involved and working in this world, it is primarily through us that his efforts are revealed! Why does the Spirit rest upon you? Jesus gives five reasons.

> **The Spirit of the Lord is on me, because he has anointed me**
> *(Luke, part of verse 18)*

May

- **To preach good news to the poor**

  What words can you share this week that will bring hope to those in poverty?

- **To proclaim freedom for the prisoners**

  Whom do you know who needs setting free from addictions that imprison them? Ask God how you can proclaim freedom to them.

- **To recover the sight of the blind**

  Will you spend time this week with people at work or in the community who are blind to the good news of Jesus? In confidence that the Spirit is upon you, pray for some of these people.

- **To release the oppressed**

  Who are the oppressed, and how can you help to release them?

- **To proclaim the year of the Lord's favour**

  Think about the favour he has shown you and thank him for all he has done in your life.

† *Merciful Jesus, thank you for your Spirit resting upon me! May I experience his overflowing from me to others. Amen.*

Isaiah 1–39

1   Enemies within and without

Notes by John Oldershaw
based on the New International Version

John Oldershaw is a Minister of the United
Reformed Church (URC) and works for the Mersey
Synod, helping churches to try different ways of worshipping God
and serving their neighbourhood. In the past he has been a local
church minister and a youth worker for the Churches of Christ and
the URC.

Introduction

The Old Testament book of Isaiah has three sections. The readings
for this theme come from the first section, chapters 1–39. It dates
from the eighth century BC, when the kingdom of Judah was at
risk both from the powerful neighbouring state of Assyria, and
from the nation's own disobedience of God. The prophet Isaiah
challenges the people with his bold statements of God's word.

Text for the week: Isaiah 1:2
Hear, O heavens! Listen, O earth! For the LORD has spoken.

For group discussion and personal thought

• In what ways have you heard God speak?

• Isaiah was a prophet who addressed people when they
   gathered together. How can people today hear the word of
   God?

• How can the church be a prophetic voice today?

Belonging

'Where are you from?' I am asked when I meet people I do not know. Sometimes the answer is the church I belong to, sometimes the town in which I live, at other times my country of origin, and at others the family of which I am part. We belong in lots of different ways. Today's passage begins by telling us about Isaiah's background, where he belongs, but then rapidly becomes a lament from God that people have forgotten that they belong to him, and he belongs to them.

> **'The ox knows his master,**
> **the donkey his owner's manger,**
> **but Israel does not know,**
> **my people do not understand.'**
> *(verse 3)*

People have been going through the rituals of worship, but neglecting what God really wants. It is not exotic sacrifices and incense that show who belongs to God.

> **'[L]earn to do right!**
> **Seek justice,**
> **encourage the oppressed.'**
> *(part of verse 17)*

These are the hallmarks of those who know that they belong to God.

We can be faithful in attending church worship, give money for the upkeep of church buildings and be constant in prayer, but still fail to hear the echo of Isaiah's voice when he said 'The Lord has spoken'.

† Lord of my life, today may I be proud of belonging to you. In my actions and words may I show your concern for all people, especially those who are poor and weak. Amen

June

An offer

Although the shortcomings of the nation are obvious, an offer is made that it does not have to be like this. There can be change; all that is required is the recognition of what is wrong, such as in this verse.

> **Your rulers are rebels,**
> **companions of thieves;**
> **they all love bribes**
> **and chase after gifts.**
> *(part of verse 23)*

This needs to be followed by repentance and a willingness to change. God's word is constantly 'This is the way it is, but it does not have to be like this, there is a better way.' The tone in these verses is one of sadness. Although accusations are made, the intention is not to condemn, but rather to encourage change.

> **'If you are willing and obedient,**
> **you will eat the best from the land;**
> **but if you resist and rebel,**
> **you will be devoured by the sword.'**
> *(verse 19 and part of verse 20)*

All the way through today's passage God is saying, 'I know what you are like, but I still care about you and want you to be true to yourselves; you can do better than this.' It has the ring of a parent talking to a teenage son or daughter, cajoling and persuading, but sadly realising that the words are falling on deaf ears.

† You know me as I am. Help me to celebrate my good points,
and to change my faults. Amen

Peace not war

There are those who argue that religion is the cause of war and conflict, but this passage gives the lie to that argument. The vision is of a faith that unites people, as they come voluntarily to the mountain of the Lord's temple and hear classic words that have been picked up in peace movements, slogans and protest songs over the centuries.

> **They will beat their swords into ploughshares**
> **and their spears into pruning hooks.**
> **Nation will not take up sword against nation,**
> **nor will they train for war any more.**
> *(part of verse 4)*

Nations still do not live according to this vision. It remains a future hope. Weapons of mass destruction have replaced spears, and we have moved little from the actual situation described here in verses 6 and 8. The people have every good thing imaginable; however, they take part in a variety of dubious practices and have ceased to walk in the light of the Lord. The day will come, declares Isaiah, when humility will replace this arrogance and pride. Judgement and hope go hand in hand in a vision that is as vital for today as it was when the words were first spoken.

† *Lord of creation, today I pray for peace, and for hope for a world where nations will use their wealth to feed the hungry and house the homeless instead of devising ever more terrible weapons of war. Amen*

June

Consequences

What a mess is described here! Parts of the land had probably already experienced terrible decline as the Assyrians carried out raiding parties, stealing goods and deporting able people. There seems to be no hope in this prophecy; there is not even any able leadership left to encourage the people and drag them into better days. All that happens is seen as the consequence of failure to live in God's way.

> **See now, the Lord,**
> **the Lord Almighty,**
> **is about to take from Jerusalem and Judah**
> **both supply and support;**
> **all supplies of food and all supplies of water.**

(verse 1)

This commentary on society, and the economic and social consequences of current behaviour, is indeed a prophetic word. It is the type of analysis that is needed today. Being a prophetic Christian voice does not make us popular. No leadership, political or ecclesiastical, likes criticism, but the consequences of pursuing particular policies need to be pointed out. The church is failing in its prophetic ministry of standing in the footsteps of Isaiah if all it is concerned about is keeping its own show on the road and preserving its buildings and traditions, come what may.

† *Lord of the church, today I pray for all those who are leaders of nations. May they have the wisdom to know, and strength to do, what is right. Amen*

At last

After the gloom, at last here is some hope. Trees are long-suffering plants. They can look dead when the temperature has been too hot or too cold or when there has not been enough rain. However, when conditions are right they burst into leaf and blossom. This is an image used by Isaiah.

In that day the Branch of the LORD will be beautiful and glorious, and the fruit of the land will be the pride and glory of the survivors in Israel.

(verse 2)

Here is encouragement for those who remain faithful to God. They may be few in number, just a remnant, but they will be rewarded and their suffering will be washed away. Connections are made to other parts of the faith story. The protecting presence of God in smoke and fire is reminiscent of the Exodus story where the people were guided by a pillar of smoke by day and fire by night. The protection from the heat of the day and refuge from the storm links with the promises made in Psalm 121. Although those remaining faithful may be few in number, they are part of the big picture of God's salvation story.

† *When I feel that I am one among very few who have faith in you, help me to remember, Lord of the universe, that I am part of a vast company of people who belong to your kingdom. Amen*

June

God's call

These two readings are among the best-known verses in Isaiah. The story of the vineyard in Isaiah 5 is echoed in the story told by Jesus in the gospels. In Isaiah 6 the prophet describes his call in the year that King Uzziah died, which was about 740 BC. Isaiah has a vision of the Lord in the temple and there is a wonderful description of seraphs (the highest order of angels) calling to one another as they worship God:

> **'Holy, holy, holy is the LORD Almighty;**
> **the whole earth is full of his glory.'**
> *(part of verse 3)*

Isaiah, knowing himself unworthy, is amazed that one of the seraphs comes to him and declares that his guilt is taken away. There is only one response for him now, obedience to God's command. 'Send me,' he says, and the result is the prophecies that we have looked at this week.

Centuries later, God's call comes in various ways: during worship, in the words of a friend – sometimes reading a newspaper can spur us into action. These are just some examples, but what is important is the readiness, indeed eagerness, to hear God's word at any time, and in unexpected ways and places. After all, the whole earth is full of God's glory.

† *Living God, as I think about your greatness and glory, help me to hear your words to me. May I have the confidence, like Isaiah, to respond 'Here am I!' Amen*

2 The hope of rescue

Notes by Sister Christopher Godden
based on the Jerusalem Bible

Having decided not to become a teacher, Sr Christopher worked for 13 years in the supply industry, coping with the arrival of computers. In 1982 she sold her house, bicycle, canoe and cat and entered the Benedictine Monastery at Talacre in North Wales. Shortly after her final profession she moved with the community to Chester, where she does her best to live according to the Rule of St Benedict and grow nearer to God.

Introduction

Our readings this week range from the time of King Ahaz (736 BC) to the eve of the return of the exiles from Babylon (c.538 BC) and are part of those sections of Isaiah known as 'The Book of Emmanuel' and 'Oracles on Foreign Nations'. Isaiah looks forward to a future king who will rule with integrity and justice, but meanwhile he faces many issues that bear a great resemblance to problems in today's world.

Text for the week: Isaiah 9:1
The people that walked in darkness has seen a great light; on those who live in a land of deep shadow a light has shone.

For group discussion and personal thought

• How can we best demonstrate our hope in God in our churches and communities today?
• The Day of the Lord will come to each of us. What do you think this means, and how can we prepare for it?
• How do we bring hope where there is none?

A hopeless mission

> Once again Yahweh spoke to Ahaz and said, 'Ask Yahweh your God for a sign' . . . 'No,' Ahaz answered, I will not put Yahweh to the test.'
>
> *(part of verse 11, and verse 12)*

Poor Isaiah. Being a prophet is no sinecure. It is his first mission since his call (*chapter 6*) and it is not going well. King Ahaz (see 2 Kings 16 for more about him) steadfastly refuses to listen to Isaiah or take his words seriously, even though he is in a desperate situation with armies at the city gate and the city under siege. Instead he sends emissaries to the King of Assyria to rescue him from his predicament. But that does not let the prophet off the hook: he must still speak the words given to him to deliver – that is his mission. It is interesting to read in verse 10 that Yahweh himself intervenes and speaks directly and personally to the king, to try and get him to listen (God never gives up, does he?). Not that that makes any difference at all, the king's response is the same: an adamant refusal to take notice.

We know the feeling of being trapped by our own mistakes or stupidity at times. It's a humbling experience. But God is humble too, only wanting us to turn to him so that he can help us sort ourselves out. Is that too much to ask and hope for?

† Let us pray for all living under siege.

Alpha and omega

**The people that walked in darkness
Has seen a great light;
On those who live in a land of deep shadow
A light has shone.**

(verse 1)

How do people who 'walk in darkness' see light? Doesn't darkness mean no light? Since 913 BC the kingdom of Israel had been split into two, the ten northern tribes forming Israel and the two southern tribes forming Judah. Now, in about 733, Isaiah looks north from Judah and sees not Israel but Assyria. Israel has become part of the Assyrian Empire. Yet the prophet sees this not as The End, but as a new beginning when a new king, of David's line, will arise and, unlike his predecessors, rule with justice and integrity.

Traditionally, today's passage is used in Christmas carol services as we rejoice in the Incarnation. How much more is it fulfilled in the death and resurrection of Jesus! Sometimes I seem to lose everything – faith, certainties, they all vanish. I enter a dark, starless night. Nothing is real. I walk the badlands hoping and longing for rescue from this place of pain, yet I know now that it is a necessary part of my journey. 'Let there be light', the first spoken words of Genesis. It is time to start again. Looking back, it often seems that in those darkest days I walked closest of all to God.

† For all who live in darkness: Let there be light.

Rise and fall

> **Does the axe claim more credit than the man who wields it,**
> **Or the saw more strength than the man who handles it?**
> *(verse 15)*

Sometimes, like just now when I tripped over the doormat, I have an uncharitable thought and the Lord pulls me up short – which enables me to stop and change my tune. The prophets were sent by God to try and stop the nations of Israel and Judah from sinning and bring them back to their senses. Often their words and actions were misinterpreted or ignored, but that did not make them any less valid.

God communicates with us in ways we can understand – in the hope that we will. Yahweh used Assyria as his tool to discipline Israel and Judah but, as sometimes happens, things began to go too far and the Assyrians overreached themselves. They thought their success was due to their own power and that they were unconquerable: 'In his heart was to destroy, to go on cutting nations to pieces without limit' (*verse 7*). Isaiah now tells the Assyrians that their excesses have earned them God's wrath. The time will come when they will learn about defeat and captivity. It will be their turn to hope and long for rescue.

† O Lord, bring hope where there is despair.

Looking forwards backwards

**That day, the root of Jesse
shall stand as a signal to the peoples.
It will be sought out by the nations
and its home will be glorious.**

(verse 10)

Isaiah looked back to the reign of King David, when Israel's fortunes were at their highest, and foresees the coming of the new king from the Davidic line who will rule over a new Israel, seen here as Eden restored. All the peoples of the world will look to this kingdom and its king and wish to be part of it.

We know the fulfilment of the prophecy came with the Incarnation and the teaching of the gospel. We also know, sadly, how far from its reality we still are. Sometimes, when life's journey seems to have taken a plunge, it is good to look back and see just how far we have travelled and how things have changed. We can also look ahead towards the end we hope to achieve. This can rescue us from self-pity, halt discouragement, and encourage us to carry on with renewed confidence and hope. It may mean hard work and hardship, which is what the returning exiles faced when they were eventually allowed home from Babylon after many years; but that is no reason for giving up.

† Let us pray for all who work with the mentally ill and outcasts of today's societies and try to bring hope where there is only despair, anguish and pain.

June

Thank you

> That day, you will say:
> Give thanks to Yahweh,
> Call his name aloud.
> Proclaim his deeds to the people.
> *(part of verse 4)*

Today's reading, marking the end of 'The Book of Emmanuel' and the return of the exiles from captivity in Babylon, contains a tremendous hymn of thanksgiving. The freed exiles look back and understand that their time in Babylon was a punishment sent by God for their unfaithfulness to him. Now that time is past, and free once again and in their own reunited land (*verses 11-12*), they sing this joyful hymn of praise to Yahweh their deliverer.

Luke 17:11-19 describes Jesus healing the lepers, only one of whom returned to say thank you. When a period of stress, worry or difficulty ends, we are sometimes so relieved that we forget to acknowledge and thank whoever or whatever brought us out of our trouble. Freed from our anxiety, we forget the past and are ready to push ahead with life. When my brother and I were young, but able to read and write, it became the rule that on the day after Christmas Day we were not allowed to play with our new toys until we had written all our 'Thank you' letters. It was a hard lesson but a good one.

† *O give thanks to the Lord for he is good, for his great love is without end.* (Psalm 135:1, Gelineau translation)

June

Hope fulfilled, hope misplaced

[T]he day of Yahweh is near . . . The day of Yahweh is coming.

(Isaiah 13, part of verses 6 and 9)

The writings of the prophets are rarely arranged in chronological order. This can seem confusing but should not obscure their message. This weekend's passages both come from a section headed 'Oracles on foreign nations'. Isaiah saw the finger of Yahweh in everything, everywhere. Our first passage is set in the period when the Judean exiles are coming to the end of their time in Babylon and will soon be allowed home. The Babylonian Empire itself will soon be no more, conquered by the Medes.

The second passage, dated some 130 years earlier, refers to a time when the Ethiopian rulers of Egypt sent ambassadors to Judah to ask them to join a coalition against the threatened menace of the Assyrians. Isaiah advises refusal. Judah's hope for rescue must be in Yahweh alone, not in Egypt or any show of arms. Every day is a Day of the Lord. Biblically, the Day always seems to involve bloodshed, even in the time of Jesus (the slaughter of the innocents and the crucifixion). We may smile when we see the man or woman carrying the poster saying 'Prepare to meet thy doom', but they do have a point. How will you stand then?

† We pray for all seeking rescue from alcohol, drugs and abuse. Come quickly to their aid, Lord.

June

3   Rewards and punishments

Notes by Anthea Dove
Based on the New Jerusalem Bible

Anthea Dove is a great-grandmother, a retired teacher, a retreat giver and a writer. She is a Roman Catholic with a strong commitment to social justice and ecumenism.

Introduction

The prophet Isaiah lived roughly seven hundred years before Jesus. By most people he was, and is, considered to be the greatest of the prophets, and he is outstanding among the Old Testament writers, in particular for his poetic language. He was highly respected in his own country and as the adviser of kings. He constantly spoke out against moral corruption and urged the people to put their trust in God. In much of his work, as in this week's readings, Isaiah emphasises God's power and speaks of him with great awe; elsewhere he writes of God's tenderness and compassion.

Text for the week: Isaiah 35:10
Those whom Yahweh has ransomed will return, they will come to Zion shouting for joy, their heads crowned with joy unending; rejoicing and gladness will escort them and sorrow and sighing will take flight.

For group discussion and personal thought

• Life in the time of Isaiah was very different from the way it is today. But can you see some similarities?

• How do you imagine the kingdom of God to be?

Reconciliation

In this passage Isaiah is foretelling the conversion of the people of Egypt, and their reconciliation with the Assyrians and the Israelites. He sees these three countries as the centre of the world, and assures people that, whatever their past sins, God will bless them with these words:

> **'Blessed be my people Egypt, Assyria my creation, and Israel my heritage.'**
>
> *(part of verse 25)*

Isaiah is clearly in awe of God and has a deep faith in him. He believes his God is just; he may deal out punishment, but he is also ready to forgive and to heal. We notice the contrast between Isaiah's concept of God here: 'Yahweh', the remote, all-powerful one, and the way Jesus experiences him: 'Abba', who is in intimate relation to him and to us. Our own understanding of God grows as we move from the Old Testament to the New.

† Lord, deepen my sense of awe in your presence.

June

Apocalypse

This strange passage paints a gloomy picture of devastation that Isaiah sees as God's punishment because people have broken the laws and their covenant with him. The whole earth has been devastated and its inhabitants destroyed; very few have survived. Then comes another, equally unhappy vision, this time of the 'city of nothingness'. In this cursed place,

> **all joy has vanished,**
> **happiness has been banished from the country.**
> *(part of verse 11)*

Then, abruptly, the picture changes and we are told of the joyous response of the people, singing to Yahweh from all the corners of the earth and giving him honour and glory.

Today, because of the advance of technology, we have seen with our own eyes pictures of utter devastation which are not punishments from God but either acts of nature, like the tsunami at the end of 2004, or the result of our inhumanity and failure to love, like the refugee camps of Darfur. The kind of thing Isaiah saw so clearly in his imagination, we see all too often on our television screens. And since every human being on the planet is our brother or sister, we have an obligation to respond.

† *Lord, let me respond to disaster as a follower of Christ. Let me share my wealth with those in distress, and let me be willing to take action on behalf of those who are oppressed. Give me the courage to challenge authority.*

Pity and mercy

Today's passage comes as something of a relief after yesterday's. Isaiah has a new and different vision, one in which most people will be blessed by Yahweh and given a wonderful feast on a mountain top. He tells us that

> **Lord Yahweh has wiped away the tears from every cheek; he has taken his people's shame away everywhere on earth.**
>
> *(part of verse 8)*

But in the same passage, Isaiah often uses the word 'pitiless'. He says that the breath of the pitiless is like a winter storm (*verse 4*), and 'you calm the foreigners' tumult' (*verse 5*). It is not clear who the foreigners are, but I am reminded of those millions of men, women and children who have been forced to flee their own country and become foreigners in a strange land, often to be met not with welcome but with a total lack of pity. Yahweh is never without pity for his children: Isaiah assures us here that he has been a refuge for the weak and for the needy in distress, a shelter from the storm and shade from the heat: words of great comfort for his people then and for us now.

† *Lord, I thank you with a full heart for the pity and mercy you have so often shown me, and I thank you for your comforting when things are difficult.*

June

Jerusalem

For us who live in the twenty-first century, there is a sad irony in reading the beginning of this passage. Isaiah is writing in triumph and with thankfulness about the glorious city of Jerusalem.

> **'This is the plan decreed: you will guarantee peace, the peace entrusted to you.'**
>
> *(verse 3)*

Alas, there is no peace in Jerusalem today. When I visited the city a few years ago, far from being a sanctuary of peace it was a place of suspicion, hostility and danger. From my lodging a short distance away outside the city walls, I had a fine view of Jerusalem, pride of the sons of Abraham, and what I remember most vividly are not the places holy to Christians, but the golden dome of the great mosque and the heartbreakingly young soldiers guarding the city gates with their guns and grim faces. Jerusalem is no longer a symbol of peace in our world; rather it is a symbol of violence and disunity. In St Luke's Gospel we read that as Jesus drew near to Jerusalem and came in sight of the city he shed tears over it and said, 'If only you too had recognised on this day the way to peace!' (*Luke 19:42*).

† *Lord, we pray for the peace of Jerusalem. Help us not to despair over the situation in the Middle East, but to do all we can to support those Israelis and Palestinians who continue to struggle for peace.*

Struggling prophet

The Old Testament prophets had a hard time of it, and Isaiah was no exception. They put all their skill and energy into trying to persuade the people to turn from rebellion against God, yet their passionate pleading was so often of no avail. At this point in his story, when the people had failed again and again to listen to his messages from God, Isaiah put Yahweh's words into writing (*verses 8-17*) and then for some reason (illness? despair?) refrained from prophesying. Just before he retired, he wrote in righteous anger:

> 'Your salvation lay in conversion and tranquillity,
> your strength in serenity and trust,
> and you would have none of it.'
>
> *(part of verse 15)*

It is not difficult to conclude from this that a prophet's lot was not a happy one! The second half of today's passage could hardly be more different. Here Yahweh is full of compassion, promising, in the eloquent and brilliant imagery which Isaiah employs both in indignation and exultation, that his people will be forgiven, blessed and healed.

† *Dear Lord, so often we too, like the Jewish people of old, fail to listen to your word. We turn away from what we know to be right, to pursue our own selfish interests. Help us to take time, however busy our lives, to listen to you in prayer and to discern the way you want us to live and the sort of people you want us to be.*

June

The coming of the kingdom

Even when Isaiah is remorselessly cataloguing the woes of those who refuse to listen to his counsel and turn away from God, we surely cannot fail to be uplifted and amazed by the beauty of his language and the inventiveness of his imagery. Isaiah was holy and wise, a courageous prophet, a lyrical poet and faithful servant of God. In the last of these readings from his work, we have two pictures of the coming kingdom: the first (*chapter 32*) a time of peace under just rulers, when God's spirit will be poured out; and the second (*chapter 35*) one of the most sublime passages in the Old Testament. It begins with the beautiful picture of the flowering desert, continues with words of encouragement that always make me smile, especially the reference to trembling knees, and soars into the glorious description of what is, in effect, the kingdom of God:

> **Then the eyes of the blind will be opened,**
> **the ears of the deaf unsealed,**
> **then the lame will leap like a deer**
> **and the tongue of the dumb sing for joy.**
> *(verse 5 and part of verse 6)*

At last the kingdom will come, at last justice will reign, and those Yahweh has ransomed will return.

† Dear Lord, we pray for the coming of your kingdom. Help us to recognise it when and where we find it, and to work for the day when the whole wasteland can rejoice and bloom because all your children are ransomed and redeemed.

Truth Through Story

1 Old Testament

Notes by Pedro Vieira Veiga
based on the New International Version

Pedro Vieira Veiga is a young pastor who lives
in Rio de Janeiro with his family. He works at
an independent Christian church in the neighbourhood of
Ipanema, though his main responsibility lies with a small group
from the nearby town of Petrópolis. He is also a psychology
and theology student.

Introduction

Many of the best-known parts of the Bible are narratives, most
of which lie somewhere between history and pure fiction. But
sometimes this is the least important thing about them, the
content of these stories is very, very rich and speaks to us of
God and of men and women who had to face many of the
same problems that we encounter. This week we shall discuss a
few of these stories, focusing solely on the lessons we can learn
from the plot and characters.

Text for the week: Genesis 9:15-16
*Never again will the waters become a flood to destroy all life.
Whenever the rainbow appears in the clouds, I will see it and
remember the everlasting covenant between God and all living
creatures of every kind on the earth.*

For group discussion and personal thought

- Have you ever had to start all over again? Is there some area of
  your life where you should? What do the stories of Adam and
  Eve and Noah tell you about such experience?
- How can we use the biblical stories not only to instruct children,
  but also to help us break free from our habitual mistakes?

What now?

The narrative of Adam and Eve's 'falling out of grace' with the Lord is one of those stories that never ceases to amaze. The garden, the serpent, God himself taking an afternoon stroll! Each of these scenes presents a rich variety of images, but every time I read this story, I find myself drawn to one particular image:

> **'Cursed is the ground because of you;**
> **through painful toil you will eat of it**
> **all the days of your life . . .**
> **By the sweat of your brow**
> **you will eat your food**
> **until you return to the ground,**
> **since from it you were taken.**
> *(part of verses 17 and 19)*

Have you ever looked back with regret to a time when things were easier and less complicated? When you knew less about suffering, or when it was easier to trust people? But we all know that this sentiment is dangerous. Even if the sun did shine as brightly as we picture it in our memories, how does that affect our present predicament? Even though the Lord took away Adam and Eve's past, he left them their present and their future. No matter how hard it was for them to start over all over again, this they *could* do. And so can we.

† Dear Lord, we thank you because love, the bond that links us to you, cannot be torn by our incapacity to understand your ways. Help us to rely solely on your love for whatever strength we need.

All living creatures

The story of Noah and the flood shows us that God too has had to start again. It couldn't have been easy for him, just as it isn't for us – but perhaps for different reasons.

> **'Never again will the waters become a flood to destroy all life. Whenever the rainbow appears in the clouds, I will see it and remember the everlasting covenant between God and all living creatures of every kind on the earth.'**
>
> *(part of verse 15, and verse 16)*

God's love is boundless, we all know that. But usually we understand this in terms of his capacity to forgive and care for *us*. This pronoun – us – can refer to our family, our friends, our neighbours, and even to Christians in general. But in this story God clearly shows his concern for all living creatures, including plants, animals and people of other faiths as well. It is often much easier to remember the differences that set us apart than the similarities that bring us together. But because of the love the Lord displayed for all of creation by saving every part of it from destruction, he is to be found not in what sets us – whoever we are – apart, but in what brings us together.

† *If all else fails, dear God, still your love for every part of your creation will hold it together. Let us cherish this love through respect and kindness for everything.*

June

Silence

In moments of grief we can often find ourselves asking where God has gone, in a desperate attempt to find a reason for our pain.

> **Naked I came from my mother's womb,**
> **and naked I shall depart.**
> **The LORD gave and the LORD has taken away;**
> **may the name of the LORD be praised.**
>
> *(verse 21)*

When Job heard the news and realised that he had lost so much, he could easily have found someone – God – to blame in order to comfort himself. Who else could have been guilty of his incredible misfortune? But instead he praised him and tried to maintain some sort of hope. He did so because he managed to keep in mind that all he had – including what was taken away – had been given to him by the same Lord that had decided to take it away.

Suffering is part of life and it should always be seen as such, just like joy. Why we suffer is indeed an important question, but definitely not as important as our attitude towards suffering. Instead of noisily losing himself as he sought a cause for all his pain, Job faced it in silence and waited, knowing that eventually it would pass – as all things we experience in this world do.

† Heavenly Father, we do not like to suffer, yet we realise that it is something we must all go through. Help us to face these occasions in the best way possible.

Doing what is right

There are times when the right thing to do isn't completely clear, but it seems that when it really counts, it usually is.

> **The king of Egypt said to the Hebrew midwives . . . 'When you help the Hebrew women in childbirth and observe them on the delivery stool, if it is a boy, kill him; but if it is a girl, let her live.' The midwives, however, feared God and did not do what the king of Egypt had told them to do; they let the boys live.**
>
> *(part of verse 15, and verses 16-17)*

One can stand against the flow of evil-doing and corruption in many different ways, but such action always leads to the same question: what are you willing to pay for it? Your respectability, your property, your safety, your life? The deeper your commitment to the ethical stance, the greater the consequences it may bring about – for better or for worse. Still, we are all responsible for doing what is right in our daily lives, even if it doesn't involve great risk. After all, just like these midwives who unknowingly saved Moses' life, we can never know all the consequences of our actions.

† Lord, we ask you to deepen our trust in you and your word, so that we will find it in our hearts to do what is right and obey your word. Teach us your ways.

June

June

Steadfastness

Loyalty isn't as popular today as it was in the past. In fact, it only seems to occur in the form of ugly extremes.

> **'My God sent his angel, and he shut the mouths of the lions' . . . The king was overjoyed and gave orders to lift Daniel out of the den. And when Daniel was lifted from the den, no wound was found on him, because he had trusted in his God.**
>
> *(part of verse 22, and verse 23)*

Today, many people join churches in search of miracles that will change their lives for ever. Sometimes these miracles happen, but sometimes they don't. Daniel's story teaches us a different path. Aware of the king's decree to pray to him and him alone, Daniel kept on praying to God with his window wide open. He didn't do so because he expected a miracle, but because he had simply decided to serve God alone. Daniel certainly hoped that God would save him from the lions, but if this hadn't happened, would he have regretted his action? The story seems to indicate that he would not, that even then he would have remained loyal. Trusting God to the end is perhaps the greatest miracle of all.

† *Dear God, some miracles are easy to see. Others are not. Clear our sight so that we may see all of them, and give us faith so that, even when we do not see miracles, we may keep loyal to you.*

It's never too late

In the first of these similar passages, Jonah is acting very foolishly. He had just seen the whole of Nineveh repent – through his preaching – and be forgiven by the Lord. Now the Lord is trying to get Jonah too to change his mind. In the second reading, David has just killed a man in order to steal his wife and is being shown the true nature of his actions by Nathan. There is a fundamental difference between the two stories, though: David recognises his folly.

> Then David said to Nathan, 'I have sinned against the LORD.' Nathan replied, 'The LORD has taken away your sin. You are not going to die. But because by doing this you have made the enemies of the LORD show utter contempt, the son born to you will die.'
>
> *(2 Samuel, verses 13-14)*

Sometimes we get so caught in the web of our own wishful thinking that it takes a serious confrontation to free us from it. Even though we then have to face up to the consequences of our actions, the story of David shows us that it is much better to do so than to remain, like Jonah, imprisoned in our own prejudices.

† *Lord, we ask you not to give up on us when we get caught up in our own lies, so that we can continue down the path you have chosen for us and lose no more time.*

June

Introduce a friend to

Light for our path 2008 *or* *Words* for today ■■■■2008

For this year's books, send us just £4.00 per book (including postage), together with your friend's name and address, and we will do the rest.

(This offer is only available in the UK, after 1 June 2008. Subject to availability.)

Do you know someone who has difficulty reading *Light for our Path*?

Light for our Path and *Words for Today* are both available to UK readers on cassette.

For the same price as the print edition, you can subscribe and receive the notes on cassette each month, through Galloways Trust for the Blind.

Please contact the IBRA office for more details:

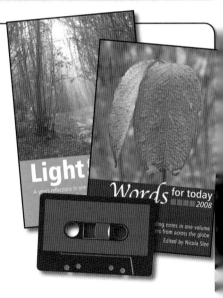

IBRA International Appeal

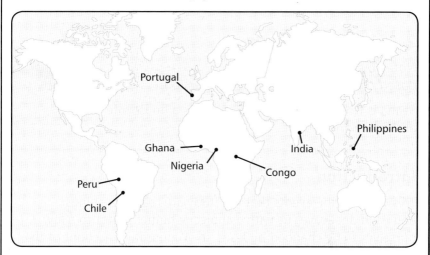

In five continents you will find Christians using IBRA material.

Some will be using books and Bible reading cards translated into their local language, whilst others use English books. Some of the books are printed in the UK, but more and more countries are printing the books and cards themselves. The IBRA International Fund works through churches, Christian groups and Christian publishing houses overseas to make these publications available.

Each year we receive more requests for help from the IBRA International Fund, with greater emphasis on helping our overseas friends to produce their own version of IBRA material.

The only money we have to send is the money you give, so please help us again by giving generously.

Place your gift in the envelope provided and give it to your IBRA representative, or send it direct to:

The IBRA International Appeal
1020 Bristol Road, Selly Oak,
Birmingham B29 6LB, Great Britain

Thank you for your help.

Truth Through *Story*

2   Stories of Jesus

Notes by Selina Samuel
based on the New International Version

Selina is from New Delhi, India. She is a housewife and a freelance editor.

Introduction

This week all the events that we study are real happenings and each one leaves us with a choice: whether or not to allow ourselves to be changed by Jesus. In Wednesday's account of the wedding in Cana, Jesus did not fill the jars with wine but filled them with water and turned it into wine. He takes us as we are and transforms us. Every event recorded was to help us, 'the insignificant people', to know and believe that we are loved by God.

Text for the week: John 2:8
Then he told them, 'Now draw some out and take it to the master of the banquet.' They did so, and the master of the banquet tasted the water that had been turned into wine.

The text for the group discussion is John 20:30.

For group discussion and personal thought

- Life is all about choices. Which criminal are you (Luke 23:39-43): the one who realises the truth about himself and seeks forgiveness or the one who continues in the face of truth to be just a criminal and to turn away from God?

- Can you share any occasion when God has turned water into wine in your life?

Stop doubting and believe

Jesus is risen! He is risen indeed! John records the details of the risen Lord so that we might believe and have life.

> **[T]hese [signs] are written that you may believe that Jesus is the Christ, the Son of God, and that by believing you may have life in his name.**
>
> *(verse 31)*

The fearful disciples sat behind closed doors. Jesus comes in through locked doors and says 'Shalom'. He asks them to see, touch and feel the marks on his hands and side. They thought their Master was dead but he is alive. Locked doors cannot stop our risen Lord.

Many of us also sit behind locked doors, especially in matters of faith, proclamation and involvement. What are some of the locked doors in your life? Unbelief? Fear of being ridiculed? Doubting whether God cares? This risen Lord Jesus can come into our lives, defying locked doors and locked hearts, and speak 'peace' to us. He spoke to the disciples, calmed them and transformed them. Resurrection is real. It is time to stop being fixated by our doubts and fears, and to experience the power of belief, confessing with Thomas, 'my Lord and my God', and being transformed into fearless witnesses of our Lord Jesus.

† *Dear God, open my mind and my understanding to recognise that God died and was resurrected and that by faith in him I can hope for a transformed life.*

June

The insignificant is significant

When God wanted to give 'good news of great joy to all people', he chose the insignificant shepherds. Yes, the wise men read the stars, the king got the news, but the shepherds had a visit from the heavenly host. He trusted them – the insignificant – with his great news. Jesus was born in a manger at the inn. The Creator of the whole world could have opted for a palace. But he chose this place which gave immediate access to rich, poor and wise alike. If he had been born in a palace, the security would not have allowed them in; he would have become the property of the rich. Now everyone, the ordinary folk, the poor and the rich, has access to him. God empowered the insignificant shepherds and they had the courage to say 'Let's go and see.' They checked out the details and then

> **returned, glorifying and praising God for all the things they had heard and seen.**
>
> *(part of verse 20)*

The content of the message gave them their significance. Our God specialises in using people like Moses with a stammering tongue, David, a shepherd boy, the fishermen, and so many like them in our times today. Can we be his willing messengers even if we feel absolutely insignificant, because our significance is in the content of the message and not ourselves?

† Dear God, help me to understand the significance of the message and to be a willing messenger. Amen

Transformed, not replaced

This is a miracle from which we can learn many lessons. Jesus validates the institution of marriage by his presence at the wedding; running out of wine could symbolically mean disaster for the marriage but, by letting Jesus provide, the celebrations continue. With Jesus in our lives the present is always better than the past; water is good and life-giving but wine symbolises abundant life; the water jugs represent the rituals of religious purification, which are also good, but we need wine. This miracle also speaks about the generosity of God, who gives them six jars of the best wine. When Jesus is involved in our lives, the quality of our lives changes. He blesses us beyond what we can ask or think (*Ephesians 3:20*). He takes our situations of hopelessness and turns them into times of dancing and joy

> **'[Y]ou have saved the best till now.'**
> *(part of verse 10)*

Notice also that the water is changed, not replaced. Jesus takes us as we are and transforms us. Many of us are not bad people. There are many good people around. Do we really need Jesus? Remember that God's family is made up of those perfected by faith in Jesus, not just good people. This new order that God is establishing is for those who let Jesus take over and so make the present better than the past.

† *Father God, please transform me so that I can have abundant life in you. Amen*

July

Revelation calls for right action

Every year Christian camps are held in mountains or retreat centres for young and old, singles and couples. The lament on the last day of most camps is usually, 'Can we stay a little longer? Do we have to go now?' Most camps are great times for both fun and revelation – about God, ourselves, our potential, and so on. It is like a touch from God.

Revelations are great but not an end in themselves. They are for renewal – and the right kind of action. Peter wanted the wrong kind of action and God had to tell him to 'Listen to my son.' Revelation equips us with his presence and glory to go back to the world of relationships at home, at work and in society, and get involved. His presence is enough for us to go down the mountain and live in obedience.

> **His face shone like the sun, and his clothes became as white as the light.**
>
> *(part of verse 2)*

July

The Celtic people talk of these experiences as the 'thin places', where the veil between heaven and earth is thin and it is easy to connect with God.

† *Help me, God, to obey you in all your revelations to us, through the scriptures, visions, dreams, the teaching of the Word and the world around us. Amen*

Is the 'towel' on your agenda?

We in Asia know how refreshing it is to wash our feet after a walk along the dusty roads. In Jesus' time it was customary for the Jews to wash their feet before reclining for their meals. The disciples were so busy fighting for positions in the coming kingdom that they forgot all about washing. The towel was the last thing on their agendas. So Jesus took the basin and the towel, and his humility and his words on leadership had a powerful effect. To be Christ-like is to serve each other.

> **'Now that I, your Lord and Teacher, have washed your feet, you also should wash one another's feet.'**
>
> *(verse 14)*

Jesus knew where he came from and where he was going. He never lost focus. We need to understand and focus on our identity and purpose in Jesus. Verse 16 says that 'no servant is greater than his master'. He picked up the towel, and we need to do that too. Ignoring our dirty feet is like trying to have fellowship with God when there is sin in our lives. We have the all-over bath when we first accept him into our lives, but after that it is a constant process of being made perfect in him.

† *Father God, help me to be in constant fellowship with you and not let any sin break that. Help me to be humble and willing to serve others. Amen.*

July

Justice and love – a sweet combination

The Sabbath is the day of rest instituted by God himself. He wants us, our servants/slaves and animals, rich and the poor alike, to rest. Economics calls it a wasted day! But our God is a just God, requiring rest for all alike. The Pharisees made 'law keeping' a rigid ritual, but Jesus knew its purpose. He is no slave of the sabbath, and in giving the sabbath law he made sure that our focus is not on ourselves (work, money and so on) but on rest and people, God and relationships.

> **'Which is lawful on the Sabbath: to do good or to do evil, to save life or to kill?'**
>
> *(part of Mark, verse 4)*

The man with the shrivelled hand needed life, not doctrine. Jesus did what he saw the Father do and so revealed the Father to us as a just and life-giving Father. By his healing on the sabbath Jesus brought life and also set our thinking right.

The cross also signifies justice and love. A criminal and a Roman soldier acknowledged Jesus. The rulers mocked. The crowds walked away shocked. Jesus asks his Father to forgive them. He broke the power of evil totally. Where do you stand?

† *Father, thank you that Jesus revealed you to us as just and life-giving. Thank you that in Jesus we too can be victors. Help me to bring life and not restrict it. Help me to choose you today. Amen*

Truth Through Story

3   Stories Jesus told

Notes by Peter Russell
based on the New Revised Standard Version

Peter Russell is a retired Methodist minister,
a father and a grandfather. He has had a
varied ministry, much of it interdenominational, in England,
Nigeria and Zimbabwe. He has been a university chaplain,
a teacher in theological colleges, convenor of the National
Affairs Committee of the Rhodesia Christian Council and
principal of the Methodist mission training college in Selly Oak,
Birmingham.

Introduction

Much of the teaching of Jesus as we have received it in the
gospels is in the form of parables. Some of these are short
word pictures, but others are recognisable stories. The telling of
stories as a way of conveying truth is found in many cultures. It
is very much part of the culture of the Bible, and of the Jewish
people of Jesus' day. The stories may be literally true, partially
true or invented. This week we shall read some of the stories
Jesus told.

Text for the week: Luke 18:1
*Jesus told them a parable about their need to pray always and
not to lose heart.*

For group discussion and personal thought

• Could these parables be retold to speak more directly to the
  twenty-first century?
• Is there an overall message in these parables?
• Which of the parables speak most closely to you?

July

Who is my neighbour?

The question the lawyer asks Jesus was much debated by Jewish scholars. God had given them the Law as the way to eternal life, but what did it mean in their own day? Many agreed with Jesus that the heart of the Law was in the commandments to love God and your neighbour (*Deuteronomy 6:5, Leviticus 19:18*), but that raised questions: 'How do I love God?' and 'Who is my neighbour?' For Jesus, love to God is shown in loving and caring for God's children, and he was prepared to break the Law when love required it, by healing on the sabbath, for example.

The lawyer now asks the second question and Jesus replies with the parable we call 'The Good Samaritan'. The Samaritans lived to the north of the Jews; the two peoples had much in common in faith and culture, but the Samaritans had opposed the re-establishment of the Jewish nation after the exile in Babylon and over the years had become traditional enemies. Many Jews thought that the Law only counted fellow Jews as neighbours, and certainly excluded Gentiles and Samaritans. So Jesus uses the Samaritan as an example of a true neighbour. Who is my neighbour?

'The one who showed him mercy . . . Go and do likewise.'
(part of verse 37)

In other words, anyone who can affect me, or whom I can affect, for good or ill.

† *God of love, help me to love my neighbours as you want me to love.*

July

Those God sends

This parable echoes Isaiah 5:1-7, where the Hebrew people are the vineyard of God, and it is about God seeking to recall the people who have turned from him. In a world without swift communication much business was done by people who were sent, and there was a considerable body of law about them. (An apostle, from the Greek word for *send*, is a person who is sent.) What sent persons did was regarded as done by the sender, and what was done to them was regarded as done to the sender, so the tenants in this story were guilty of crimes against the landlord.

The best person to send was a son, but he needed to be a 'beloved son' (*verse* 6), meaning a son whom the father could trust. Used of Jesus it means that he is one who speaks for God, and does God's will.

He had . . . a beloved son. Finally he sent him to them.
(part of verse 6)

There is much in the Old Testament about the Jews turning from God and ignoring his prophets, and that is reflected in this parable; it also reflects the concern of the early Christians about the rejection of Jesus. If God's people reject him, his work will not be left undone: he will give the vineyard to others. There will be a new people of God, Christ's people.

† Help me to know and hear those you have sent.

July

Forgive us as we forgive

We have to remember that parables do not have to correspond in every detail with the truth they are illustrating: a parable is often told just to make a single point. The way the king behaves in this parable cannot be said to resemble the way God behaves towards God's people. The central figure of the parable is the servant who does not respond to his master's generosity.

> **[O]ut of pity for him, the lord of that slave released him and forgave him the debt.**
>
> *(verse 27)*

The amount the slave owed to the king was enormous – about a hundred and fifty thousand times a day's wage for a labourer. What the other slave owed was a hundred days' wages. Having been forgiven the enormous amount, the slave could afford to be generous; he could have shown his gratitude by a generous act of his own. By his actions he shows that he does not understand forgiveness, and the need for forgiveness in personal relationships. The point of the parable is that the unforgiving can make themselves unforgivable.

† *Help us to forgive, so that we may receive the fullness of your love.*

Will not God grant justice to his chosen ones?

The point of this parable is that the godless and uncaring judge in the end listened to the petition of the poor widow because of her persistence. How much more will the loving and caring God hear those who plead to him! Once more we have a parable in which not every detail represents the reality it is teaching about.

> '[W]ill not God grant justice to his chosen ones . . . Will he delay long in helping them? I tell you, he will quickly grant justice to them.'
>
> *(part of verses 8 and 9)*

It would be wrong to think that God will always give us whatever we ask for. The experience of Christians through the ages contradicts that idea. Though St Paul prayed for health, it was not granted to him, but he did receive the assurance of God's loving care (*2 Corinthians 12:8-9*). If we do not get exactly what we ask for, it may be because God knows our need better than we do, or because someone else has a greater need than ours, or because we have to fit in with a greater plan. But in this parable Jesus tells us that it is not because God is like an uncaring judge. He hears us and cares about us.

† Give me, loving God, the assurance of your care for me.

July

195

Two men went up to the temple to pray

Like the parable we read yesterday, this is a parable about our relationship with God. Pharisees were part of the religious establishment, people who took seriously the need to obey the Law given to God's people, and so studied it and applied it to everyday life. This particular Pharisee in fact went beyond what the Law required, fasting *twice* a week, and giving tithes on *all* he had. This led him into spiritual pride: when he goes into the temple he thinks more about himself than about God – see how often the word 'I' comes into his prayer!

Tax collectors, on the other hand, worked for the Roman rulers of the Jews. They were despised as traitors, and regarded as unclean because of their contact with the Romans. Yet,

> **this man went down to his home justified rather than the other.**
>
> *(verse 14)*

This tax collector knows he has no claim on God; he simply puts himself into God's hands, and because of that he is justified. The Greek word for 'justified' was a legal term meaning 'acquitted' or 'found not guilty': in Christian thinking it meant 'not guilty in the sight of God', and so 'accepted by God'. He is accepted by God because he comes knowing his insufficiency and need.

† God be merciful to me, a sinner.

Room for all

The story of the cunning manager in Luke 16 is a puzzling parable: verses 8-13 look like sayings of Jesus added to the story by Luke to suggest ways to understand it. Did the master – or, as some translations say, the Lord – really think the manager had done well? In fact he is commended not for honesty or dishonesty but for forethought (*verse 8*): the followers of Jesus must plan ahead, but they must be faithful to their Master.

Our second parable is one of the best known and best loved. Jesus told this lovely parable to remind those who tried to keep God's law that God also loves and has room for those who do not. It has sometimes been hard for the church to recognise the mercy of God. Of course God wants people to obey his word and act in love, but he also welcomes those who have failed but want to come back to him. Both his sons, the faithful and the prodigal, are loved.

> **'Son you are always with me, and all that is mine is yours.'**
>
> *(Luke 15, verse 31)*

It is not always easy to think that those like the thief on the cross (*Luke 23: 42f*) who have repented at the last minute are alongside those who have striven to do God's will all their lives; but, sinners as we are, we should rejoice that God has room for all.

† *Help me to do your will, and forgive me when I fail.*

July

197

3   Teaching in parables

Notes by Kate Hughes
based on the New Revised Standard Version

For Kate's biography see p.56

Introduction

In chapter 13 of his gospel, Matthew collects together some of
the stories Jesus told about the kingdom of heaven. He used these
parables to teach people how to prepare for the coming of the
kingdom, what they needed to do to enter it, and how glorious
a thing it was – worth any cost. Throughout this chapter there is
an underlying theme of *hearing*: before you can act on what Jesus
says, you have to hear it and understand its meaning; in the same
way, you need to see and understand his actions as signs of the
kingdom.

Text for the week: Matthew 13:16
Blessed are your eyes, for they see, and your ears, for they hear.

For group discussion and personal thought

• What is the difference between looking and seeing, and
  listening and hearing?

• Discovering buried treasure, tracking down a precious
  pearl. What would be your picture of what discovering the
  kingdom of God is like?

The sower

'Let anyone with ears listen!'
(verse 9)

Someone described a parable as 'an earthly story with a heavenly meaning'. The parables that Jesus told always begin from familiar situations, firmly rooted in everyday life. Everyone in his audience would have been familiar with the sight of a sower flinging his seed over the fields. They would also have been familiar with the end results – patches of bare ground, some crops choked with weeds or with withered stems, and fields of healthy plants heavy with grain. In a way, Jesus is describing how the different people in the great crowd would receive his words. Some would listen, nod their heads, say 'Nice story', and then forget his words. Others would listen in puzzlement and wonder what Jesus was getting at. Some would get excited but then get sidetracked by other things. And others would understand, and ponder how they could become good soil for the word of God's kingdom. The difference between them would stem from whether they were merely listening to a story, or really trying to hear what God's messenger might be saying to *them*.

It is a matter of expectations: do *we* expect to hear God speaking to us – through parables, through the words of others, through events, through reading, through prayer? Do we have an ear for the word of God?

† *Open our ears, Lord, we want to hear Jesus, and let his words change us.*

July

Not just listening but hearing

'For to those who have, more will be given, and they will have an abundance; but from those who have nothing, even what they have will be taken away.'

(verse 12)

I used to work for a large theological distance learning programme based in Johannesburg. We sent our students feedback questionnaires, which included questions about writing essays. Some of our students were older people who hadn't written an essay since they left school 30 years earlier, and in answer to the question 'How long did it take you to write this essay?' they would answer 'All my spare time for four weeks!' And then one day, all their study, research and effort would come together and they would begin to write good, well-researched essays which only took them a few days' work. And from then on, the more essays they wrote, the better they did.

It's much the same with listening to Jesus. Once we make the effort to really *hear* him, it becomes increasingly easy to understand his words and put them into action. But those who don't really listen to him and therefore don't *hear* him, can't make sense of his words and eventually give up trying and walk away. The first group are able to receive more and more; the others lose what they already have.

† *Lord, help us not just to listen to you but truly to hear what you are saying, through your written word, your spoken word and your actions.*

Explaining the parable

Scholars suggest that this explanation of the parable of the Sower was not given by Jesus, but provided later by the early church and incorporated into his gospel by Matthew. Jesus certainly gives the impression that he doesn't explain his parables, but uses them to challenge those who are merely listening and not hearing (see yesterday's reading). But whoever provided the explanation, it can help us to understand and act upon the parable.

> **But as for what was sown on good soil, this is the one who hears the word and understands it, who indeed bears fruit.**
>
> *(part of verse 23)*

The words of Jesus challenge us. Do we hear God's word of the kingdom? Do we act as if we are citizens of the kingdom and bear fruit? Or do other things divert and distract us: letting 'the evil one' get at us, falling away in the face of suffering and persecution, or allowing worldly cares and making money to absorb us? Do we need to make any changes to our lifestyle to make our soil more fertile and so better able to receive God's seed?

† *Lord, you scatter your seed over the whole world and give everyone the opportunity to respond. Show us how we can become fertile soil and bear fruit.*

July

Dealing with evil

The next parable also starts from a familiar scene. The farmer sowed good seed, but when the plants began to grow they were all mixed up with weeds. It looked a mess, but with young plants it would be impossible to pull out the weeds without damaging the wheat as well. This is not a situation that the farmer either intended or welcomes – something has gone wrong or, in the words of Jesus, 'An enemy has done this.' So the farmer instructs his slaves to leave the field alone:

'Let both of them grow together until the harvest.'
(part of verse 30)

For most of us, rooting out evil is not our task. Zealous crusades against those who are considered wrongdoers have resulted in massacres, witch hunts, persecution, suffering and injustice. It is God's responsibility, not ours (though he may call specific individuals to help him, like the reapers in the parable), and he will deal with it in his own time and in his own way. Our task is to resist evil with God's help, so that it cannot hurt us. As citizens of the kingdom, we have all the help we need to walk through the world unharmed (though not necessarily unaffected) by its evil. This requires a faith in God's love and power which, starting small, can grow to mighty proportions, like the mustard plant which provides shelter for the birds (verse 32).

† O Lord, increase our faith.

Memorable stories

Jesus told the crowds all these things in parables; without a parable he told them nothing.

(verse 34)

Again, an explanation is provided for the 'parable of the weeds in the field', either by Jesus himself or by the first Christians. But Jesus was a good teacher: he knew that a short, memorable story about a well-known situation would catch people's attention and be remembered much more easily than a longer sermon about the end of the age. He wanted his listeners to go away and think about the story that had stuck in their minds, and then, quietly and without fuss, spread it through their families and neighbours, the poor and the wealthy, like yeast working through flour and liquid to produce bread.

The explanation given to the disciples, by contrast, is bare and rather abrupt: this represents this, that represents that, this is what will happen, the righteous will shine like the sun, and that's it! Information for the mind, but perhaps not so much for the heart as the farmer with his slaves looking at his weedy field, or the woman mixing her daily bread. Which of the parables in this chapter stick most firmly in *your* mind?

† *Thank you, Lord, for your parables, which give us vivid pictures to take away, think about, and ponder in our hearts. Help us through them to respond to your invitation to be part of your kingdom.*

July

The glory of the kingdom

Saturday's reading begins with two very short parables which say a great deal. Other parables in Matthew 13 have described our need to receive the seed of the kingdom and the precautions we need to take to remain safely within the kingdom. The pictures of the field with its buried treasure and the beautiful pearl bring home the glory of God's kingdom. To be part of it is worth any price, any hard work, any sacrifice:

> **On finding one pearl of great value, he went and sold all that he had and bought it.**
>
> *(verse 46)*

Is that how you feel about the kingdom of heaven? What does the kingdom mean to you in practice? Is it just a vague concept, or is it something you long for and work for, and pray 'Your kingdom come'? Can you see signs of the kingdom in your daily life? Or do you, like the people of Nazareth in Sunday's reading, not recognise the kingdom breaking in on what is familiar and ordinary? They could not accept that the carpenter's son could be the bearer of the kingdom (verse 55); they listened to his teaching and were astonished, but they did not really hear what he was saying. Their preconceptions made them deaf. Do you hear – or simply listen?

† *Lord, open my eyes and ears to the evidence of your kingdom in my daily life, so that I can catch the excitement of discovering buried treasure or possessing a thing of great beauty.*

4 John the Baptist

Notes by Yordan Kalev Zhekov
based on the New Revised Standard Version

Yordan Kalev Zhekov is an Evangelical Christian born in Bulgaria. He holds a Doctor of Science degree in the field of theology from the Catholic Faculty of Theology of the University of Ljubljana, Slovenia, and has served as a minister of God's word in various churches and communities in Bulgaria, Romania, Slovenia and Croatia.

Introduction

What makes someone's biography? The current boom in biographies, ranging from political figures to singers, footballers and reality TV celebrities, makes this a challenging question. Is it the sleazy gossip about an embarrassing truth, the tactical moves towards infinite wealth, or the meaningful content of one human life? John the Baptist's biography is very short in all the gospels, but it reveals a life of knowledge, purpose, determination and devotion in someone who perceived and fulfilled God's plan for him. This week we follow Matthew's account of John's identity, ministry and message, the response it brought, his encounter with Jesus, his end and the memory he left.

Text for the week: Matthew 11:11
Truly I tell you, among those born of women no one has arisen greater than John the Baptist; yet the least in the kingdom of heaven is greater than he.

For group discussion and personal thought
- How does the biography of John the Baptist encourage you to follow Jesus Christ more closely?
- What are the most important events you would include in your own biography?
- Why was John's identity, ministry and message so important for Israel, the gospel writers and their original audiences?

July

The ministry

John the Baptist appears on the scene to break God's long silence towards his people. The place of his appearance is the desert, with its prophetic significance of the divine deliverance of the people. John's proclamation underlines his prophetic ministry and reveals its nature.

'Repent, for the kingdom of heaven has come near.'
(verse 2)

This announcement of the closeness of God's presence demands urgent action from the people, underlined by the character of the messenger.

John's ministry fulfils the words of Isaiah about the coming deliverance from exile (*Isaiah 40:3*). His appearance reveals his role as the Messiah's forerunner in the character of Elijah (*2 Kings 1:8*), whose coming was clearly predicted (*Malachi 3:1; 4:5*). John's ministry had a massive impact on the people; their positive reaction stemmed from their expectations and their understanding of John's role, which further underlined its significance and importance. John was completely involved in, and entirely devoted to, his ministry of preparing the way for Jesus. His whole way of life, words and actions, even his clothes, reveal only one goal, the fulfilment of his ministry for Jesus and the people of Israel.

Are we, as Christ's followers, as devoted to the ministries he has given us in our families, churches and communities? Do we resemble John in his devotion and passion to his ministry? Do our actions and speech reflect the Word of God?

† *Jesus, help us to invest ourselves in the ministries you have given us.*

July

The message

John's message becomes more specific when he turns to a particular group of his audience. The prominent scholarly and religious authorities of Israel came to John with mixed attitudes. The deceitful nature of their predominant reaction is reflected in the words of John, who does not hesitate to identify their real nature. They were fleeing from God's coming judgement like vipers from a fire, but their inner thoughts reflected self-sufficient rejection of John's baptism.

He is adamant that their salvation depends, not on their descent from Abraham, but on their righteous deeds, the fruit of their repentance. Only a positive response to his baptism will prepare them to face the Messiah. The words of John are addressed to his entire audience and define his preparatory role and Jesus' saving ministry.

> **'I baptize you with water for repentance, but one who is more powerful than I is coming after me; I am not worthy to carry his sandals. He will baptize you with the Holy Spirit and fire.'**

> *(verse 11)*

John's listeners must decide their destiny: salvation or judgement. They are to make their choice in the light of the coming Messiah. They can experience his salvation through repentance and deeds of righteousness, or reject him and condemn themselves to the fire of his eschatological judgement. This choice is still relevant for everyone today who hears the gospel.

† Help us, Lord, through our life of faith to choose Jesus' salvation.

July

The encounter

The culmination of John's ministry is his encounter with Christ. This was a profound historical moment for John, for Israel and for humanity as a whole. It is John's recognition of his need in the face of Jesus' appearance that reveals his understanding of Jesus' identity. Obediently, he accepts completely the desire of Jesus to be baptised: the Messiah has come to fulfil God's plan for the salvation of his people and he identifies with them through baptism. He is going to experience all the struggles and difficulties of their life and give his life for their salvation. This inauguration of Jesus' mission is stamped with God's approval through the verbal recognition of Jesus' divine sonship and the appearance of the Holy Spirit.

> **And when Jesus had been baptized, just as he came up from the water, suddenly the heavens were opened to him and he saw the Spirit of God descending like a dove and alighting on him. And a voice from heaven said, 'This is my Son, the Beloved, with whom I am well pleased.'**
> *(verses 16-17)*

The scene recalls the creation of the world in the presence of God's Spirit (*Genesis 1:2*), but this creation is of a new humanity through the saving mission of Jesus. Have we become part of that new humanity? A simple act of faith in Jesus and repentance for our sins will bring about this miracle.

† Dear Jesus, forgive us our sins and make us new people.

The person

Caught between his knowledge of the Messiah's victory over the powers of evil and his reality as a victim of those powers, John needs reassurance. In giving it, Jesus does not undermine John's identity and mission but underlines its significance. The answer confirms Jesus' messianic ministry but also describes the paradox of the kingdom of God – the now and not yet. The eschatological end has begun but is not yet completed. The unrighteous are convicted of sin but not yet finally judged. They are offered salvation, but evil still dominates the world.

John is the first to experience the paradoxical nature of God's kingdom, welcoming the Messiah in his life and yet suffering injustice and martyrdom at the hands of the wicked. The power of evil cannot overshadow the greatness of John's identity and ministry. However, John's outstanding position cannot be compared to the glorious reality of God's kingdom brought by the Messiah, which is experienced by those who accept it.

> **Truly I tell you, among those born of women no one has arisen greater than John the Baptist; yet the least in the kingdom of heaven is greater than he.**
>
> *(verse 11)*

The pain of our daily sufferings should not overshadow the reality of God's kingdom and God's love towards us revealed in Jesus, but strengthen our faith in him – our Saviour.

† *Help us, Lord, to go through the troublesome, evil reality of this world with complete devotion to Jesus.*

July

The response

The opposition of the religious authorities to Jesus increased in fury throughout his ministry. He follows up on their latest challenge with a parable reflecting the response of Israel to John's message and ultimately to himself. Through the replies of the sons to their father, Jesus identifies two groups which contrast radically.

Like the first son who initially offensively disobeyed his father but then drastically changed his attitude and obeyed him, the depraved part of the community, the tax collectors and the prostitutes, negated God's law through their immoral life but accepted John's message.

The prominent part of the Israelite community, the religious leaders, resembled the second son both in his complete verbal agreement with the father and his eventual disobedience when they completely rejected John's message. Moreover, they refused to change their attitude as the first son did.

> **For John came to you in the way of righteousness and you did not believe him, but the tax collectors and the prostitutes believed him; and even after you saw it, you did not change your minds and believe him.**
>
> *(verse 32)*

Empty words without supportive actions show religious vanity. How much are we people of our words? Do we accompany our confessions of faith in Jesus Christ with corresponding deeds of righteousness? All the elements of our daily life require consistency between our words and our deeds.

† Dear Lord, help our faith in Jesus to be expressed and acted upon.

Death and remembrance

The death of John the Baptist was as glorious as his ministry and at the same time as brutal as the evil world in which he lived. The figure of his executioner, Herod Antipas, embodied this evil in the wickedness of his character and deeds. He recognised the prophetic nature of John's identity and ministry and their eschatological culmination in Jesus (14:1-2). This brutal murder ended John's life, but it also defined his victory over the powers of evil. Through his life John announced the coming of Messiah and through his death he foreshadowed the death of Jesus.

After his transfiguration, Jesus defined the role of John as that of the forerunner, the prophetic Elijah whose ministry and message prepared the way for his own work. This is how he was to be remembered.

> **Elijah has already come, and they did not recognize him, but they did to him whatever they pleased.**
> *(chapter 17, part of verse 12)*

The selfish distortion of the divine message by those who possessed knowledge of the scriptures had ended John's life and was leading to the violent death of Jesus as well. Their missions, however, were gloriously completed in the fulfilment of God's plan of salvation. Our knowledge and understanding of God's Word should not be an obstacle, but guidance for the salvation of others.

† *Dear Lord, help us not to selfishly misuse your Word, but to use it for the benefit of others.*

July

Violence and War

1 War

Notes by Helen Van Koevering
based on the New Revised Standard Version

Helen has now worked for several years with the
Anglican Church in northern Mozambique (which
knew three decades of war until peace in 1992). More recently,
she has been involved as an ordained priest in training clergy and
lay women for ministry.

July

Introduction

The Bible hides nothing of the highs and lows of human
experience, the raw history of the people of God in their
relationship with the living God. Many stories are graphic in their
description of human failure and sin, destruction and hatred,
conflict and war, but through them we discern God's way, God's
light, God's love in the midst of the deepest valleys of human life,
even the dark valley of war. We can learn to recognise God's heart
for peace. Where Jesus wept for Jerusalem, we weep for those
areas of our world today where peace is not known, where conflict
continues, where the life of God is denied – and our readings this
week give us suggestions for those things that will make for peace.

Text for the week: Luke 19:41-42
*As he came near and saw the city, he wept over it, saying, 'If
you, even you, had only recognised on this day the things that
make for peace! But now they are hidden from your eyes.'.*

For group discussion and personal thought

• What have you learnt about peace in the midst of war this
week?

• What is your responsibility for bringing about the 'things
that make for peace'?

212

Strength from teamwork

The wilderness journey of the Israelites was full of challenges – survival in the desert, quarrels amongst themselves and threat of attack from other tribes through whose lands they passed. Each challenge was an opportunity to learn more about both themselves (and us) and their (and our) God. When the Amalekites appeared to make an unwarranted attack on the Israelites, Moses recognised immediately the need to call on the Lord throughout the conflict, and he chose to do just this, standing on a hill in view of the fighting with the staff of God raised in his hand. But it necessitated teamwork.

> **Moses' hands grew weary; so they took a stone and put it under him, and he sat on it. Aaron and Hur held up his hands, one on one side, and the other on the other side; so his hands were steady until the sun set.**
>
> *(verse 12)*

Moses raised his hands to call on the Lord for his people and inspire morale. Even in a conflict which has deteriorated into war, we need to remind ourselves and others of God's limitless presence and power, and our own need for the support, counsel and care of others – teamwork.

† *God, even in our dark days, remind us of your presence and love for us and all creation – and help us to be living reminders to others. Thank you for my friends, colleagues and family; may our leaders know the support and encouragement of teams around them too. Amen.*

July

The way of the warrior

'Do not lose heart, or be afraid, or panic, or be in dread of them; for it is the LORD your God who goes with you, to fight for you against your enemies, to give you victory.'

(part of verse 3, and verse 4)

In today's reading, we can recognise that God's ways are not our ways. Humanitarian concerns are paramount, even in the midst of war, and there is a certain protocol to follow to ensure wholehearted commitment to the battle. And there is this protocol because there is God, the Creator, who is with us and alongside us, and the battle is the Lord's – whatever the battle.

For some in southern Africa, living in areas of conflict, weakness and poverty, the image of Christ as warrior for his people has been described, carved, painted and voiced. To trust in Christ fighting for the weak, and bringing victory out of suffering, is a powerful image for those in the midst of suffering who know their weakness. It has presented an alternative vision to living in discouragement, fear and shock – a vision of living out patience, empathy and forgiveness during both the suffering in war and the rebuilding after war.

† Lord, you have provided the way above other ways, and we are accompanied by the warrior of the way. In him is our vision of a different life – open our eyes to this life, no matter the circumstances in which we find ourselves. Amen.

Ecological concerns

If you besiege a town for a long time, making war against it in order to take it, you must not destroy its trees by wielding an axe against them. Although you may take food from them, you must not cut them down. Are trees in the field human beings that they should come under siege from you?

(verse 19)

War has its roots in human failure and human hatred, misused power and misplaced priorities. It is the result of broken human relationships, neither welcome nor sought after. But how many times have we irreparably damaged the innocent earth during our wars? Remember the devastation of the world wars; look at the terrible disaster of the Vietnam War; never forget the horror of the utter destruction of Hiroshima by a nuclear bomb! In some places, the destruction of the land during wartime has brought further suffering in peacetime – sometimes the land has never recovered. But even in the absence of war, we are wreaking havoc on creation, as natural disasters around the world are highlighting for us. Concern for the natural world is in the Creator's heart – let it be in ours too.

† Creator God, stir us to greater concern and activity to preserve and maintain the beauty and provision of our world. All creation is precious in your sight, and we praise you. Amen.

July

Being in God's plan

The book of Judges reveals a man true to his name – Gideon, whose name ('smiter') stands for man in all his fearful, heavy-handed individuality. Gideon always seemed to need signs from God to act confidently on God's word: first with meat and leavened bread, then a fleece, and now with a dream interpreted by an unbeliever:

'I had a dream, and in it a cake of barley bread tumbled into the camp of Midian, and came to the tent, and struck it so that it fell; it turned upside down, and the tent collapsed.' . . . When Gideon heard the telling of the dream and its interpretation, he worshipped; and he returned to the camp of Israel, and said, 'Get up; for the LORD has given the army of Midian into your hand.'
(part of verse 13, and verse 15)

Then, with amazing courage and confidence, Gideon armed his smaller army only with trumpets, jars and torches. The noise of trumpets and breaking jars so frightened the Midianites, that the battle was won easily after a leaderless retreat to the Jordan.

The Old Testament may emphasise God as the warrior for God's people, but in Gideon's non-violent victory we catch a glimpse of the divine plan to send God's Son, Jesus Christ, the one who was to turn the world upside-down (or rightside-up) as Prince of Peace.

† *Give me courage and wisdom, Lord, to recognise the peace that passes all understanding, but which Jesus gave the world. Amen.*

In his name

'You come to me with sword and spear and javelin; but I come to you in the name of the LORD of hosts, . . . that all this assembly may know that the LORD does not save by sword and spear; for the battle is the LORD's and he will give you into our hand.'

(part of verse 45, and verse 47)

David and Goliath's story is well known, and David's bold faith in the living God has much to teach us all. It wasn't that he denied the danger of Goliath, but that David saw the threat from the perspective of the living God. It is not through great armoury or many weapons, nor through allowing fear of an enormous threat to determine our own action, that battles are won. Our choices are crucial – either we can run in fear or attack in powerful fury, or we can allow calm, confident experience in our living God to confront the threat. As an evangelist once said, 'David teaches us that we can either scream "Help, he's so big - I can't do this!" or "Wow, he's so big – I can't miss!"' Fear and lack of confidence so often lead to war, and recognising this is the first step towards the alternative of peace.

† *Lord, may we know your living presence and act as David teaches us – with courage, confidence and the love that casts out all fear. In your name, Amen.*

August

Know God's best

'O LORD, how long shall I cry for help,
and you will not listen?
Or cry to you, 'Violence!'
and you will not save?'

(Habakkuk, verse 2)

As he came near and saw the city, he wept over it,
saying, 'If you, even you, had only recognised on this day
the things that make for peace! . . . you did not recognise
the time of your visitation from God.'

(Luke, part of verses 41 and 44)

To recognise 'things that make for peace', whether in the threat
of war or in its midst, is to recognise that the root of these
'things' lies in the knowledge of God's best for all creation,
God's plan of salvation through Jesus. Salvation calls us to
repentance and forgiveness; to transformed relationships; to
sacrificial action in order to be channels for God to turn the
world upside-down, beginning with us. To cry out to God, to
lament the violence, chaos and disorder of war, is to cry with
God and be reawakened to know God's best, God's purpose
and plan. Then, with lives open to recognise God's presence,
the power of the Spirit and God's perfect law fulfilled in Jesus,
we have 'things of peace' to give the world: the peace, justice
and love of God.

*† Jesus, you cried for Jerusalem, and you cry for us in the
violence of our wars. Teach us and our nations' leaders those
things that make for peace, the peace you intend for us all.
Amen.*

August

IBRA International Bible Reading Association

1020 Bristol Road, Selly Oak, Birmingham B29 6LB, Great Britain

Order form for 2009 books

Name: _____

Address: _____

_____

_____

_____Postcode: _____

Telephone number: _____

Your order will be dispatched when all books are available. Mail order only (post included).

Code	Title of Book	Quantity	Unit Price	Total
	UK customers			
AA0822	Words For Today 2009	£8.25		
AA0821	Light For Our Path 2009	£8.25		
AA0823	Light For Our Path 2009 large print	£12.00		
	Overseas customers in Europe			
AA0822	Words For Today 2009	£11.00		
AA0821	Light For Our Path 2009	£11.00		
AA0823	Light For Our Path 2009 large print	£17.50		
	Overseas customers outside Europe			
AA0822	Words For Today 2009	£13.00		
AA0821	Light For Our Path 2009	£13.00		
AA0823	Light For Our Path 2009 large print	£19.00		

Payments in pounds sterling, please.
Please allow 28 days for delivery

Total cost of books	
Donation to IBRA Fund	
TOTAL DUE	

☐ **I enclose a cheque (made payable to IBRA)**

☐ **Please charge my MASTERCARD/VISA/SWITCH**

Card Number: ⬚⬚⬚⬚⬚⬚⬚⬚⬚⬚⬚⬚⬚⬚⬚⬚ **Issue Number:** ⬚⬚

Expiry Date: _____

Security number (last three digits on back): _____

Signature: _____

The INTERNATIONAL BIBLE READING ASSOCIATION is a Registered Charity

International Bible Reading Association

Help us to continue our work of providing Bible study notes for use by Christians in the UK and throughout the world. The need is as great as it was when IBRA was founded in 1882 by Charles Waters as part of the work of the Sunday School Union.

Please leave a legacy to the International Bible Reading Association.

An easy-to-use leaflet has been prepared to help you provide a legacy. Please write to us at the address below and we will send you this leaflet – and answer any questions you might have about a legacy or other donations. Please help us to strengthen this and the next generation of Christians.

Thank you very much.

International Bible Reading Association
Dept 298, 1020 Bristol Road
Selly Oak
Birmingham
B29 6LB
Great Britain

Tel. 0121 415 2977

Fax 0121 472 7575

2   Violence

Notes by Iain Roy
based on the Good News Bible

Iain Roy is a retired minister of the Church of
Scotland with a background of ministry in an
area of urban deprivation, and industrial chaplaincy. A former
moderator and clerk of Ardrossan Presbytery, he is regularly
engaged in public worship.

Introduction

Violence is a reality of life today, both in society and within
the home and family. Crime, sectarian and ethnic conflicts and
the misuse of political power can all lead to violence. Even the
church has its own sad history of violence when it has failed
to recognise the individual freedom of both believer and non-
believer. Christ shows us that violence is not God's way. Christ's
strength lay in weakness. His power is love, the slower but
surer way to effect change in human lives.

Text for the week: 1 Samuel 24:4-5
*They said to him, 'This is your chance!' . . . But then David's
conscience began to trouble him, and he said to his men, 'May
the Lord keep me from doing any harm to my master, whom
the Lord chose as king!'*

For group discussion and personal thought

- Are there any points of conflict within your own local
  community which create violence? Is there anything the church
  fellowship could do to help resolve these situations?
- Identify areas of violence in the world today and resolve to pray
  for some of them regularly.
- What personally angers you? Could this lead you to violence?
  We need to understand and counter the violence that can be
  latent in any of us.

August

Brother versus brother

Some of the most savage human conflicts have been civil wars when brother has been ranged against brother, and families divided.

> 'Do you think you are going to be a king and rule over us?' his brothers asked. So they hated him even more because of his dreams and because of what he said about them.

(verse 8)

Joseph's brothers were almost guilty of the heinous crime of fratricide. What saved them from it was his brother Reuben's intervention. Yet, even selling him into slavery was an act of violence against his person.

The strange irony of their act, however, was that in the long run it was their own salvation. Joseph's meteoric rise to power in Egypt put him in a position to save his family and his people when famine threatened their survival. His magnanimity negated their violence to him. He offered them instead forgiveness and compassion, a different basis on which to live life together, the alternative way Christ offers us, the way of love.

† Lord, negate the violence and hatred that still beset our world, and show us and all humankind the other way – the way of love, forgiveness and compassion.

The spiral of violence

The Old Testament world was a violent world, as Samson's actions here show.

> Samson prayed . . . 'God give me my strength just once more, so that with this one blow I can get even with the Philistines for putting out my two eyes.' So Samson took hold of the two middle pillars holding up the building . . . He pushed with all his might, and the building fell down on the five kings and everyone else. Samson killed more people at his death than he had killed during his life.
>
> *(part of verses 28-30)*

It would be wrong for us to conclude that violence is no longer a very real element in life today. Abuse of women and children, sectarian, political and criminal violence, even in some countries the violence of the state against the citizen are real issues in the modern world. What the Samson story shows is that violence begets violence: the persecuted can so easily become the persecutor, the victim of violence the perpetrator of it. Violence is a spiral from which there is no release unless humanity chooses another way to relate to others, the way of forgiveness and reconciliation, Christ's way.

† Lord, help us to defeat the violence of this world, sometimes latent even within ourselves, by strengthening in us the sense of human worth and dignity revealed in Jesus Christ.

August

Learning from life

Long-held beliefs are always difficult to counter. Christ found it difficult to change the persistent belief in his society in a correlation between human sin and illness and death.

> 'What about those eighteen people in Siloam who were killed when the tower fell on them? Do you suppose this proves they were worse than all the other people living in Jerusalem? No indeed!'
>
> *(verse 4, and part of verse 5)*

The eighteen were not guilty as charged. They were innocent victims, yet they died. The sad fact of illness, violence and war is that they are no respecter of persons. Like the rain from heaven they fall on good and evil alike. Religion and religious people have constantly struggled with this fact of life. The book of Job in particular reflects that. On a day when we remember the atomic bombing of Hiroshima, we do well to remember the lessons of history, life, and religion: that the innocent are always as likely to suffer as the guilty. It is best to live our lives by love, which 'does not keep a record of wrongs' (*1 Corinthians 13:5*).

† *Father, we remember all the innocent of every day and age in their suffering and we pray that the lessons of history and the love of Christ may keep us from repeating the violence of past days.*

August

Weakness and strength

David is the strangest mixture of a man – capable both of great love and great violence. Here his followers urge him to violence.

> They said to him, 'This is your chance! The LORD has told you that he would put your enemy in your power and you could do to him whatever you wanted to.' David crept over and cut off a piece of Saul's robe without Saul's knowing it. But then David's conscience began to trouble him, and he said to his men, 'May the LORD keep me from doing any harm to my master, whom the Lord chose as king!'

(verses 4-5, and part of verse 6)

Here we see David as we must often see ourselves – as a creature of conscience. What to do in life is not always clear-cut. David's internal struggle and debate led him to spare Saul and let God be his judge. David's restraint in turn led Saul also to see things in a different light. It is never weakness to forgive. It is strength. It is not procrastination to think before we act, not if it brings us nearer to that mind which was in Christ, ever ready to forgive and to love.

† Lord, give us a healthy conscience so that we think before we act and are influenced by your great love for all humankind.

August

Cost of discipleship

We sometimes forget within the Church the price others have paid for us to have faith. Stephen is only the first in a long succession of Christian martyrs.

> **the members of the Council listened to Stephen, they became furious and ground their teeth at him in anger . . . Then they all rushed at him at once, threw him out of the city, and stoned him.**
>
> *(verse 54, and part of verses 57 and 58)*

Even today violence is a price some pay for faith. It should make those of us who do not have to pay such a price more willing to consider what is asked of us in our Christian discipleship. As Dietrich Bonhoeffer put it, there is a 'cost of discipleship'. The faith that demands little gives little. The faith that asks much of our time, our talents, our resources, offers us far more from Christ's love than we can ever give from ours.

† Christ, help us to meet what you ask of us day by day with a good heart and a willing spirit, knowing that whatever we give to you can never match what you give to us.

The sustaining fellowship

The man who did violence to the Christians – as Saul – had violence done to him as the Christian Paul. It was for him part of the pilgrimage between these two names, *his* cost of discipleship.

> **Some Jews . . . won the crowd over to their side, stoned Paul and dragged him out of the town, thinking that he was dead. But when the believers gathered round him, he got up and went back into the town.**
>
> *(Acts, part of verses 19 and 20)*

The reading from Hebrews shows that Paul was only the latest in a long line of those who had violence done to them for their beliefs. What helped Paul to persevere in discipleship, despite the violence, was the fellowship of the Church, the communion of the saints – the love and support of others. Most of us need to work harder at this aspect of our faith: to be more aware both of what we receive from others and also what we can give to others. Great movements such as Christian Aid and Amnesty International base their work on this sense of mutuality. We impoverish our faith when we see it too narrowly as 'my' faith and not 'our' faith, the gift of Christ to us.

† *Give us a sense of our place and worth in the fellowship of the Church and the communion of the saints so that we are strengthened by receiving from others and challenged by what we can give to them.*

August

Romans 9–16

1   Israel in the purpose of God

Notes by David Huggett
based on the New Revised Standard Version

For David's biography, see p.119.

Introduction

If you usually communicate with friends and family by email
you may find it difficult to grasp how anyone could write a
letter as long as Romans. Even more difficult to understand
is how its deep theology and intricate arguments could be
absorbed by those listening to the letter being read in public.
Yet Romans has been a life-changing book for many over the
centuries since it was written. The theme that runs throughout
is that of God's lordship. Against that background Paul, a Jew
who has become a Christian, wrestles with the question of why
the Jewish people have rejected Christ. In so doing he raises a
number of important issues for us today.

Text for the week: Romans 11:29
The gifts and the calling of God are irrevocable.

For group discussion and personal thought

- The Church in the West has declined dramatically in recent
  years, losing much of its influence in society. What steps
  could you suggest to remedy this situation?

- What pictures, other than Paul's image of the olive tree,
  could you suggest to illustrate the relationship between Jews
  and Gentiles?

- It has been suggested that 'the pew makes the preacher'.
  What do you understand that to mean? How important do
  you think preaching is in our multimedia society?

God is merciful

Some people seem to have it all – as we might be tempted to say, they have all the 'luck'. Paul knows how privileged the Israelites are when it comes to spiritual matters (*verses 4 and 5*). So it is all the more puzzling that they should reject the one who was their own Messiah. The puzzle is solved in part when we realise that a person does not become a child of God by belonging to a particular race or nation (*verse 6*).

In recent years great strides have been made in the study of human genetics, and some scientists seem to believe that we have a gene for everything – from obesity to religion. But being a child of God doesn't depend on genetics, or on the colour of our skin, or the place we were born. It is all to do with God's mercy:

It depends not on human will or exertion, but on God who shows mercy.

(verse 16)

The word 'mercy' is one of those lovely words to describe God's compassionate treatment even of those who resist him and, like Peter, deny him. Israel's story in the Old Testament is a story of God's recurring mercy.

† *Thank you, Lord, for your mercy in accepting me just as I am. Help me not to take advantage of that.*

August

God knows best

When I was a child I did not always appreciate the decisions my parents made. It was even worse when I queried some decision, only to get the reply, 'Because I said so.' To me that seemed no answer at all. When I became a parent I understood. There are some things you just know, or you realise that an explanation would be far too difficult for a child with much less knowledge or experience to understand. That is a healthy lesson for us to learn in our relationship with God. As Paul points out:

> **[W]ho indeed are you, a human being, to argue with God? Will what is moulded say to the one who moulds it, 'Why have you made me like this?'**
>
> *(verse 20)*

We would really like to have an answer for every question. But it's not like that. There are, however, certain things about God of which we can be quite certain: he is just, he is merciful, and as to the way he deals with his people, whether Jews or Gentiles, he knows what he is doing.

† *Lord, help me to hold firm to the things that I do know now, and help me to trust you for the things I do not know or do not understand.*

August

Simple fact – simple faith

What is the basis of a true relationship with God? Israel had made the mistake of believing that they were 'chosen' because of their genetic inheritance and zealous keeping of the law (*verses 2-3*). We may not make that mistake, but many still feel that they have to contribute *something* to their salvation. Society encourages us to believe that we must grow up impressing people, so that they think well of us. Parents, teachers, friends must all be impressed by how good, clever, lovable and beautiful we are. So when it comes to God we think the same is true: we must do something to impress him and make him willing to accept us. Nothing could be further from the truth. The gospel is simple:

> **[I]f you confess with your lips that Jesus is Lord and believe in your heart that God raised him from the dead, you will be saved.**

(verse 9)

'Jesus is Lord' seems to have been the original and the only necessary creed of the early Christian church (see also *1 Corinthians 12:3* and *Philippians 2:11*). As Paul explains in the rather curious verses 6 and 7, you don't need to go to any lengths to reach God (heaven or hell), because Jesus has already come to earth as Saviour and conquered death through his resurrection. All we need is to turn to him in faith and acknowledge his lordship.

† *I believe in my heart that Jesus is Lord. Help me to confess it with my lips.*

Preaching and listening

Paul placed a very high value on preaching, indeed he was passionate about it (*1 Corinthians 9:16*). It was not a lesser part of a service of worship, to be endured – as it sometimes is today. Preaching is a heavy responsibility which requires careful and thorough preparation both intellectually and spiritually. But here Paul makes it clear that there is also a heavy responsibility laid on hearers:

> **Faith comes from what is heard, and what is heard comes through the word of Christ.**
>
> *(verse 17)*

Not everybody has had the opportunity to hear the gospel. However, Paul says, that is not an excuse the Israelites can make. The point is that it matters *how* we hear. If you have ever played the party game Chinese Whispers you will know how a message whispered in one person's ear can become very different as it is passed on. We can too easily filter out the things we don't like hearing, or interpret the message according to our own preconceived ideas. As well as praying for the preacher we need to pray for ourselves as we listen and as we read.

† Father, I thank you for all the ways that you speak to me. Help me to be attentive and careful in all my listening.

God never gives up on us

The way the nation of Israel treated God is a sordid story. Who could blame God if he wanted nothing more to do with them, especially when they finally insult him by rejecting Jesus? Will he reject them then? No way, says Paul. God continues to work out his master plan in spite of having to work with the most unlikely material. In fact Israel has always been, and will remain, part of God's eternal purposes of redemption.

> So I ask, have they stumbled so as to fall? By no means!
> But through their stumbling salvation has come to the
> Gentiles.

(part of verse 11)

Jesus' ministry was mainly to the Jews, and Paul began his ministry to the Jews, normally preaching in the synagogues, until the time when their rejection of the gospel on offer led him to say 'We turn to the Gentiles' (*Acts 13:46*). God used their refusal to expand his offer to all.

A large and thriving church near where I live suffered quite a serious split. A small number of the members left and joined a tiny struggling church that was on the brink of closure. Now both churches are strong and flourishing. God can use our stumbles to fulfil his purposes.

† Thank you, Lord, that you are not disturbed by our folly, nor
limited by our partial understanding. Encourage us to believe
that even when we feel like the 'remnant' of Israel, you will
work out your glorious plans for your people.

The mystery of God's purposes

The Gentile Christians could have thought themselves superior to the Jews who had rejected and even crucified the Lord. Paul reminds them more than once that he is a Jew, and so, he could have added, was Jesus. So he warns his Gentile readers: 'Do not become proud, but stand in awe' (*verse 20*), because in fact they owe a great deal to Israel: great spiritual leaders like Abraham and Moses, and the revelation of God himself and his plan of redemption for all.

The mystery of God's purposes is only slowly unfolding. Like a good murder mystery story, the clues are there but it is only on the last page that we can look back and see how everything fits together. It would be so nice to understand it all now, but even Paul, with his great theological mind, will only see the whole when he looks back on it. For the moment we must accept that God's ways and thoughts are far above ours (see *Isaiah 55:8,9*). We cannot make God more manageable or confine him in our little theological boxes. Our worthy response must surely be,

> **O the depth of the riches and wisdom and knowledge of God! How unsearchable are his judgements and how inscrutable his ways!**
>
> *(verse 33)*

† *'The love of God is broader than the measures of our mind'* (F W Faber). *Thank you, Lord.*

2 Living the Christian life

Notes by Sheila Giffard Smith
based on the New International Version

Sheila is a retired teacher, specialising in dyslexia. She was for some time in charge of a Sunday School and now leads a Bible study home group. She has published two devotional books, having enjoyed regular morning Bible study and prayer for many years. She is still writing, feeling 'driven' to share her faith and insights. She lives in Surrey, England.

August

Introduction

In these three chapters from Paul's Letter to the Romans, the apostle turns from the deep theology of the previous eleven chapters to practical advice for all Christians. Unsurprisingly, he reflects Christ's own teaching. There are exhortations and prohibitions. All the passages are basically about relationships within the Christian community – our attitude to one another's differences, weaknesses and strengths and the ways in which we can be pleasing to God and considerate to others. He gives us a route map of certain areas, indicating the path to follow in our walk with God, and a way to discover his blessing. This section began with the words, 'Be transformed' (*Romans 12:2*), and as we endeavour to live like Christ, how we need to pray for this transformation!

Text for the week: Romans 12:16
Live in harmony with each other.

For group discussion and personal thought

• What should a Christian do about a church member who is constantly undermining/misleading another?

• How can we show sincere love in our church?

• What is the best way to resolve disputes?

Be transformed

This passage begins with the word 'Therefore', referring to the truth in previous chapters which have abundantly demonstrated God's mercy in bringing Gentiles to faith in Christ. Our part is to serve the Lord with our whole being as 'living sacrifices'.

> **Do not conform any longer to the pattern of this world, but be transformed by the renewing of your mind.**
>
> *(part of verse 2)*

Rather like a butterfly chrysalis, we cannot stay in that stage for ever: we must leave it behind, dry out our wings and fly! We need not go on with the same old habits and limitations; God's intention now is that we should grow in knowledge of his good and pleasing will.

The rest of the passage explains how necessary this is for the body of people we call the Church. We all have different gifts, just as bodily parts all have particular functions, and we need to accept in humility what we are fitted for and where we are needed. It would hardly be useful if everybody volunteered to do the flowers, say, and nobody was willing to read the lesson, lead the prayers, deal with the collection, and so on! By God's grace we are enabled to serve in our own particular way, whether this is in a church service or in everyday life.

† Lord God, help us to serve and please you in the way you desire, and to do so cheerfully and with humility.

Costly love

What is sincere love? In the Christian sense it is not an emotion, but active love. These verses spell out in detail how true love does not depend on our feelings, but is self-sacrificial. It is the outworking of the 'spiritual act of worship' that the apostle speaks of (*verse 1*) – and it is intensely practical, and humbling too.

> **Hate what is evil; cling to what is good. Be devoted to one another in brotherly love. Honour one another above yourselves.**
>
> *(part of verse 9, and verse 10)*

Paul sets before us an almost impossibly high standard of conduct in our interaction with others, and this we can achieve only with true humility. We are not to think too much of ourselves, as we read yesterday (*verse 3*); nor are we to be proud (*verse 16*). Does this mean 'being a doormat' and letting people walk all over us? Well yes, in a way – but not as a sign of weakness and resignation, but of strength in our service to the Lord, putting others first, even our enemies! We are called to live in a way that goes against our instinctive, worldly nature in order to ensure that there is harmony. For this we need to keep our spiritual life in good order – joyful in hope, patient in affliction and faithful in prayer.

† *Lord God, help us in our prayer life, for only as we pray shall we learn your will and find the strength to do it.*

Unwilling submission

This passage is, at first sight, terribly difficult to accept. Consider this extract:

> **Everyone must submit himself to the governing authorities, for there is no authority except that which God has established . . . rulers hold no terror for those who do right, but for those who do wrong.**
>
> *(part of verses 1 and 3)*

Thinking of evil men who have ruled throughout the ages, and certainly in recent times, it is impossible to realise that they were, and are, appointed by God, and that we need not be frightened of them. Are they all really God's servants to do us good (*verse 4*)?

It is probable that the misuse of power was not in Paul's mind when he wrote this passage. To rebel against good rulers instituted by God would of course deserve punishment. But sound Christian theologians maintain that if laws are put in place which contradict God's law, civil disobedience becomes a Christian duty, possibly resulting in dire consequences, even death. We have examples in the Bible, and in more recent times, of such rebellion by Christian believers. For example, when the apostles were brought before the authorities after disobeying the command not to preach in the name of Jesus, they answered, 'We must obey God rather than men!' (*Acts 5:27-29*). What courage they showed, for they risked severe penalties and possibly death!

† *Lord God, please guide us in all our conduct. Teach us to discern and obey your laws above all others.*

238

Wake up!

'Clothe yourselves with the Lord Jesus Christ.' Paul is indicating that as far as possible we must bear Christ's image – dress in his spiritual clothing, as it were. When children play at dressing up, they not only look like the one they mean to be, but they behave like that one. So it is with us: when we are clothed with Christ we want to be recognised as Christians and to behave like him. What will he find us doing, thinking, saying, when he comes again? What will he want to find? Certainly, he will expect us to be leading good and upright lives, worthy of him. He will expect us to be obeying all the Ten Commandments. The main emphasis in this passage is our relationship with our fellow Christians – fulfilling the law of love.

> **Love does no harm to its neighbour. Therefore love is the fulfilment of the law.**
>
> *(verse 10)*

There is only one debt that may be outstanding in the eyes of Christ, and that is 'the continuing debt to love another' (*verse 8*). Shortly before Jesus was crucified he said to his disciples, 'A new command I give you: Love one another . . . By this all men will know that you are my disciples' (*John 13:34*). It is as if love is an article of clothing that makes all disciples recognisable.

† *Lord Jesus, throw your cloak of love around us so that we may reflect your image.*

August

Don't tread on other people's toes!

'Why shouldn't I do this? I'm not doing anything wrong.' We may often find ourselves thinking like this, and we may be perfectly entitled to pursue a particular interest or desire. I went to Yoga classes for a while, but a friend was really upset, feeling that I was dabbling with the occult. That was not, in fact, the case: I was benefiting from healthy exercise and relaxation. But I stopped going for her sake. If what we do goes against another person's religious principles, we should not indulge in that course of action.

Paul's point is that we should respect other people's different beliefs, especially if their faith is weak. One major issue for the Jews was the law regarding dietary restrictions, and another concerned certain sacred days.

> **One man considers one day more sacred than another; another man considers every day alike . . . He who regards one day as special, does so to the Lord. He who eats meat, eats to the Lord, for he gives thanks to God; and he who abstains, does so to the Lord and gives thanks to God.**
>
> *(part of verse 5, and verse 6)*

We Christians may not agree about everything, and this is natural. But strong Christians undermining the faith of the weak are not acting in love, no matter how convinced we are of the rightness of our choice.

† *Lord, give us discernment so that we avoid being stumbling blocks to other Christians.*

'You are what you eat!'

This slogan might describe the bulk of chapter 14; yet in fact it is a trivial matter. Much more important in the contention arising from the many Jewish taboos concerning food and drink – and this involved Christian Jews – are Christian relationships.

> **For the kingdom of God is not a matter of eating and drinking, but of righteousness, peace and joy in the Holy Spirit.**

(verse 17)

Christians may legitimately differ, but we cannot live in isolation; we are accountable to each other and to God, and all are on an equal footing before God. The important point Paul makes is that Christians should respect each other's beliefs, abstaining from anything that might cause a weaker Christian to stumble, however much we feel that what we do is right. This is the sincere love described in 12:9.

On the other hand, if we consider that what we do is wrong, then for us it is wrong. 'If in doubt, don't' is good advice, with which the apostle apparently agrees (*verse 23*). To sum up, we are to be peacemakers, building up individuals, not judging them. What we believe and do is between us and God, and he alone is Judge.

† *O Lord, give us greater love and respect for each other in our differences, and help us to build bridges, not dig ditches.*

August

Romans 9–16

3 Final exhortation and greetings

Notes by Robert Draycott
based on the New Revised Standard Version

Robert Draycott is a Baptist minister who is currently Chaplain of Eltham College, London. Previously he served as a minister in Northamptonshire and as a missionary in Brazil.

Introduction

How lovely it is to be welcomed into someone else's home, especially when we are weary after a long journey. Our welcome is also special when our hosts have never even met us before and may also be crossing barriers of language and culture. This idea of welcoming people into our homes is our 'way in' to these concluding chapters of Paul's letter to the Romans. He had been welcomed into many homes on his missionary journeys. He looked forward to being welcomed in Rome. Paul had never visited that city before but he knew that he was writing to the Christians in Rome, rather than to – as we often tend to say – the church at Rome

Text for the week: Romans 15:7
Welcome one another, therefore, just as Christ has welcomed you, for the glory of God.

For group discussion and personal thought

- What have you learnt from Christians of other traditions?

- Whom do you need to ask for help? Are you the sort of person that people feel able to approach when they need help?

Welcome one another

Christians today, with their separated denominations, are not so different from the Christians in Rome to whom Paul wrote. This message of welcome, despite real differences and disagreements, is just as important now as it was then. The Christians in Rome naturally tended to meet with like-minded friends – which is often the basis of our separations today.

Modern Christians tend to idealise the early church, imagining that everything was harmonious and united. This can lead to discouragement and disillusion with the church today, and we lay the blame for its failings on other people, rather than ourselves. With good psychology, Paul appeals only to the 'strong', which is how most of us see ourselves.

> **We who are strong ought to put up with the failings of the weak, and not to please ourselves. Each of us must please our neighbour for the good purpose of building up the neighbour . . . Welcome one another, therefore, just as Christ has welcomed you, for the glory of God.**
>
> *(verses 1-2 and 7)*

We all know people from different denominations in our neighbourhood, at work, in our own families. Recognise them as fellow Christians, welcome them as fellow Christians, treat them as fellow Christians!

† *Lord, we thank you for kind people who have offered us hospitality. Help us in our turn to welcome both friend and stranger. We also pray for your healing love in those situations where Christians find it difficult to love their fellow Christians.*

Written to be heard

Paul's letters were written to be read aloud. The shorter letters would have been heard in their entirety. A longer letter such as Romans would probably have been divided into two or three sections, and today's passage is clearly part of a much larger section.

> **I myself feel confident. . . that you yourselves are full of goodness, filled with all knowledge, and able to instruct one another. . . I have written rather boldly by way of reminder, because of the grace given me by God, to be a minister of Christ Jesus to the Gentiles. . . I have reason to boast of my work for God.**
>
> *(part of verses 14-17)*

In isolation Paul appears unattractively boastful; but in the wider context of his letter, he has 'reason to boast' and reminds his hearers of his credentials. He knows he has written 'boldly' but his authority comes from the grace given to him.

Many Christians apparently do not read the Bible regularly, which is puzzling when we ourselves find this such a helpful practice. We can feel superior to them, imagining ourselves 'closer to the Lord', 'the strong'. We should share Paul's confidence that our fellow Christians – even those who differ from us – are 'full of goodness . . . and able to instruct one another'.

† When I imagine myself to be better than other Christians, remind me of my own faults and failings. Help me to see the goodness in other people.

By way of you to Spain

Today's reading may explain Paul's purpose in writing to the Christians in Rome: he longs to see them on his way to Spain.

> I do hope to see you on my journey and to be sent on by you, once I have enjoyed your company for a little while. . . I will set out by way of you to Spain; and. . . I will come in the fullness of the blessing of Christ.
>
> *(part of verses 24 and 28, and verse 29)*

Paul understood human nature, and how easily people can be misunderstood or misinterpreted. He is afraid that some will cynically say 'He is not really interested in seeing you – he just wants a stop-off on the way to Spain.' That was true, but not the whole truth: Paul also genuinely wanted to visit Rome to see a good number of friends. It really was a case of 'by way of you to Spain'.

Contrary to his enemies' opinion, Paul was not really proud and boastful. He knew just how much he needed friends, and their help. He was clearly worried about his visit to Jerusalem – rightly, according to Acts 21 and 22. He knew that asking for help often gets people on 'our side', showing them that we too are vulnerable.

† *We give thanks for our friends, especially those we didn't know we had who helped us in time of need. May we in our turn be true friends.*

August

Paul's appeal

Paul has specific fears about his forthcoming visit to Jerusalem:

> **I appeal to you, brothers and sisters. . . to join me in earnest prayer to God on my behalf, that I may be rescued from the unbelievers in Judea, and that my ministry to Jerusalem may be acceptable to the saints.**
> *(part of verse 30, and verse 31)*

Paul refers here to three groups: 'unbelievers', 'the saints', and 'you'. To the unbelievers, Jews who were not Christians, Paul was a traitor who had not simply deserted his Jewish faith and practice but claimed that Christ was the true fulfilment of Judaism. Paul rightly feared for his life from them. 'The saints' were the Christians in Jerusalem who greeted Paul warmly (*Acts 21:17*), though Acts tells us that that there were some quite important differences and disagreements between them and Paul. On some things they had agreed to disagree, on other points they had compromised. But they still retained the bonds of Christian love and fellowship – true saints do not exclude and reject fellow Christians over what are really trifling differences. Addressing 'you', Paul seems remarkably confident of support from people, some of whom he doesn't know. He is very positive, assuming the best, inviting a positive response from the Roman Christians, appealing to their better nature – still a very effective strategy.

† *Forgive us, Lord, when we assume the worst about people and situations. Help us to think the best of people and thus encourage them.*

August

Friends

Here Paul mentions a whole host of friends, 30 people in all, 27 by name, beginning with Phoebe.

> **I commend to you our sister Phoebe, a deacon of the church at Cenchreae, so that you may welcome her in the Lord as is fitting for the saints, and help her in whatever she may require from you, for she has been a benefactor of many and of myself as well.**
>
> *(verses 1-2)*

Phoebe was probably sufficiently well off to be travelling to Rome on business, and Paul may have entrusted his letter to her. Next Paul mentions Prisca (*verses 3-5*). We know something about Prisca (or Priscilla) and her husband Aquila from Acts 18, and here we are told that they hosted a house church.

In verse 7 Paul sends greetings to 'Andronicus and Junia, my relatives'. Most scholars now agree that Junia, like Phoebe and Prisca, was a woman (although her name has been translated as if it were a man's name). This is highly significant for two reasons. Firstly, it reminds Christians today of the importance and value of the ministry of women in the early church, however divisive an issue we may make of it. Secondly, this passage should help defend Paul against the charge of misogyny, of which he is often accused.

† *Lord, we give thanks for all who have ministered to us. Bless all those, women and men, who are engaged in the challenge of ministry.*

August

From names to the name

Paul knew the value of teamwork and his dependence on his colleagues and friends, as this final chapter makes clear. Timothy, in particular, stands out as 'my co-worker'. Paul also depended on Tertius, his scribe, to whom he dictated his thoughts. A third person named is Gaius, 'who is host to me'. Timothy, Tertius and Gaius remind us of the different roles that Christians today can take. Some are leaders and speakers like Timothy. Others are more like Tertius: dealing with the 'nuts and bolts', practical people. Then others are like Gaius, with resources that they share generously. We need all three types, we need to know our own capabilities, and not envy those with different but equal gifts.

Then Paul moves from names to the Name, from the human to the divine:

> **Now to God who is able to strengthen you according to my gospel and the proclamation of Jesus Christ . . . to the only wise God, through Jesus Christ, to whom be the glory for ever! Amen.**
>
> *(part of verse 25, and verse 27)*

The letter began (*1:3*) and now ends with a reference to the gospel proclamation about God's Son, Jesus Christ our Lord. We began this week with the call to welcome one another. We end it with a reminder to welcome the Lord Jesus Christ.

† *Thank you, Lord, for the strength that comes from our faith; when we falter on the road, encourage us so that at the last we may be welcomed home.*

1   The benefits of wisdom

Notes by Anthony Loke
based on the Revised Standard Version

Revd Anthony Loke is an ordained minister with
the TRAC Methodist Church in Malaysia and a
lecturer in the Old Testament in the Seminari Theoloji Malaysia.
He pursued doctoral studies from the University of Wales. His
wife has an M. Theol in Christian Education. They have two
teenage children, aged 17 and 15.

Introduction

The first nine chapters of the Book of Proverbs lay the
foundation for those embarking on the journey to know
more about life and how to be equipped for the journey. They
contain fine descriptions of 'Lady Wisdom', and the benefits
and delights she bestows upon those who diligently seek her.

Text for the week: Proverbs 8:33-35
Live in harmony with each other.

For group discussion and personal thought

• Why do the ancient Hebrews personify Lady Wisdom? Likewise,
  why is foolishness spoken of as Lady Folly?

• What is the place of wisdom in the family setting? How can
  wisdom be passed down from one generation to the next?

September

Proverbs 1:1-19

The beginning of knowledge

The fear of the LORD is the beginning of knowledge; fools despise wisdom and instruction.

(verse 7)

The traditional author of the Book of Proverbs is King Solomon (*verse 1*), although there are also other authors mentioned such as Agur, Lemuel, 'the wise', and 'the men of Hezekiah'. The first nine chapters, consisting of longer poems, are placed before the actual proverbs in chapter 10 onwards. They serve as an extended introduction to prepare the reader to enter into the world of the proverbs and use them fruitfully. Verses 2-6 give seven reasons why one should study the proverbs and verse 7 sums up the purpose of the book.

Then the book itself begins with an exhortation to young men to heed their parents' teaching (*verse 8*). The first warning is to beware of being enticed by 'sinners', because young people are susceptible to wrong influence, especially by their peers. Finding acceptance by the gang is a powerful temptation. Being young, naïve and inexperienced, they can be led astray by bad elements. What is heartbreaking is that they may not know the consequences ahead of them and yet choose to plunge themselves headlong. The father's advice tries to make them aware of the connection between actions and consequences. It is wiser to 'look before you leap'.

† Lord, help us to heed the advice of those who are older and wiser than us, so that we may learn from their mistakes and avoid repeating their errors. Amen.

The right choice

But he who listens to me will dwell secure and will be at ease, without dread of evil.
(verse 33)

Here we find personified Wisdom portrayed as a street evangelist, for she calls out to everyone. She will receive two responses: some will reject her (*verse 24*) but some will listen to her (*verse 33*). Those who reject her are called the 'simple ones' (*verse 22*) (i.e. the simpletons or the naïve). Because they reject wisdom, they will bring trouble upon themselves (*verses 26-27*) and eat the fruit of their foolish ways (*verse 31*). Wisdom does not need to condemn them because they have already condemned themselves by their own waywardness and complacency (*verse 33*; compare *John 3:18*, 'whoever does not believe stands condemned already').

Those who heed Wisdom's voice find her pouring out her heart to them and making known her thoughts (*verse 23*). They will find safety and ease (*verse 33*). Thus, one of the most important things to do in life is to make the right choice. To heed wisdom is to do the right thing and make the right choice, while to reject wisdom is to become wayward and complacent like the fool (*verse 32*). The bottom line is simply this: 'If you find wisdom, you will find life'.

† Lord, help me not to close my ears to the voice of Wisdom, otherwise I shall bring destruction and calamity upon myself. Amen.

September

Searching for wisdom

For the LORD gives wisdom;
from his mouth come knowledge and understanding.
(verse 6)

The father gives good 'fatherly' advice to his son (*verse 1*).
This advice is applicable to all young people as they embark on
life's journey. Wisdom is highly extolled in chapters 2 and 3. In
chapter 2, to turn one's ears to wisdom is to actually discover
the fear of the Lord and find God's knowledge (*verse 5*). It
is to understand what is right, just and fair (*verse 9*); to be
saved from wicked men (*verses 12-19*); to be saved from the
adulteress (*verse 16*) and to walk in the ways of good men and
the paths of the righteous (*verse 20*).

Seeking for wisdom is likened to searching for precious
minerals, but the moral benefits of wisdom far outweigh
the difficulties involved in searching for it (*verse 4*). Wisdom
becomes our moral safeguard to protect and guard us from
all temptations (*verse 11*), to deliver us from evil speech
(*verse 12*), to help us from walking the paths of evil (*verses
12-15*), and protect us from illicit relationships (*verses 16-19*).
Unfortunately, many people give up their quest for wisdom far
too easily. 'When the going gets tough, the tough get going.'

† Lord, help me not to be weary in seeking for Wisdom but
to diligently pursue her so that I can walk in her right paths.
Amen.

September

The benefits of wisdom

**Trust in the LORD with all your heart,
and do not rely on your own insight.**
(verse 5)

Chapter 3 presents further benefits of wisdom. It will prolong your life and bring prosperity (*verse 2*). It will be like a garland or necklace that embraces us (*verses 3, 22*; compare *4:9*). It will help us win favour with God and man (*verse 4*). It will also help us to put our trust in God and acknowledge him (*verses 5-6*). There is always an inherent danger that we will choose to rely on our own insight and try to be 'wise in our eyes' (*verse 7*). In doing so, we will take 'our eyes' off the Lord.

The benefits of wisdom can be seen in its application. For example, if we are wise, we will not hoard the things we have received from the Lord but gladly honour him with our substances (*verse 9*). The result will often be more blessings from God. Wisdom can be learnt even through godly discipline (*verses 11-12*). It may seem painful when God chastises us but ultimately we will learn to be wiser people. It is because God loves us that he disciplines us. 'Spare the rod, spoil the child.'

† *Lord, teach me to trust and rely on you and not on myself, so that I may always walk under your constant guidance.*

September

Finding wisdom

> Happy is the man who finds wisdom,
> and the man who gets understanding,
> for the gain from it is better than gain from silver
> and its profits better than gold.
>
> *(verses 13-14)*

The 'happy' man is the one who finds wisdom. Like the writer of Psalm 1, the wisdom teachers sought to show that material things ultimately do not satisfy as wisdom does. Wisdom is portrayed as a hard-won possession, more profitable than gold, silver or rubies (*verse 15*), because wisdom makes us a richer person than money ever can.

Wisdom is also portrayed as a 'tree of life' in verse 18 (compare *Psalm 1*). The image of a tree in the Old Testament is often a graceful picture of God's sources of renewal and blessing (for example, the tree of life in the garden of Eden in *Genesis 2:9* and the tree in *Revelation 22:2* whose leaves bring healing to the nations). The blessed man is the one who, through wisdom, walks rightly before God.

The emphasis is on attentive listening to the advice of parents as well as grandparents (*chapter 4, verse 3*). These represent the accumulated wisdom of the generations who have gone before us. We neglect that deposit of wisdom to our own peril and loss.

† Lord, help me to heed good advice from those who have gone before me, so that I may walk the right path. Amen.

September

Finding life

For he who finds me finds life
and obtains favour from the Lord;
but he who misses me injures himself;
all who hate me love death.

(verses 35-36)

To get the undivided attention of the young men, the ancient Hebrew teachers resorted to personifying wisdom. They spoke of Wisdom as a 'person' who is like an evangelist, calling and beckoning the 'simple ones' and 'foolish men' to follow after her (*verse 21*). Wisdom is also portrayed as a master workman involved in creation with God from the very beginning (*verses 22-31*). Lastly, Wisdom appeals to her children to listen to her and find her (*verses 32-36*).

In chapter 9, Wisdom is spoken of as a fine lady dwelling in a magnificent house, and a gracious hostess offering her guests the best menu (*verses 1-2*). Those who turn in to her house find life (*verse 4*) and walk in the way of insight (*verse 6*). As a contrast to this figure of Wisdom, there is a counterpart, Lady Folly or Foolishness, who is described in the second half of chapter 9 as wanton and loud-mouthed; those who enter her house are on the road to the place of the dead.

† *Lord, give me always the grace to hear both the sweet voice of Wisdom and the alluring voice of Folly, to recognise the difference, and to choose the life that Wisdom offers. Amen.*

September

Proverbs

2 A sampler of sayings

Notes by Corneliu Constantineanu
based on the New International Version

Corneliu Constantineanu is a Romanian
Pentecostal who grew up under the communist
regime. After taking an engineering degree, he has devoted his
life to the study of theology and a teaching ministry, trying to
integrate the Christian faith with the social and political realities
of everyday life. He holds a PhD in New Testament and teaches at
the Evangelical Theological Seminary in Osijek, Croatia, where he
serves as Dean of Graduate Studies. He is also the pastor of the
International Church in Osijek. Corneliu is married to Ioana and
they have two daughters, Anamaria and Carmen.

Introduction

Wisdom is not about mere information or pure knowledge.
Rather, it has to do with understanding and insight, instruction
and discipline, righteousness, justice and equity, prudence and
discernment, learning and skills. It is the ability, even the art,
of living well and skilfully in all circumstances of life. Wisdom
is always linked to God, as its true source and foundation.
Proverbs stresses that a wise life gives precedence to God. This
week's readings show us the practical benefits of wisdom, and
will hopefully inspire us to pursue it earnestly in order to live
truly and authentically.

Text for the week: Proverbs 24:14
*Know also that wisdom is sweet to your soul; if you find it,
there is a future hope for you, and your hope will not be cut
off.*

For group discussion and personal thought

- If wisdom is so important for a fulfilled and happy life, what
  practical actions can you take to search for it?

Wisdom brings joy to parents

There are, indeed, many benefits of wisdom and we see in our text today that wisdom means doing the right thing at the right time (*verse 5*), accepting guidance in life (*verse 8*), having a great love for knowledge (*verse 14*), and so on. Significantly, this entire section begins with a proverb that deals with home, the first place where wisdom is imparted and gained. Wisdom is thus intimately associated with family relationships:

> **A wise son brings joy to his father,**
> **but a foolish son grief to his mother.**
>
> *(verse 1)*

Those of us who are parents know that children can bring enormous satisfaction and joy, or deep sorrow and hurtful pain. That is why consideration for parents is an essential mark of wise living. This is a very important aspect of life, especially today, when the very concept of family is in great jeopardy and family life is increasingly disregarded. Although it may not always be possible, living as we were meant to live means having considerable regard for our parents, caring for and loving them, and showing it in concrete and tangible ways.

† *Lord, help us to live wisely, as we were created to live, by showing our consideration and love to our parents, if this is possible.*

September

A wise person accepts the advice of others

There is plenty of evidence that human beings are prone to self-deception. It is with this reality in view that we find, throughout the Bible, repeated warnings against the 'deceitfulness of the human heart'. And perhaps the easiest way to deceive ourselves is to make our own opinion the sole basis for our vital decisions in life. According to our reading today, it is only the fool who bases his conclusions on his own judgement and finds it right 'in his own eyes':

> **The way of a fool seems right to him,**
> **but a wise man listens to advice.**
> *(verse 15)*

It is the mark of wisdom to listen to advice and it is the only way a person can resist deception. The psalmist was also very much aware of this danger and so he comes with his self-examination before God – and this is an excellent example for our prayer:

† *Search me, O God, and know my heart; test me and know my anxious thoughts. See if there is any offensive way in me, and lead me in the way everlasting (Psalm 139:23-24).*

Choosing the better option

True wisdom, as described in Proverbs, enables us to exercise right judgement when we are confronted with a necessary choice. Sometimes it can only be a choice between two evils, and the wise will opt for the lesser of the two. But at other times there is a choice between two good alternatives, and true wisdom will enable us choose the better option:

**Better a little with the fear of the LORD
than great wealth with turmoil.
Better a meal of vegetables where there is love
than a fattened calf with hatred.**
(verses 16-17)

These 'better' sayings reverse conventional wisdom and overturn accepted norms and values. Wealth and riches, normally considered a benefit, have a negative connotation here. Not that they are wrong in themselves, nor is poverty a virtue in itself. The key emphasis, however, is on the fact that, despite life's problems, one can have an ultimately truthful, meaningful and wise life by choosing what is better: the values of justice, peace and love, all crowned with the first and most important element, the fear of the Lord. This is a wonderful reminder to all of us, in our increasingly materialistic world, that happiness does not come from possessions but from a contented heart, in perfect harmony with ourselves, our Creator, the world and our neighbours. True wisdom enables us to know the difference.

† *Dear Father, we pray that your wisdom will guide us through the innumerable decisions we make every day, and help us always to make the better choice.*

September

Listening, understanding and discerning

How often do we fail to listen? Or answer before we listen? Or jump to conclusions based on a one-sided report? Today's reading tells us that this is not the mark of wise living!

> **He who answers before listening –**
> **that is his folly and his shame . . .**
> **The heart of the discerning acquires knowledge;**
> **the ears of the wise seek it out . . .**
> **The first to present his case seems right,**
> **till another comes forward and questions him.**
> *(verses 13, 15 and 17)*

The fool thinks his own view is right and does not to listen to others. The wise, by contrast, are not simply open to learning from others but are always searching for knowledge, understanding and discernment. To really understand and know, you have to enquire and go beyond what 'seems right' at first sight, and refuse to be impressed by a single view or perspective. It also means listening to others and entering into dialogue with them, in genuine communication. We all have our own story and want to be truly listened to. We must fight against the temptation to 'dismiss' others or base our opinion on superficial impressions, and listen to the other side of the story. This is what true wisdom teaches us.

† *Dear Lord, help us to be open and sensitive to the needs of others; give us your wisdom to understand and discern the truth when we listen to the stories of others and to be genuinely concerned for their wellbeing.*

Training and disciplining children

It can be said that individuals, and even entire nations, are judged by their attitude towards children. As we have seen, Hebrew wisdom literature placed a high value on family life in general and on children in particular. Children were the glory of their parents and grandparents, and their training and correction were emphasised:

> **Train a child in the way he should go,**
> **and when he is old he will not turn from it . . .**
> **Folly is bound up in the heart of a child,**
> **but the rod of discipline will drive it far from him.**
> *(verses 6 and 15)*

In order for children to reach their potential at a later stage, parents are charged with a great responsibility for their early education and discipline. It is indeed in the early years of childhood that the most important traits of one's character are formed and shaped, and so parents have a huge responsibility to direct and train, as well as discipline, a child's basic impulses. Only by doing this can we give our children a chance and have hope, not doubt, for their future. This is one of the most essential contributions that parents can make to the future of their children and their society.

† *Dear Father, we thank you for the gift of children and for the joy and happiness they bring to our lives. Help all parents to do everything they can to train their children in the ways of wisdom and the fear of the Lord.*

September

The effects of wisdom

In Proverbs 24, the wise man enumerates the advantages of wisdom, summing them up in verse 14:

> [W]isdom is sweet to your soul;
> if you find it, there is a future hope for you.
> *(part of 24, verse 14)*

In Proverbs 31, the value of wisdom is personified in the ideal wife. In radical contrast to the contentious woman whose company is undesirable, and the wicked woman who leads young men into sexual immorality, this chapter describes the incomparable qualities of a wise wife: she is fully trusted by her husband who is, because of her, respected by the community; her constant preoccupation to do good, speak with wisdom and teach with kindness display her wonderful moral qualities; she is diligent and proficient in all her work, provides for her family, manages her household skilfully, and meets the needs of the poor and needy. What other response should she get but one of blessing and praise from her children, husband and community:

> Her children arise and call her blessed;
> her husband also, and he praises her:
> 'Many women do noble things, but you surpass them all'. . .
> let her works bring her praise at the city gate.
> *(verses 28-29 and part of verse 31)*

† Our heavenly Father, we thank you for all that wisdom gives to us in our daily lives, in our homes and at work. May your Holy Spirit help us to grow in wisdom in all we do.

Colour in the Bible

1   Not all black and white

Notes by Elisa Gusmão
based on the New International Version

Born in Brazil, where, as a teenager, she was a youth leader in the Presbyterian Church of Copacabana, Elisa moved to the UK with her Scottish husband in 1987. She works as a translator and serves the United Reformed Church as an elder and lay preacher. Between them, Eric and Elisa have six children and five grandchildren living in England, Switzerland, Canada, the USA and Brazil.

Introduction

We love colours. Archaeologists have discovered that five hundred thousand years ago our ancestors were already using colours to adorn their bodies. We also attribute symbolic meanings to each colour – which are not always the same. For example, in the Bible, white is not always associated with purity and goodness; it is also a symbol of death and hypocrisy – as we shall see further on. Equally, black can describe beauty in one passage, and have negative connotations in another. Let's then have a look at our palette!

Text for the week: Mark 9:2-3
[H]e was transfigured before them. His clothes became dazzling white, whiter than anyone in the world could bleach them.

For group discussion and personal thought

• Have you ever tried to pair up the Beatitudes (Matthew 5) with the 'Woes' (Matthew 23)? How do they shed light on each other?

• Painters and writers can use colours for different effects in their work. What are three different meanings of the colour white in the Bible?

• Discuss the reasons for human suffering.

263

Pride versus humility

Miriam and Aaron were accusing Moses because of his Cushite wife Zipporah, daughter of the Priest of Midian. In Exodus 18:19 we find Moses' father-in-law giving him advice on how to represent the people before God – by sharing his responsibility with other Israelites. This would put Aaron and Miriam's political power in danger, so it is understandable what Moses' dark-skinned wife had to do with their claim to stand as prophets alongside Moses (*verse 2*). Aaron and Miriam's proud love of power contrasts with Moses' humility. It is he who benefits from a unique intimacy with God.

'When a prophet of the LORD is among you,
I reveal myself to him in visions,
I speak to him in dreams.
But this is not true of my servant Moses;
he is faithful in all my house.
With him I speak face to face,
clearly and not in riddles;
he sees the form of the LORD.'
(verse 3 and verses 6-8)

Moses' modesty goes together with his Midianite connections, while Miriam and Aaron's pride results in a skin disease that made her temporarily look *white* 'as a stillborn infant'.

† *God, who rejoices in pious hearts, give me the humility of Moses, so I can cast aside childish human ambitions of power, and enjoy deeper intimacy with you.*

September

Iniquity versus purity of heart

If we compare the terrible 'Seven Woes' in this chapter with the Beatitudes in chapter 5 of Matthew, we see how they are connected. Whilst the Beatitudes praise those who do good, here the Scribes and Pharisees are admonished for being and doing evil.

> **'Woe unto you, teachers of the law and Pharisees, you hypocrites! You are like whitewashed tombs, which look beautiful on the outside but on the inside are full of dead men's bones and everything unclean. In the same way, on the outside you appear to people as righteous but on the inside you are full of hypocrisy and wickedness.'**
>
> *(verses 27-28)*

The white paint on tombs might look good but it was not for decoration: it warned passers-by not to come too close to the corruption within.

Hypocrisy was what the Pharisees were good at – that human ability to look good and sound holy, whilst planning and doing exactly the opposite. Their acts, coming from wicked hearts, lacked love and were marked by injustice and greed. Today, as always, it is the heart that matters. God 'does not look at the things man looks at. Man looks at the outward appearance, but the Lord looks at the heart' (*1 Samuel 16:7*). The sixth Beatitude stands in opposition to today's reading: 'Blessed are the pure in heart, for they will see God' (*Matthew 5:8*).

† *'Create in me a pure heart, O God, and renew a steadfast spirit within me' (Psalm 51:10).*

September

Sin versus communion with the true God

Learn to do right!
Seek justice,
encourage the oppressed.
Defend the cause of the fatherless,
plead the case of the widow.
'Come now, let us reason together,'
says the LORD.
'Though your sins are like scarlet,
they shall be as white as snow;
though they are red as crimson,
they shall be like wool.'

(verses 17-18)

In Isaiah's time, colours were not applied to materials the way we do today in our modern industries. Blue fabrics, for instance, were obtained with an indigo dye, while crimson and scarlet were the result of another dye, extracted from a small worm found in some leaves. The colour in fabrics or wool double dipped in this dye was permanent.

So is sin: irremovable by our own efforts. Sin is the condition transmitted to each human creature born since time immemorial; we cannot change it using our own inner resources. Searching for help, we may find many 'gods' in the shape of obsessions and addictions of all kinds, but, sooner or later, they will all disappoint us. It is in our encounter with God, so well revealed in Jesus, that the whole scenario changes. Our life finally makes sense and we have a future.

† Creator God, come and be present in my soul, make it white as snow, and lead me to seek justice and peace for the good of my fellow human beings.

A dazzling promise

Years ago, my whole family used to go for short breaks to my parents' house in a forestry reservation up in the hills near Rio. There, we walked, cooked on a coal stove, and spent our evenings reading by a gas lamp or playing games. Outside, in the pitch-black sky, we could see thousands of stars. When it was time to return, no one felt like going home . . .

There he was transfigured before them. His clothes became dazzling white, whiter than anyone in the world could bleach them. And there appeared before them Elijah and Moses, who were talking with Jesus. Peter said to Jesus, 'Rabbi, it is good for us to be here. Let us put up three shelters – one for you, one for Moses and one for Elijah.'

(part of verse 2, and verses 3-5)

On the mountain, Jesus suddenly looked different, even his clothes were bright. There, the whole family was also present: the Father's voice, the Son, and the Spirit – in the cloud. To complete the picture, Moses represented the law, and Elijah the prophets! No wonder Peter did not want leave that fearsome, but wonderful place. For there the disciples had a glimpse of who Christ really was, and of the kingdom to come.

† *Father, whose promises we discern in the Bible, help us to remain faithful, labouring daily for the establishment of the kingdom. We ask you in the name of our Lord, Jesus Christ. Amen.*

September

267

Love in black and white-gold

Dark I am, yet lovely,
O daughters of Jerusalem,
dark like the tents of Kedar,
like the tent curtains of Solomon.
Do not stare at me because I am dark,
because I am darkened by the sun . . .
My lover is radiant and ruddy,
outstanding among ten thousand . . .
His mouth is sweetness itself;
he is altogether lovely.
This is my lover, this is my friend,
O daughters of Jerusalem.
(chapter 1, verse 5 and part of verse 6;
chapter 5, verses 10 and 16)

Christians regard this 'Greatest of Songs' (the meaning of the title) as prefiguring the union between Christ the bridegroom and his church. But we can also see the book as a dialogue between a man and a woman, expressing their feelings for each other. The Shulamite has her skin darkened from labour in the vineyard, imposed by her brothers. In contrast, her bridegroom's body is white 'like polished ivory' (*chapter 5, verse 14*). Their love, reminiscent of divine love, 'burns like blazing fire, like an almighty flame' (*Song of Songs 8:6b*). The inclusion of this collection of poems in the Bible is an evident blessing, not only on human love, but on love between people of different origins.

† *'O Light Invisible, we praise thee! Too bright for mortal vision . . . Praise and glory be unto thee; let my mouth, my soul, and all creatures together, praise and bless thee.'*

(Thomas à Kempis (1379–1471), The Imitation of Christ*)*

Black and white

'Yet when I hoped for good, evil came;
when I looked for light, then came darkness . . .
My skin grows black and peels;
my body burns with fever.
My harp is turned to mourning,
and my flute to the sound of wailing.'

(Job, verses 26 and 30-31)

The author's picture of Job's desperation is impressive. Job's disease and fever, his loneliness and the depressing sound of his music form a very dark picture. Dark equals gloom, black means unwholesome. It is only after a lot of protesting that Job has an encounter with God, and, finally, recovers his health and property. On the other hand, if we look at our second reading, we see black and white in a very positive way. These two colours were used by Jacob to settle his account with his wily father-in-law Laban, after fourteen years of excellent work for him:

'Let me go through all your flocks today and remove from them every speckled or spotted sheep, every dark-coloured lamb and every spotted or speckled goat. They will be my wages.'

(Genesis, verse 32)

† *Lord of the rainbow, teach me to love the world and the creatures you created. Grant me the wisdom to see that there is always light beyond the darkness. Amen.*

September

269

Colour in the Bible

2 Green, purple and red

Notes by Iain Roy
based on the Good News Bible

For Iain's biography see p.221.

Introduction

Scotland, my native land, is sometimes thought of as dull, grey and rainy. But there is nothing dull about Scottish art. Colour is in fact a particular characteristic of Scottish painting past and present. What that art reveals is not just how important colour is for conveying a sense of place and person, but also for conveying mood and feeling. The Bible has this same sense of the importance of colour to convey the deep things of the spirit.

Text for the week: Revelation 4:3
All round the throne there was a rainbow the colour of an emerald.

For group discussion and personal thought

- On a piece of paper make three well-spaced slashes of the colours green, purple and red. For each colour, identify a biblical passage which gave you tranquillity in a time of difficulty (green), enriched your life (purple), and stands out as a spiritual highlight for your life (scarlet). Share your passages in your group.

- Discussion is only one method to explore biblical truth. Try reading the creation story in Genesis and selecting suitable music to reflect each day of creation, then make a disk or tape of the music to serve as background to a reading of the creation story, either on your own or as part of a group. You could also make a back-drop for the reading from cut-out pictures or painting to represent the days of creation. You could then share your reading with a group to which you belong (in church, at Sunday School, at prayer group and so on.).

A green and pleasant land

Green, especially in countries blessed with a plentiful supply of rain, is the most common colour of the landscape.

> '[F]or all the wild animals and for all the birds I have provided grass and leafy plants for food' . . . 'Now you can eat them, as well as green plants.'
>
> *(part of verses 30 and 3)*

What always surprises, however, is the sheer variety of shades of green. It makes it one of the most difficult of all colours for artists to represent. The Creation story in Genesis is perhaps best seen like a painting. It is not a scientific account of creation. It reflects the world as the writer saw it in his day and we see it in ours – a green and pleasant land, a place of beauty and provision, God's gift to us for us to cherish and preserve.

† Lord, in the midst of all that is ugly and wrong in our world, help us to retain a sense of the world's beauty and your provision. Help us to be good stewards of its resources.

September

271

The calm of green

Two psalms above all others have gripped the imagination of my Scottish countrymen and women: Psalm 121 and this Psalm, 23. It is not difficult to understand why. There are few places in Scotland far from hills or mountains, and green is the ever-present colour of our landscape.

> **He lets me rest in fields of green grass**
> **and leads me to quiet pools of fresh water.**
> *(verse 2)*

This psalm is often used at weddings and funerals, two quite different experiences which both bring change to our lives. What the psalmist saw in the image of the shepherd and his sheep and the tranquillity of the pasture was a reflection of the relationship God has with us. As the shepherd gives to his sheep, God offers us nurture, moments of tranquillity and reflection to restore our spirits and calm our fears, blessing in good days, refuge in difficult days.

† Lord of the quiet places, give us a place of calm in the midst of our busy lives, where we can remember who we are and more especially who you are, the God who loves us – always.

A rich colour

Thanks to science and technology the modern painter can easily purchase a variety of colours. It was not always so.

There was once a rich man who dressed in the most expensive clothes and lived in great luxury every day. There was also a poor man named Lazarus, covered with sores, who used to be brought to the rich man's door, hoping to eat the bits of food that fell from the rich man's table. Even the dogs would come and lick his sores.

(verses 19-21)

The colour purple in the ancient world was made from the shells of molluscs and was rare and expensive. The rich colour we call 'purple' therefore became the colour of rank and wealth. We can be sure the rich man here wore purple; Lazarus by contrast was barely clothed, his sores exposed. The picture is eloquent. It depicts the social gulf between the two men.

But in heaven there is role reversal. God's love has no such social distinction. God does not value us for what we have, but for who we are and for what, with his love and grace, we might become. In his presence our only need is humility.

† *Father, help us to look beyond the things we can see easily to the things that are more difficult to see – the worth in each of us rather than the faults, the potential in all of us only waiting to be released by your spirit and grace.*

September

All dressed up

Dressing up is a game children play. Leave a box of old clothes in a room and a child's imagination can travel far and wide.

> **The soldiers took Jesus inside to the courtyard of the governor's palace . . . They put a purple robe on Jesus, made a crown out of thorny branches, and put it on his head.**
>
> *(part of verse 16, and verse 17)*

To be dressed up by someone else, however, is a different thing. It smacks of compulsion, the necessity to conform. The purple robe put on Jesus, far from conferring status on him, conferred ridicule. The soldiers, like so many others of his day and ours, misunderstood him. Their game over, they stripped the purple robe away and clothed him again in his own clothes, the garments which really declared his kingship – the humility of God seen in a man, dressed in the clothes of ordinary men: God come to love his world and all within it, not in kingly robes but the clothes of every day.

† *Lord Christ, help us to see you where you really are, in the midst of life itself, in ordinary things and in ordinary people.*

A lively colour

My son is a director of a company that manufactures pigments. His advice to me when I buy a car is, 'Get red. It will keep me in business!'

> While [Tamar] was in labour, one of [her twins] put out an arm; the midwife caught it, tied a red thread round it, and said, 'This one was born first.'
>
> *(verse 28)*

Red, or its near relation scarlet, is certainly a colour that catches the eye. You notice it. That is why I buy red cars, not to please my son but because I think it a safe colour to drive. The midwife in this incident used scarlet for its distinctiveness, marking the firstborn. The mother of these children could well have been described as a 'scarlet woman', now rather an old-fashioned English phrase to describe a woman of dubious moral values. But this 'scarlet woman' is like the heroine in the American novel, *The Scarlet Letter*, a woman more sinned against than sinning. Judah, her father-in-law, treated her unfairly, then sexually abused her. This child and his twin were the result. It is a colourful story but like so many biblical stories it is the questions it asks of us as much as the answers it gives that are really important.

† Christ, help us to see that life is not all black and white, especially in human living. Help us to look long and deeply before we rush to judgement of others.

September

The colour of salvation

Colour coding is one of the tools of modern retail marketing that conveys essential facts about the product. In Joshua 2 the red cord in Rahab's window was a code. She had helped the spies of Israel as they reconnoitred Jericho. In return they promised safety for her and her family. This scarlet cord was their lifeline.

The cross is often worn as jewellery, without the colour that stained the original – the scarlet of Christ's blood. The real cross was, as its blood proclaims, a place of sacrifice where Christ gave his all so that we should never doubt his love for us.

Our final reading gathers all the colours together. Rainbows still fascinate and surprise us when they appear.

> **All round the throne there was a rainbow the colour of an emerald.**
>
> *(Revelation, verse 3)*

The rainbow was a significant symbol to Jew and Gentile alike – in Genesis 9 it is a sign both of the end of the flood and of God's covenant with Noah. The book of Revelation is not easy to interpret, but this symbol speaks to us still: the rainbow with all its colours, an evocative sign of God's undying love for us, his people. Its colours joyfully proclaim the faith that gives courage, the hope that overcomes fear, and the love that helps us win through difficulties.

† *Father, when all is dark, give us light. Let your love chase away our gloom, and enable us to see all the colour of a life lived in trust of you.*

September

5 People in need

Notes by Anne Roberts
based on the New International Version

Anne Roberts trained as a geographer and
taught in Uganda for two years. She worked
in church teaching and administration for twenty years and is
now a teacher in further education, a church administrator and
freelance writer. She lives in Bolton in north-west England with
her husband Howard.

Introduction

My time in Uganda was rewarding, difficult – and life-
changing, as I discovered God's faithfulness to us even when
we fail. Then for twenty years I worked happily for a large
Anglican church. The leaving was not so happy and the years
since have once again emphasised God's faithfulness, whether
faith is strong, weak or even non-existent – precisely what this
week's mix of passages teaches us. By looking at Jesus in these
scenes we see the Father and we know what God is like.

Text for the week: Matthew 8:2
*Jesus reached out his hand and touched the man. 'I am willing,'
he said. 'Be clean!'*

For group discussion and personal thought

• Looking back over your own Christian journey: can you recall
times of no faith, little faith and much faith? Thank God for
them all and consider what you learned in each.

• Take time to 'see' Jesus as Matthew portrays him, on the
roads, hills, fields, lake and in the towns, drawing all people
to himself; especially see him doing this when lifted up on the
cross and raised to glory.

Faith is honoured

A man with leprosy came and knelt before him and said, 'Lord, if you are willing, you can make me clean.'

(verse 2)

This man was, by law, an outcast, for the protection of those who might contract his skin disease if they came into physical contact. The man probably thought that the disease was a punishment for sin – hence his fear that the holy man would want to see him continuing to suffer, rather than heal him. How could such a situation fail to cut right to the heart of the compassionate Saviour? How we have misunderstood and misrepresented our heavenly Father, whose nature is love! He wants us to walk free of our sin, not be ground down by it.

The centurion saw things differently. He recognised Jesus' authority and moral integrity. He would not be deceived into thinking that Jesus agreed with any notion of sickness being a punishment for sin. He was also humble and recognised Jesus' superiority.

'Lord, I do not deserve to have you come under my roof. But just say the word, and my servant will be healed.'

(part of verse 8)

In his response to the centurion's faith, Jesus dispelled a further misunderstanding. The covenant God had made with Abraham and his descendants was special, but it was not exclusive. God opens his heart of healing and forgiving love to all who seek it.

† Lord, I need you to touch me with your healing love. Thank you that you are willing.

From fear to faith

The disciples were overwhelmed with fear when the great storm blew up; Jesus slept through it all. What they expected him to do is unclear, but they woke him anyway.

'Lord, save us! We're going to drown!' He replied, 'You of little faith, why are you so afraid?'
(part of verses 25 and 26)

Perhaps there was a gentle smile on his face as he watched their reaction to the sudden calming of the waves at his command. They hadn't seen him do this kind of thing before and it was time to teach them more about the extent of his authority. He would not be impatient with them, as his words might at first suggest.

The demon-possessed men they met on the other side of the lake were beyond belief or unbelief. The demons were in charge of them – but not irreversibly.

The demons begged Jesus, 'If you drive us out, send us into the herd of pigs.' He said to them, 'Go!' So they came out and went into the pigs.
(verse 31 and part of verse 32)

The townspeople's material wellbeing was far more important to them than the spiritual wellbeing of the demon-possessed, and they were furious at this threat to their livelihood. They were blind and deaf to the power and love of the one whom God had sent to save them all.

† Lord, so much around us demonstrates your power and love. Dispel my darkness as I turn and look and believe.

September

Faith to believe

Step by step, Jesus shows the people who he is. The proof is not in his words but in their consequences. This poor man could not bring himself for healing and had probably lost all hope, convinced that his paralysis was the result of sin. So his friends brought him.

> **When Jesus saw their faith, he said to the paralytic, 'Take heart, son; your sins are forgiven.'**
>
> *(part of verse 2)*

These words are an assault on the sensitivities of those who believe, quite rightly, that only God can forgive sins. Jesus has taken to himself something of God's authority. This is blasphemy – or else he has the right to do it. His next words demonstrate that he does have that authority:

> **'Get up, take your mat and go home.'**
> *(part of verse 6)*

Whatever the initial cause of the man's paralysis, it is guilt which has held him in its grip. He recognises that Jesus is no blasphemer and receives the gift he is offered. Theological arguments apart, he feels the consequences of Jesus' words in his body – and he is free. The crowd saw what was going on and believed. It is important that we too believe: Do I still feel guilt for my sin? Do I believe that God, through Jesus, has dealt with all my sins? If so, I am a new creation and can live it.

† *Loving Saviour, by your Spirit invade every area of my being and fill it with your forgiving love.*

Equal in God's eyes

Throughout the gospels we sense Jesus moving freely among all sorts and conditions of people. They all want to be near him and he wants to be with them and share God's good gifts with them. Again today we see two contrasting individuals. One is a confident synagogue ruler (Mark and Luke), heartbroken at the death of his daughter. The other is a woman ashamed to declare her condition in public. He is in the top league spiritually and she is ritually unclean. Again, Jesus loves them equally and moves in compassion towards them both.

> **Jesus turned and saw [the woman]. 'Take heart, daughter,' he said, 'your faith has healed you.' And the woman was healed from that moment . . .**
>
> **[H]e went in and took the girl by the hand, and she got up.**
> *(verse 22, and part of verse 25)*

The extent to which society is divided varies greatly in the world of the twenty-first century. Any Christian who is comfortable with existing divisions has failed to understand that it was precisely to heal these divisions that Jesus came. The good news is for the privileged and the downtrodden, the sinner and the saint. Once we acknowledge our sin and our need of forgiveness we are on level ground with all the rest – whoever they are. And Jesus raises us all up to the same height, as the truth sets us free.

† *Thank you, heavenly Father, that we are all precious in your sight.*

October

Beware of unbelief!

Jesus was even willing to give time and attention to those who thought themselves morally and spiritually superior to him. It is easy to dismiss such people and fall into the trap of feeling superior to them. Jesus knows each of their hearts. Some are proud and set in their thinking. Others simply want to be sure that no one is deceived and that God's law is upheld. Jesus took time to teach them, pointing out the inconsistencies in their thinking and the danger they were in.

> **'[I]f I drive out demons by Beelzebub, by whom do your people drive them out? . . . But if I drive out demons by the Spirit of God, then the kingdom of God has come upon you.'**
>
> *(part of verse 27, and verse 28)*

They were in danger of being so hardened against him and his teaching that they would speak against the Holy Spirit who inspired his words and empowered his deeds. This cannot be forgiven, because it is a denial of the presence of God when he is so obviously at work.

Reading these notes indicates openness to the truth with which God wants to enlighten us. Sometimes it is hard to understand why those around us are not equally open. God understands and we must never give up praying for them and being willing to help them into the truth and out of danger.

† *Lord, open our eyes to your truth always, as we guard our hearts against unbelief.*

Jesus meets all our needs

They were heady times. Jesus has walked on water and so has one of his disciples. Five thousand had been fed with five loaves and two fish. A Gentile woman pleads with the Son of David to free her demon-possessed daughter, and . . .

Great crowds came to him, bringing the lame, the blind, the crippled, the dumb and many others, and laid them at his feet; and he healed them. The people were amazed . . . And they praised the God of Israel.

(chapter 15, verse 30 and part of verse 31)

Jesus engages with all who come and meets them at their point of need. People need food – he feeds them. Peter is too sure of himself – Jesus both humbles and encourages him. The Gentile woman believes that if Jesus is who he seems to be, his blessings are for her as well as for Israel. Jesus confirms her in this belief. As God's Servant, he brings good news to the poor, freedom to prisoners, sight to the blind and release for the oppressed (*Luke 4:16-21*). Some are warned of the danger of unbelief but none is condemned. Little faith is encouraged, much faith rewarded. We need to look around us every day with Jesus' eyes and recognise everyone as the object of his love, condemning no one, recognising our own need of his forgiving love.

† Dearest Lord Jesus, how would we not love you, who have loved us – all – so much? We praise the God of the whole world!

October

283

6   Questions put to Jesus

Notes by Lesley George Anderson
based on the New Revised Standard Version

Lesley G Anderson is the President of the United
Theological College of the West Indies, Jamaica,
and Chair of the Praesidium of the Caribbean Conference of
Churches. He is also a member of the World Council of Churches
Pentecostal Joint Consultative Group.

Introduction

Jesus was a highly regarded teacher with excellent teaching
skills, who lived what he taught. Consider the responses of
Jesus to the questions put to him. Examine carefully the gist
of his teachings in them. Some are regarded as 'hard sayings'
because they are surprisingly shocking. Their intent is to keep
us from walking willingly and knowingly into sin. Aim to have a
complete understanding of them and accept with humility his
instructions to live as his disciples.

Text for the week: Matthew 18:4
*'Whoever becomes humble like this child is the greatest in the
kingdom of heaven.'*

For group discussion and personal thought

• Why are we called to live humble lives like Jesus? What are
  some of the challenges of living a life of humility? Why did
  Jesus find it necessary to use a child as a way of explaining
  humility?

• List some of the ways that Jesus exemplified humility in his
  life. How difficult is it to live a life of humility when fame,
  money, honours and self-advancement all seem so attractive?
  Do you agree that humility is about being truly great?

• Read Philippians 2:1-11; how can you put Matthew 18:1-9
  into practice in your life?

Why do you eat with tax collectors and sinners?

The Pharisees felt themselves to be better than others. They glorified themselves and their own righteousness. They therefore excluded themselves from the table and condemned Jesus for eating with tax collectors and sinners. Jesus overheard their petty remarks and said:

'Those who are well have no need of a physician, but those who are sick. Go and learn what this means, "I desire mercy, not sacrifice." For I have come to call not the righteous but sinners.'

(part of verse 12, and verse 13)

So Jesus comes and offers himself to us as the Great Physician who is able to meet all our mental and physical illnesses. We who are sinners also sit down and eat with Jesus. The bread we eat reminds us of his broken body; the wine we drink reminds us of his poured-out blood. The table reminds us of our unity in Christ and our togetherness as a family. Since we are sisters and brothers in Christ, who died for us on Calvary's cross, the table is not to be used to exclude people, create divisions, set boundaries and make distinctions of any kind. In Christ the excluded and marginalised in our society are valued and accepted at his table of fellowship.

† *Lord Jesus, in response to your call to follow you, give us open minds to accept each other at your table. Amen.*

October

Why do your disciples not fast?

In response to this fascinating question, Jesus responds:

> 'The wedding guests cannot mourn as long as the bridegroom is with them, can they? The days will come when the bridegroom is taken away from them, and then they will fast.'

(part of verse 15)

Jesus, the Bridegroom, has come. With his coming was the coming of the kingdom of God. He therefore reigns as King! Jesus, the Bridegroom, is the Saviour who lived, died and was resurrected to save us from our sins. The piece of unshrunk cloth and the new wine in this passage represent the reigning power of Christ in the world. The Spirit of the Bridegroom is here. This is the new wine and the old wineskins of Judaism cannot contain it. The old wineskins represent Old Testament fasting as a way of relating to God. The new wine demands new fasting, for Christ, the Bridegroom, in dying on Calvary's cross, has given us new life. Our sins have been forgiven. Death has been conquered. He lives for ever more. The Spirit is sent. The wine is new! We need to discover the power of God in this new wine of the Spirit and become beautiful vessels, like the decorative ones I have seen in Argentina, Brazil, Costa Rica and Panama!

† Lord, fill us with your Holy Spirit that we may pour out our lives in service to others. Amen.

October

Is it lawful to cure on the sabbath?

On pastoral visits to the House of Refuge in Port-of-Spain, in the West Indies, I was introduced to people suffering from all kinds of illnesses and deformities. They were ministered to with love, care and gentleness every day of the week. Christ healed the man with the withered hand on the sabbath. He was disabled and physically challenged to use his hand to make a living for himself. Christ's curing of the man offended the Pharisees. So he answered them:

> **'Suppose one of you has only one sheep and it falls into a pit on the sabbath; will you not lay hold of it and lift it out? How much more valuable is a human being than a sheep! So it is lawful to do good on the sabbath.'**
>
> *(verses 11-12)*

It was the mind of Christ not to let opportunities for service to others be inhibited by prejudices. He was God's servant reaching out to the afflicted and distressed in their time of need. The sabbath was for worship and works of charity, meeting the needs of the sick, the suffering poor, those living with HIV/AIDS, the dispossessed: generally, doing good to others on the basis of love. We too need to be restored from our withered nature. We need that new life which only Christ can offer!

† O Lord our God, we stretch our hands to you in prayer. Teach us that in acts of mercy, a human being is more precious than a sheep! Amen.

October

Why do your disciples break the tradition of the elders?

The scribes and Pharisees were from Jerusalem, the holy city, and, as religious intellectuals, should know better than others. However, this was not the case: they were worse. They were enemies of the gospel of Jesus Christ: 'They are darkened in their understanding, alienated from the life of God because of their ignorance and hardness of heart' (*Ephesians 4:18*). They appeared to have no genuine love for God. God is 'near in their mouths yet far from their hearts' (*Jeremiah 12:2*). In response to their question Jesus answered them with another question:

> **'And why do you break the commandment of God for the sake of your tradition?. . . You hypocrites!'**
>
> *(verse 3 and part of verse 7)*

We must be careful not to make accusations or assumptions and charge others with being guilty of breaking the laws of society. We can bring greater guilt upon ourselves by breaking the laws of God.

† O Lord, help us not to make rash judgements about others. Teach us how to avoid the Pharisaic spirit of pride and self-righteousness. Amen.

Who is the greatest in the kingdom of heaven?

Jesus lived and preached a life of humility (*Philippians 2:1-11*) and was careful to commend and encourage this way of life to his disciples and followers. Yet, it was the disciples who raised the question: 'Who is the greatest in the kingdom of heaven?'(*verse 1*), perhaps because they were arguing about it among themselves. Andrew, the first to be called to be a disciple of Jesus; Peter, the chief spokesman, with the keys already in his hands; Judas, the treasurer, in whom his colleagues had so much confidence; Jude, a blood relative of Jesus; John, the beloved disciple; and the others – all felt specially called to privilege and greatness. But Jesus called a child to him and stood him in front of them, and said:

> **'Truly I tell you . . . whoever becomes humble like this child is the greatest in the kingdom of heaven.'**
> *(part of verse 3, and verse 4)*

Christians are not called to be childish. They are called to be childlike in their openness, their trust, their reliance on others to supply their needs, their delight in the world. Many people today are seeking fame, glory, money, honours, and greatness. Do we understand Jesus' teaching about the kingdom of heaven?

† Lord, help us to live truly humble lives. Amen.

What must I do?

The two questions in these passages both deal with right conduct. The first asks about divorce, and Jesus' answer is that marriage is an institution ordained by God, and what God has joined together we should not separate. People today divorce for many reasons, including incompatibility, unfaithfulness, cruelty and abuse. In this passage, to divorce and remarry for any reason other than unchastity is to commit adultery (see *verse 9*).

In response to the second question (*verse 16*), Jesus said:

> **'Why do you ask me about what is good? There is only one who is good. If you wish to enter into life, keep the commandments.'**
>
> *(verse 17)*

To be rich was considered a blessing from God. To be poor was considered punishment for sin. Jesus was clear that it is hard for a rich man to enter the kingdom (*verse 23*). A camel going through the eye of a needle (*verse 24*) is physically impossible, but highlights the need for humility. 'Then who can be saved?' (*verse 25*). People like the rich young man who are blessed with money? No! He refused to sell all and follow Christ. He loved his money more. To be saved is to 'enter the kingdom' or 'obtain eternal life'. It is not by wealth, but by grace that we are saved through faith in Christ!

† Lord, keeping your commandments is not enough; help us to receive your grace with empty hands, like little children, not like adults who think they are rich already. Amen.

1 The ocean of chaos

Notes by Alec Gilmore
based on the New Revised Standard Version

Alec Gilmore is a Baptist minister with 20 years of pastoral experience and 30 years in writing, lecturing and publishing. His latest book is *A Concise Dictionary of Bible Origins and Interpretation* (Continuum, 2007).

Introduction

If you want to see God in creation the ocean may seem an unlikely place to start, and the 'chaos' connection hardly helps. With tidal waves, burst river banks and floods, we all know the force of water out of control, nature gone berserk. Fortunately few of us experience such disasters personally but the underlying feelings are not uncommon. Think of an occasion when you felt like a tiny boat on a massive sea. Call it your 'ocean of chaos moment'. Use it as a backcloth to these readings. Move between the biblical 'ocean of chaos' and your own story to penetrate some of the pictures that the Bible offers, and so enrich your experience.

Text for the week: Psalm 77:16
When the waters saw you, O God . . . they were afraid; the very deep trembled.

For group discussion and personal thought

- Re-examine your own 'ocean moment' in the light of Genesis 8:13-22. How did you feel immediately afterwards? How does that experience enrich your appreciation of this story?

- Reflect on the story of the Flood in the light of climate change and a shortage of fossil fuels. How do you see the judgement of God and where can you find the Noah family?

- When faced with a situation like that of Jonah, what cargo did you have to throw away? What positives emerged?

October

God limits the ocean

In an 'ocean moment' it is difficult to pin responsibility for what happened on any human being. Insurance companies call it an 'Act of God'. Those who escape 'thank their lucky stars' or use whatever phrase comes to mind. Many will rally round and help the victims in whatever way they can, but probably all in their more reflective moments will reluctantly concede that it was a tragedy and there was nothing anyone could have done about it. Accidents happen. Some are not preventable.

This psalm could be helpful in two quite different situations. One is the moment of anxiety. When terror strikes, these words can be a way of pulling yourself together, like making an affirmation of faith, shouting as you go into battle or thumping your chest to build up the adrenalin though your knees are shaking. The other is the moment of tranquillity when you are simply thankful that even in the depths of uncertainty you still have a gut feeling that everything is going to be all right. God has it all under control. Over the centuries he has demonstrated it. Over the years you have found it true. Now, even in crisis, you can still say,

**You set a boundary that they may not pass,
so that they might not again cover the earth.**
(verse 9)

† Father, when terror threatens I trust in you. When terror strikes, grant me the trust to battle through.

The heavens open in judgement

Long before Psalm 104 was written, there was a faithful man wise enough to see that the world which he took for granted might not continue for ever, and with so much beyond his control it might be wise to take a few precautions. His contemporaries said 'It will never happen.' One day, it did.

In the six hundredth year of Noah's life . . . all the fountains of the great deeps burst forth, and the windows of the heavens were opened.

(part of verse 11)

Disaster, on a large scale. Traditionally a story of God's judgement on a wicked world, and widely used to discourage the wicked, it has probably been more effective in producing guilt among survivors and observers than in changing anybody's way of life. Try seeing it as a judgement *for* good rather than *against* evil, with positive rewards for the wise who *see* what is happening, *hear* what events are telling them, and *prepare to adjust* their way of life. See God as one who saves rather than destroys. Notice his attention to detail to ensure that a remnant of everything he created will continue, with a chance of a new beginning despite the worst that the forces of evil can throw at it. Hostage victims and survivors from prisons and concentration camps often testify to the way in which God still saves and renews.

† Lord, thank you for my own 'ocean moment', for what was saved and what was renewed, and for the new beginning.

October

Life renewed on earth

God said to Noah, 'Go out of the ark, you and your wife, and your sons' wives with you. Bring out with you every living thing. . . so that they may. . . be fruitful and multiply on the earth.'

(verses 15-16 and part of 17)

Imagine that day for Noah and his family. Thankful. Relieved that it was all over. They had come through safely and could now begin to rebuild their lives. Lots of 'new year resolutions', no doubt. How might their feelings have changed towards the people who had been destroyed? They had never liked some of them anyway. Now they had got what they deserved.

But then, when they moved around and saw the bodies, did their hearts begin to beat with a different rhythm? No doubt their thankfulness gave them an urge to make more of their life and develop a new set of values. What about the animals? Noah must surely have wondered why he had to take all that menagerie with him. A few, of course. Surely not all. But did he feel differently after living with them at close quarters for so long? They must have become part of his family. Maybe he learned to appreciate some he had never noticed. Perhaps they all had to be there because they needed each other and God needed them all.

† Father, help us to see ourselves as part of your creation, with a duty to care, but not to rule. Amen

Fear of the deep

We have moved on several hundred years from the days of Noah. Nothing like that has happened since. Now we have a different problem. A storm at sea, and even seasoned mariners fear the end has come.

> **Then the mariners were afraid, and each cried to his god. They threw the cargo that was in the ship into the sea, to lighten it for them. Jonah, meanwhile, had gone down into the hold of the ship and had lain down, and was fast asleep.**

(verse 5)

The Jews never liked the ocean, and always lurking in the background was that mythical sea monster, Leviathan, symbol of chaos, defeated by Yahweh at creation but never quite destroyed and always liable to raise his ugly head.

Unlike Noah, for Jonah there is no escape, and after a series of traumatic but not ultimately disastrous events he finishes up in Nineveh as God intended, having learnt two lessons. First, the realisation that there are forces in the world entirely beyond his control and we are always liable to become their victims. Second, the importance of using knowledge, experience and whatever else is at hand to minimise the damage. Some precious cargo may have to go, fundamental questions be asked and sacrifices made, for only then do we begin to discern more clearly what God is up to.

| Father, when there is no way out, help me to draw on the resources you have given me and then wait patiently for your time.

October

God provides . . . a way through the sea

Where does God feature in all these disasters? Is he entirely outside them so that we have to beg for some kind of deliverance? Or is he in them with us, sharing our sufferings and frustrations? Perhaps his intentions are also being thwarted, things not working quite as intended, too much human interference. But if so, is God helpless as we are, or does he have some cards up his sleeve?

The psalmist sees God as being at the heart of it, and the ground of his belief is that God has worked so many wonders in similar situations. He almost sees God as a swimmer, living in the ocean chaos, handling wave after wave, and like the salmon swimming upstream against the strongest current, so that even the waters tremble when they see him coming. But between us and him there is one crucial difference. Whereas we are always 'under' and need lifting up, the psalmist sees God as always in control. He always knows where he is putting his feet down and his every step is a move in that direction.

> **Your way was through the sea,
> your path, through the mighty waters;
> yet your footprints were unseen.**
>
> *(verse 19)*

We cannot always appreciate those 'footprints', but we can always believe that they are there.

† Father, in the darkest moments when I can see nothing, give me the strength to continue to trust, and wait.

Jesus calms the storm and walks on the lake

Those who have no problems with miracles will have no difficulty with these two stories. If Jesus is Son of God then he must demonstrate his control over the forces of nature. Sceptics may want to look elsewhere for the meaning. For both groups two points are worth reflection. First, whatever the force of the storm it seems not to have been a problem for Jesus. He slept through it, but when the cries of the disciples penetrated his unconscious

> **he woke up and rebuked the wind and the raging waves; they ceased, and there was a calm.**
>
> *(Luke 8, verse 24)*

The warm response of one who is not afraid has a calming effect on others. Any crisis needs a calm and steady hand and where that happens the hand of God is at work. Secondly, walking on the water is different. This time he is *not* there. The disciples need to know that he *is* there and still in control. So think of it as a vision in which Jesus says, 'I am' *(NRSV margin)*, the very words that God used to Moses *(Exodus 3:13)*. In other words, 'Remember your God; and all those stories and psalms about his control over wind and storms.' Two words only, but enough to bring hope and courage to a group of terrified men.

† *Father, next time I am on the point of panic, reassure me of your presence and your power.*

Seeing God in Creation

2 The tree of life

Notes by Anthea Dove
based on the New Revised Standard Version

For Anthea's biography, see p.168

Introduction

This is One World Week. It is an opportunity for us to deepen
our conviction that each human being, whichever part of the
globe they inhabit, whatever their race or creed, belongs to
one family, the family of God. Equally, this week is our chance
to renew and strengthen our commitment to making this
beautiful planet a safer, healthier and above all, fairer world,
where everyone has an equal share in its resources. Today the
earth is torn apart by violence and terror; so many of our sisters
and brothers live in fear, die needlessly of hunger or disease,
suffer in extreme poverty. It is a sober truth that the nations, all
nations, are in need of healing.

Text for the week: Revelation 22: 2
*On either side of the river is the tree of life with its twelve
kinds of fruit, producing its fruit each month; and the leaves of
the tree are for the healing of the nations.*

For group discussion and personal thought

• For you, what does a tree symbolise most powerfully?

• What aspect of One World Week strikes you as the most
important?

October

Responsibility

The writer of the book of Genesis imagines the earth at the beginning of time: God's creation, a world of beauty and innocence. He tells us that God planted a garden:

Out of the garden the LORD God made to grow every tree that is pleasant to the sight and good for food, the tree of life also in the midst of the garden, and the tree of knowledge of good and evil.

(verse 9)

Sadly, we know that in this story innocence does not last. A woman and a man were guilty of destroying it. The irony is that thousands of years after this story was written, men and women continue to destroy God's beautiful creation. The magnificent rainforests of South America are still being hacked down, exquisite coral reefs are being destroyed, and rivers, once shining and rich in resources, have become polluted and dull.

The cause of all this is greed, for money and for power. Unless enough of us have the determination to stop it, this wonderful gift from God that is our planet will self-destruct. It is a terrible legacy to leave to the generations that come after us: a waste land, a treeless desert.

† *Dear God, Creator of the universe, we thank you for all you have given us: for the beauty of this earth, for trees and rivers and flowers. We pray for ourselves, that we may become responsible stewards of creation.*

October

Fruitfulness

The first psalm uses the imagery of trees to describe people of integrity:

> **They are like trees**
> **planted by streams of water,**
> **which yield their fruit in its season,**
> **and their leaves do not wither.**
> *(part of verse 3)*

Trees have many different qualities. Usually they are beautiful; nearly always majestic and strong. Sometimes, when we walk through quiet woodland, the soaring branches of the trees remind us of a cathedral or a holy place. And trees are fruitful: it is satisfying to pick apples or plums from the tree rather than the supermarket shelf, and I remember the pleasure I felt when I discovered a mango tree in my garden in India. For some people, trees literally mean life: the coconut tree provides food and oil, and fibre and leaves for building homes. For the writer of Psalm 1, what mattered most in a tree was its fruitfulness. And Jesus said to his disciples, 'I appointed you to go and bear fruit, fruit that will last' (*John 15:16*). Paul, writing to the Galatians, says, 'the fruit of the Spirit is love, joy, peace, patience, kindness, generosity, faithfulness, gentleness and self-control' (*Galatians 5:22-24*). Of course, this seems like a tall order, but these are goals to aim for if we want to be fruitful people, and people of integrity.

† *Dear Lord Jesus, teach us to value the talents you have given us and use them so that we may bear fruit for your sake.*

Integrity

Today we continue to think about fruitfulness. What does being fruitful actually mean for you and me? I believe we must take care not to equate fruitfulness with success. I don't need to ask myself, 'What have I achieved?' or 'What sort of impression do I make on others?' Nor is it necessary or helpful for me to compare myself with my neighbour. Luke says,

'No good tree bears bad fruit, nor again does a bad tree bear good fruit, for each tree is known by its own fruit.'
(verse 43 and part of verse 44)

The fruitfulness that God asks of us comes from deep within. It is the result of our being at rights with God and also with ourselves. So when we are secure in our faith that God loves us, and concerned to do good not for ourselves but for him and for others, we will find that we are able to be courageous, generous people who are genuinely motivated by love. All of us act, at least from time to time, with mixed motives, and all of us quite often get things wrong, but if we are open and honest before God, we will not go far astray, and we will be people of integrity.

† *Dear Lord, keep me true to you and true to myself. Show me the way to be fruitful, so that I may take a part in the building of your kingdom.*

October

Acts 5: 27-32

Cross and tree

'The God of our ancestors raised up Jesus, whom you had killed by hanging him on a tree.'

(verse 30)

I remember that I was rather shocked the first time I came across this way of describing the cross on which Jesus died. My thoughts about the cross had all been negative: a dreadful piece of dead wood. On the other hand, my thoughts about trees were all positive: trees are beautiful, living, fruitful symbols of life. However, on reflection, I realised that the cross is full of potential. It is a symbol of death, but also of redemption.

The ancient art of the Celtic Christians sometimes shows Jesus as Christ the King, still on his cross, but wearing a kingly crown and protected by angels. It is as though the cross, which was once a tree, is again transformed from dead wood into a living, flourishing tree. It has become the tree of salvation. Perhaps that is why the crosses hanging in our churches and on our walls at home are reminders, yes, of the cruel death of our Saviour, but are also symbols of forgiveness and hope and life made new.

† *Lord Jesus, Christ, when you hung upon your cross, you called on your Father, saying, 'Father, forgive them, they do not know what they are doing' (Luke 23:34). Forgive us, too, for the many ways we fail in love, and teach us to forgive others with humility and generosity.*

The healing of the nations

It is appropriate that we are reading this particular extract from scripture today, because it is United Nations Day, when we celebrate the fact that we all live in one world.

> **On either side of the river is the tree of life with its twelve kinds of fruit, producing its fruit each month; and the leaves of the tree are for the healing of the nations.**
> *(part of verse 2)*

The United Nations Organisation was set up with the hope of bringing about the healing of the nations, of ending discord and promoting peace, of declaring the human rights of every man, woman and child. Like every human institution it is fallible, and in moments of crisis sometimes seems unable to function. Like other human institutions, it is in urgent need of reform.

Because the United Nations is a coming-together of all the countries of the world, it is represented by people of widely different faiths and none, but its core values are the same as the ones that Christians hold dear: tolerance, justice and integrity. The United Nations, in all its enterprises, needs our prayers, our support and our enthusiasm.

† *Loving Father, our world is troubled, and we human beings, your children, have made it so. We ask your blessing on the work of the United Nations, on all who work for better health and education for the poorest, and all who work for justice and for peace.*

October

The kingdom of God

'It is like a mustard seed that someone took and sowed in the garden; it grew and became a tree, and the birds of the air made their nests in its branches.'

(Luke, verse 19)

In Saturday's reading from Luke's Gospel, Jesus compares the kingdom of God to a mustard seed. The kingdom of God is like the mustard tree because it comes into being through small acts of kindness, compassion and love, and gives comfort to the needy, shown by the image Jesus gives of the tree sheltering the birds in its branches. In Sunday's reading from Isaiah we have the wonderful image of what it will be like when the kingdom of God comes:

The wolf and the lamb shall feed together,
the lion shall eat straw like the ox;…
They shall not hurt or destroy
on all my holy mountain, says the LORD.

(part of verse 25)

No more violence or disharmony, only peace, joy and love. This is such a sad contrast with the real world as we know it today, but Isaiah's poetry lifts our hearts and our hopes, and inspires us to pray and work for God's kingdom to come.

† Our Father, who art in heaven, hallowed be thy name, thy kingdom come, thy will be done on earth as it is in heaven.

October

3 Dust to dust

Notes by Kavula John
based on the New Revised Standard Version

Kavula John is a Methodist minister based in
London. As well as having pastoral charge of
two churches, she is Chaplain to a Methodist Homes residence.
She was born and brought up in a village in Kenya.

Introduction

My dad had not been well during half term. On Monday
morning I was getting ready to go back to my boarding school.
When I went to say goodbye we held hands for a while and
then he said: 'This hand is flesh and blood. You can hold it
today. There will be a time when it will not there anymore
for you to hold. This life is not permanent, it is quite simply
limited.' I remember thinking, as I walked the seven miles back
to school, that I should never take for granted the life and
time that God had given me. I should smile and be courteous
to the people I met on the way, because it might be our last
encounter.

That chat with Dad and walk back to school have stayed with
me on my journey of faith. We should be careful with each day,
and with those we meet, for it will never come again. This life,
in this world, is only for a while, and with God's help we should
do our best with it.

Text for the week: Psalm 90:12
So teach us to count our days that we may gain a wise heart.

For group discussion and personal thought
• Why is it helpful and encouraging to know that we are dust?

Human life is brief

All life begins with God. Recognition of God as Creator is at the heart of the Judeo-Christian tradition. Here the psalmist reflects on the shortness of human life on earth. Life on earth is seen as consisting not only of a process of growing and flourishing but also of diminishing and returning, returning to the dust from which it came. It is passing and impermanent. And this entire process of birth, growth, decline, death and decay is in God's hands. From one perspective, it might seem as if God is angry and has set out to destroy all that he has made. Therein lies the challenge to human understanding. We should be under no illusion that

> **The days of our life are seventy years,**
> **or perhaps eighty, if we are strong.**
> *(part of verse 10)*

It is by reflecting on the briefness of life and its speedy end that we can grow in wisdom and in understanding the significance of human life.

† *Lord, forgive me for the times when I have forgotten that my life has a purpose within your plan. You have granted me life and I pray that in your mercy you will also grant me wisdom to live my days as I ought. Amen.*

God remembers we are dust

God is loving and kind to us. He shows this by forgiving us
when we fail, for he knows we are only human. Being human
is being vulnerable, but our God understands that this is our
human condition. God offers us unconditional forgiveness,
heals us and loves us with love that knows no bounds. And
with confidence we can join the writer of this psalm:

**Bless the LORD, O my soul . . .
who forgives all your iniquity,
who heals all your diseases, . . .
who crowns you with steadfast love and mercy.**
(part of verses 2-4)

We see that it is God's blessings that sustain us and make
us healthy and strong like the eagle, as the psalmist says.
In Hebrew thought, the eagle is a powerful metaphor for
strength, freedom and prosperity.

At the same time, the psalmist urges us not to forget that
God is also a just judge who watches over his people for
their protection. From his great love come unlimited mercy
and compassion, so he rightly deserves to be called the
'Father' of all people, for he knows us through and through
as children of the dust. The more we become aware of our
mortality and sinfulness, the more we should remember that
God understands our condition and is merciful and forgiving
towards us.

† *Thank you, God, for all your goodness to me. Always remind
me to trust you, for it is because of you that I am. Amen.*

October

In a dry and weary land

All life is vulnerable. There is nothing perhaps more devastating to life on earth than a prolonged drought which eventually turns the land into dry, arid desert. The ancient Hebrews were surrounded by desert and knew only too well that where the desert was made to bloom God was at work. In our reading for today, the psalmist has such an image in mind as he contemplates life without God. A life without God's love is like a traveller walking in a dry land without water.

> **[M]y flesh faints for you,**
> **as in a dry and weary land where there is no water.**
> **So I have looked upon you in the sanctuary,**
> **beholding your power and glory.**
> *(part of verse 1, and verse 2)*

We receive God's love and fulfilment through prayer and openness to his Spirit, and the result is an explosion of sheer joy and praise and thanksgiving.

But notice, too, that we don't only experience God's company in holy places such as sanctuaries or chapels. We meet him wherever we are: in the noisy city, the quiet countryside, the big forest, and in the dry lands where rain has failed. This makes us ever mindful of his loving presence and protection.

† *Lord, teach me your ways and lead me into them by your Holy Spirit, so that I may be refreshed in body, mind and soul. Amen.*

October

Under judgement

Drought is a terrifying thing: without mercy it sweeps away life. When the rains fail, people are in grief. Their wellbeing is affected and they experience great suffering. The prophet Jeremiah mourns from the depth of his spirit as he foretells a drought for the people of Israel, a great drought that will ultimately bring to nothing all meaningful existence. He sees this as a consequence of the people's disobedience towards their God and he prays to God to bring a change:

> [Y]ou, O LORD, are in the midst of us,
> and we are called by your name;
> do not forsake us!
> *(part of verse 9)*

Jeremiah grieves over the breakdown of Israel's covenant relationship with God. The people needed to recognise how bad the situation was. Only then would they cry out to God and plead not to be abandoned.

Jeremiah's message should be a warning for our own times. For example, if we neglect God's covenant in nature and continue to cause massive environmental damage, we place the whole of creation in danger of falling apart. We should not wait until disaster has struck before seeking reconciliation with our Maker.

† *Loving God, you have called me to be your child and I take my place with joy. Remind me when I stray from your path and quench your spirit. Revive me again and again and let your living water flow and fill my soul so that I may rise and praise you with confidence and strength. Amen.*

October

The land flourishes under God's care

God's role in creation and his continuing care of what he has created is the highlight of this psalm. He is the one who sustains the natural world according to his covenant and who is present at all times, watering and enriching the earth. Water on a dry land changes it from barrenness to growth. Growth means life for all.

> **You visit the earth and water it,**
> **you greatly enrich it;**
> **the river of God is full of water.**
> *(part of verse 9)*

The Holy Spirit is God's gift of water to us, an ever-flowing river full of refreshment. By opening our lives to God, we invite his Spirit to flow through us, watering us and renewing us. If the Spirit of God is in us, then we will be full of productivity and will bear those fruits of the Spirit: 'love, joy, peace, patience, kindness, generosity, faithfulness, gentleness, and self-control' (*Galatians 5:22*) and not only will we be blessed but others will be touched and blessed through us.

† *There are many times, Lord, when I feel down and empty. I pray today that you will renew and revive me by your Spirit. Help me to trust myself fully to you and use me for your glory. Amen*

Jesus writes in the dust

The people in the temple were eager to hear Jesus' teaching, but then he was confronted by some religious leaders determined to catch him out. Would Jesus follow the Law and approve the stoning of a woman caught in adultery? No. Jesus understood their true intent and responded in a way that went deeper than words. Writing in the dust was a prophetic gesture which could be interpreted as 'Remember that we have come from dust and return to dust, for we have all sinned.' His opponents understood his message.

> **'Let anyone among you who is without sin be the first to throw a stone at her.'**
>
> *(part of John 8, verse 7)*

The accusers departed and Jesus assured the woman of forgiveness – a sign of a new kingdom with new values which overrode the Law as the Pharisees and scribes knew it.

The challenge for us, as for those scribes and Pharisees, is not to judge others so readily but to cultivate the loving, merciful and forgiving values of the kingdom of God. To do this, the parable in Luke tells us, we need to prepare our soil to receive God's seed, so that it is no longer barren dust but productive and fertile ground.

† *Lord, your truth has often been wasted on me, when I have been judgemental and critical of others and not allowed the seeds of your kingdom to grow in me. Forgive me, and transform the dust of my humanity into the fertile soil of your kingdom. Amen.*

November

Readings in Matthew

7 Teaching in Jerusalem

Notes by Christian Glasgow
based on the Good News Bible

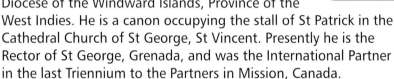

Christian E Glasgow is an Anglican priest in the Diocese of the Windward Islands, Province of the West Indies. He is a canon occupying the stall of St Patrick in the Cathedral Church of St George, St Vincent. Presently he is the Rector of St George, Grenada, and was the International Partner in the last Triennium to the Partners in Mission, Canada.

Introduction

Our passage this week falls in the section of Mathew's Gospel which highlights Jesus' teaching in Jerusalem. It takes us through a series of contrasting movements. It begins with Jesus commending the authority and principles of the scribes and Pharisees, while condemning their deeds. It continues with his angry pronouncement of judgement and punishment on the religious leaders followed by his compassionate lament for Jerusalem and ends with a discourse on the end of the age – reading the signs of the time.

Text for the week: Matthew 24:35
'Heaven and earth will pass away, but my words will never pass away.'

For group discussion and personal thought

- Jesus denounced the hypocrisy of the scribes and Pharisees. Are you preaching one thing and practising another? Is your spirituality just an outward show? How are you being a catalyst for the growth and development of those around you?

- The disciples of Jesus were curious to know the signs that would signal the end of time. Does the world today share a similar curiosity? If so, how?

Do as I say, not as I do

A teenager attending a secondary school in Grenada returns home from school one evening and is met by her mother who is in quite a rage because she has just found out that her daughter, her only daughter, is pregnant. The teenager is subjected to a tirade about her immoral behaviour, about what is acceptable and expected from her; and her mother even quotes scripture to reinforce her point. While all of this is going on, there is confusion in the teenager's mind. 'What's the big fuss about?' She does not understand why her mother is carrying on like this. After all, her mother has four children by four different men and never went to secondary school, and this is only the teenager's first pregnancy. 'So what's the big deal?'

> '[Y]ou must obey and follow everything they tell you to do; do not, however, imitate their actions, because they don't practise what they preach.'
>
> *(verse 3)*

We all find ourselves in a position of leadership at one time or another. This passage reminds us that 'action speaks louder than words'. It also challenges us to let our deeds coincide with our proclamations and admonitions.

† *Lord, help us as leaders to be mindful of the impact of our actions on those whom we lead, and keep us ever conscious of the necessity to lead by example.*

November

I will not, and I will not let you

In St Vincent a young priest is called to his first church. He enters this parish full of zeal and excitement, ready to move mountains. However, he encounters a congregation well entrenched in traditions, rituals and ceremonies that are very superficial. He embarks on a teaching programme designed to enlighten the parish and move it forward. The priest's goal is to take the parish from a maintenance and static mode to a missionary and dynamic one, based on the belief that worship without active service leads to spiritual ghettoes. The custodians of the church object and lead a boycott.

> **'You hypocrites! You lock the door of the Kingdom of heaven in people's faces, and you yourselves don't go in, nor do you allow in those who are trying to enter.**
>
> *(verse 13)*

Rituals, ceremonies and traditions are not meant to be ends in themselves but tools/aids pointing us beyond – to God. When this is the case, worship is transformed from mere ritualistic observances to a practical expression of service to humankind. We need, therefore, to encourage what gives meaning to our worship, enhances our relationship with God and fosters the unity of human beings.

† *Teach us, good Lord, to understand that it is mercy you want, not sacrifices.*

Decoration or declaration

In many Caribbean islands it is fashionable for people to adorn themselves with gold or silver jewellery which very often incorporates religious symbols. One day a pastor, coming through the airport in St Lucia, saw a fashionably dressed young man sporting several gold chains around his neck, one of which bore a beautifully decorated Celtic cross. This surprised him somewhat because he knew that the young man was a notorious drug dealer. The pastor approached the young man and, pointing to the cross, asked 'Is this for decoration or is it a declaration?'

> **'You hypocrites! You are like whitewashed tombs, which look fine on the outside but are full of bones and decaying corpses on the inside. In the same way, on the outside you appear good to everybody, but inside you are full of hypocrisy and sins.'**
>
> *(part of verse 27, and verse 28)*

Our religious piety must be more than an outward show. What we say or do must be as a result of our total surrender to the will of God – genuine action, not pretentious show to impress others. Human beings may be impressed by the outward appearance but God sees and knows what is on the inside.

† *Help us, Lord, to remember that you are the all-seeing and all-knowing God.*

November

315

'One day, one day congoté'

In Grenada some people still use a French patois, which is really a combination of broken French and English, to express deep emotions in a colourful manner. A young man was ambushed on his way home from a night of frolicking. However, his alleged assailants were acquitted on the day of trial for lack of conclusive evidence. In response to this outcome, his family was seen pointing their fingers at the acquitted men and heard passionately shouting 'One day, one day congoté'. Meaning: ' So you are getting away, but one day you will pay for your crimes.'

> **'You snakes and sons of snakes! How do you expect to escape from being condemned to hell?'**
>
> *(verse 33)*

This passage reminds us that even though we may get away with things for a while, the time will come when we will be judged by God. It therefore challenges us to live ever mindful that we cannot do what we want for as long as we want.

† *Father, help us to live daily seeking to do your will so that by your grace we may pass from death to life.*

Reading the signs of the times

In the early part of the year 1979, residents in St Vincent observed that animals were behaving strangely. Domestic animals were very restless and skittish. The local wildlife began migrating from the mountains and entering villages and even the capital, Kingstown. People wondered at this strange occurrence. The elders who had experienced the 1902 eruption of the La Souferre volcano simply said that the volcano is 'acting up' and will erupt soon. Lo and behold, on 13 April 1979, Good Friday, Vincentians awoke to the eruption of La Souferre.

> 'Tell us when all this will be, . . . and what will happen to show that it is time for your coming and the end of the age.'
>
> *(part of verse 3)*

Jesus, in response to his disciples' request, teaches them how to discern the signs of the times in order to unmask false messiahs. In a sense, the followers of Jesus are challenged to be like the prophets of old who, reading the signs of their time, were able to 'forth tell' the future.

† Lord, keep us attuned to the happenings around us so that we may discern your messages.

Timeless words

During this week, we have reviewed some of Jesus' teachings in Jerusalem and, as we scrutinise the several episodes, we find his words to be timeless. For if we reflect on contemporary experiences we see the same double standards in our midst. There exist the same stumbling blocks even within the church, with those who are stuck in tradition not willing to move and seeking to prevent others from growing. Even among our contemporary religious leaders there are sheep in wolves' clothing and pretenders who seem to be getting away with their charade. Just as Jesus' words are proved to be timeless in our contemporary experience, so too his prophecy of judgement must be understood as timeless.

> **'Heaven and earth will pass away, but my words will never pass away.'**
>
> *(verse 35)*

Our challenge in our sojourn here is to become familiar with the teachings of Jesus and to live by them daily as we await his second coming, for in them there is eternal life.

† *O Lord, open our ears to hear your word; open our eyes to see your signs; and strengthen us to follow where you lead so that at the last we may by your grace attain eternal life.*

8   Teaching about the End

Notes by Alec Gilmore
based on the Revised English Bible

For Alec's biography see p.291.

Introduction

We have no idea what is going to happen tomorrow or how important today is going to be in the overall pattern of our life. And so we also have no idea of the impact of our words, thoughts and actions on those around us, for their future as well as for ours. Therefore we are called to live every day with a sense of the presence of God — beginning each day with the reassurance that it offers; continuing with the checks and balances it provides; and concluding with a sense of forgiveness for the times we have missed the mark, and thankfulness for the forgiveness of others.

Text for the week: Matthew 24:46
Happy that servant if his master comes home and finds him at work!

For group discussion and personal thought

• Do I live each day as if it were my last or as if it were my first? Is my natural instinct one of caution and wariness or confident abandon and adventure?

• When was the last time you had a sudden surprise (or shock) that made you question something you had always believed without question? How did you respond?

• Ponder your unachievable goal, your vision that can never be realised, and work out ways of maintaining it as a springboard and encouragement rather than a frustration.

November

Awaiting the End

Several stories towards the end of Matthew can be read against the background of a Jewish society living in fear or hope (according to your viewpoint) of the kind of cataclysmic 'end' which today might be described as regime change. Some saw Jesus as the anointed one to bring it about. When it failed to happen, the early church interpreted the stories more in terms of a Return (or Second Coming) and over the years they have come to be seen as teaching about the End.

For the most part Jesus was cautious about such enthusiasms and tried to calm things down when he said,

> 'About that day and hour no one knows, not even the angels in heaven, not even the Son; no one but the Father alone.'
>
> *(verse 36)*

That, together with the fact that circumstances today are so different, suggests that it might be more helpful to think of now, and waiting, rather than expectation or speculation. His words are a reminder to us to pay more attention to where we are, to appreciate the eternal significance of every day, to learn to watch and wait, always aware that every thought, decision and action is a moment of judgement. Sometimes a very familiar story comes alive in a new way when we look at it from a different perspective or ask a different set of questions.

† Father, help me to see every day as a series of moments in which to bring honour to your name.

Sprints and marathons

In this story, try beginning with the arrival of the Bridegroom. Who (or what) is he? See his coming as that great moment of celebration that is just around the corner. It could be debt cancellation, the end of world poverty, the achievement of world literacy, or something much more ordinary. Everyone must be in on it.

Now, the bridesmaids. The problem is not really the failure to think ahead or a lack of resources. Both groups had planned and prepared and all had oil in their lamps. The difference was in attitude and intention. Five were so excited by the anticipation and only had eyes for the celebration. The others were wise enough to prepare for delay, disappointment and the possibility of a long haul. So what happened?

> **'As the bridegroom was a long time in coming, they all dozed off to sleep. But at midnight there came a shout: "Here is the bridegroom!"'**
>
> *(verse 5 and part of verse 6)*

Then the real difference became apparent. One group had organised themselves for this moment and were ready. The others had lost interest, allowed themselves to be distracted and were caught unawares, unable to seize the moment of opportunity when it came. The difference is between short-termism and the long haul, the sprinter and the marathon runner.

† *Father, when the fulfilment of my dream seems long delayed, give me a sense of calm to wait your time. Meanwhile, help me to ensure that when the moment comes I have everything ready.*

November

The risk of losing

The heart of this story is a willingness to take responsibility, even risks, with something that is precious; something we do not own but simply hold in trust. The most precious thing that we all hold, and the only thing for which we can be wholly responsible, is our self – our integrity, values, beliefs, convictions and faith. And we do not own ourselves; we live our lives 'in trust for God'.

The first man had gifts in abundance. In the interests of serving his master he was willing to use them, trade them and risk them as he shared them with others. In doing this he found that, far from losing them, he saw them change, mature and increase in value and (when his master returned) his own life enriched as a result. The second man was more limited but did likewise. The third man was fearful and apprehensive. With his limitations you may feel he had a right to be. So he decided to risk nothing, protect it exactly as it was and share it with no one, and the little that he had wasted away. Why? Because it is a law of the spiritual life that

> 'everyone who has will be given more, till he has enough and to spare; and everyone who has nothing will forfeit even what he has.'

(verse 29)

† *Father, show me today how to share myself with others, not for reward but out of love for them and for you.*

Surprise, surprise!

Two groups of people with a common problem but with quite different consequences. One group did not know how to recognise God (Christ) in their neighbour. Preoccupied with traditional religious signs and symbols, they failed to see responding to human need as part of God's plan. The other group failed to recognise him in their own day-to-day events. Preoccupied with doing what they naturally felt to be right, they failed to see such common, basic human things as an expression of their faith. What they had in common was the element of surprise: when the truth came home to them, leading to disbelief, followed by questioning it even when it was staring them in the face.

> **'Lord, when was it that we saw you hungry . . . or thirsty . . . a stranger . . . or naked   ill or in prison?'**
>
> *(part of verses 37-39)*

We could argue endlessly about the rights and wrongs of the two approaches, but perhaps what both have to learn is that the time to be most aware of God is when he takes us by surprise.

† *Father, forgive me for all those times when I take you for granted, assume you are where I think you are, want what I think you want and will do what I expect. Cushion me, I pray, against the shock of discovering otherwise, but at the same time give me (many) a surprise and open my eyes to see.*

Either–or

A trick question. The Herodians would support the tax, the Pharisees hated it. The Zealots refused to pay. Those who did pay were regarded as collaborators. The details are not our problem and there is little point in pursuing them. Jesus was not making a statement about disestablishment or tax law in the twenty-first century. Think of it rather as an 'either–or' story and relate it to something in your own experience. You *or* me. Us *or* them. Right *or* wrong.

Consider how different your chosen topic looks when you try to see it from the opposite point of view. Ask yourself how many problems are the result of such polarisation, or why we feel the need either to build walls to protect our point of view or to demonise others. Jesus once again starts in a different place. Not either–or. Not even both–and. Just somewhere else. First, give the emperor his due, but then . . .

> **'Pay to Caesar what belongs to Caesar, and to God what belongs to God.'**
>
> *(part of verse 21)*

The first bit is clear and straightforward. Then comes the sting in the tail for all parties, in a comment that raises another question that nobody was asking: what sort of taxes (dues) are you paying to God?

† *Father, whenever I find myself in an either–or situation, deliver me from quick and easy solutions until I have seen my prejudices through the eyes of 'the other' and heard the question you really want me to answer.*

Who is my neighbour?

The Pharisees do Jesus the honour of calling him 'Teacher', possibly showing respect for his credentials because from the beginning he had demonstrated loyalty to the temple: as a baby, a 12-year-old, and on numerous other occasions. Nevertheless, he had spent the previous three years responding in very different, unfamiliar and untraditional ways to people – to women, to victims, to rejects, to other faiths, races and traditions – and always demonstrating that 'the love of God is broader than the measures of our mind'. What he quotes is on the side of the angels:

> **'"Love the Lord your God with all your heart, with all your soul, and with all your mind . . . [and] love your neighbour as yourself."'**
>
> *(part of verses 37 and 39)*

But the last five words stir up a hornet's nest. Who is this neighbour? Superficially it meant Jews – people like them. Unlike Luke's account (*10:29*), nobody asks the question. There is a deafening silence. Jesus seems to say: 'Go away and think about it.' Then, when you find him, 'Love him as yourself.' That really is a tall order. Imagine lavishing on your neighbour all the love and care that you lavish on yourself! Verses 41-46 seem to confirm the point that some questions are better not asked.

† Thank you, Lord, for an impossible target but a wonderful vision and objective. Inspire me with the thought of how even a few steps in that direction could transform my personal relationships and change the world.

Music in the Bible

1 The power of music

Notes by Aileen Khoo
based on the New International Version (NIV)
and the New Living Translation (NLT)

Aileen Khoo has worked in the Methodist Church
in Malaysia for 33 years. Currently she is Director of Christian
Education at Trinity Methodist Church, Petaling Jaya. She
particularly enjoys leading Bible studies, especially experimenting
with participatory Bible study methods.

Introduction

Music is mentioned many times in the Bible, suggesting to us
its importance and power in its use in worship, for expressing
joy, as a means to subjugate, to punish, and to accompany
prophesy, to serve and to encourage. Much of our personal
theology is shaped by music. In times of stress or crisis, hymns
often flash across our minds even before scripture. In each
of this week's notes, I suggest music for you to listen to and
hymns for you to sing. Let us sing and make music to the glory
of God!

Text for the week: Psalm 150:6
Let everything that breathes sing praises to the LORD!

For group discussion and personal thought

• How does music help you in your relationship with God?

• Do you find music in church worship a hindrance or a help?

• What is your favourite hymn, and why?

Sing praise to God

Let everything that breathes sing praises to the LORD!
(verse 6, NLT)

Creation praises God. Only human beings need to be reminded to praise God. Just listen to the birds and animal noises, and you may hear the whole of creation sing. Psalm 150 has seven different musical instruments in concert, praising God. When we praise God we join the heavenly host: 'Therefore with angels and archangels and all the company of heaven we laud and magnify thy holy name.' We are created to sing praises to God.

For Martin Luther, music was a power for life and order. 'O for a thousand tongues to sing my great redeemer's praise', composed Charles Wesley on hearing his friend Peter Bohler exclaim 'Had I a thousand tongues, I would praise God with them all.' Inscribed on the composer Heinrich Schutz's tomb are the words 'The Christian singer of Psalms – a joy for foreigners, for Germans a light.' Psalms are for singing, singing is for worship and to worship is to live.

- Listen to: 'Psalm of David' by Heinrich Schutz

- Sing:
  'Let All the World in Every Corner Sing' by George Herbert
  'O for a Thousand Tongues to Sing' by Charles Wesley

† *My heart is confident in you, O God; no wonder I can sing your praises with all my heart! Wake up, lyre and harp! I will wake the dawn with my song. (Psalm 108:1-2, New Living Translation)*

November

Sing the almighty power of God

The Lord is my strength and my song.
(verse 2, NIV)

Having seen the Egyptians, their formidable enemy, perish in the Red Sea, Miriam and all the women danced with tambourines in praise of God for their safe passage. God had caused his people to triumph. Some of King David's psalms were composed when he was in trouble and greatly distressed 'but David found strength in the Lord ' (*1 Samuel 30:6*) – perhaps through singing. Paul and Silas, with their backs bleeding, chain-bound, sang hymns in prison (*Acts 16:25*). Whenever Luther was discouraged he would say to his companions 'Come, let us sing the 46th psalm.' The composer Franz Joseph Haydn, when faced with obstacles, said that something within him whispered, 'There are but few contented and happy individuals here below; everywhere grief and care prevail, perhaps your labour may one day be the source from which the weary and worn . . . may derive a few moments of rest and refreshment', and while composing *The Creation*, 'daily I fell on my knees and asked God for strength'.

- Listen to: *The Creation* by Joseph Haydn

- Sing:
  'On Eagle's Wings' by Michael Joncas
  'We, thy People, Praise Thee' by Kate Stearns Page

† *It is good to praise the Lord and make music to your name, O Most High, to proclaim your love in the morning and your faithfulness at night, to the music of the ten-stringed lyre and the melody of the harp. (*Psalm 92:1-3, NLT)

Sing the greatness of the Lord

'As soon as you hear the sound of the horn, flute, zither, lyre, harp, pipes and all kinds of music, you must fall down and worship the image of gold that King Nebuchadnezzar has set up.'

(verse 5)

Read the whole passage aloud, feeling its solemnity and repetitive rhythm, especially the five repetitions of 'that he/King Nebuchadnezzar has set up'. The passage starts and ends with King Nebuchadnezzar. God is left out. The Jews were required to bow down before the image King Nebuchadnezzar had set up to re-educate and indoctrinate. He, like Stalin, Hitler and Mao, knew the power of music for good or evil. All great movements and revolutions have been accompanied by music and patriotic songs. Martin Luther's chorale 'A mighty fortress is our God' helped spread the Reformation. He used the power of hymns to enable God's word to dwell among people.

This passage is a powerful reminder to all who elevate the glory and power of their nation above that of the sovereign Creator. In the end, all his musical instruments could not save Nebuchadnezzar, who learnt the hard lesson that only the Most High rules over all kingdoms and gives them to whomever he chooses.

- Listen to: 'A Mighty Fortress' (Cantata no. 80) by J S Bach

- Sing: 'A Mighty Fortress is our God' by Martin Luther

† Sing to the Lord, for he has done glorious things; let this be known to all the world. (Isaiah 12:5, NLT)

Sing the goodness of the Lord

I will put an end to your noisy songs, and the music of your harps will be heard no more.

(verse 13)

The people were bringing substandard, rotting sacrifices to the Lord. Bells and other musical instruments have been associated with churches calling people to worship. How can we call people to worship God if our deeds are corrupt? Martin Luther believed that music ruled the entire creation and was given to humankind. God has given us voices and words, therefore it is our duty to praise God. Luther's desire to worship God inspired him to translate Latin hymns into the vernacular so that the congregation could sing in worship.

Music is an offering by the congregation. We may not be world-class singers but anything less than our best is not honouring God. With confidence we know that God has removed our sins 'as far as the east is from the west' (*Psalm 103:12*). This should make us sing his goodness!

- Listen to: 'Lord God of Abraham' and 'If With All Your Hearts', from *Elijah* by Felix Mendelssohn

- Sing:
  'Out of the Depths I Cry to You' by Martin Luther
  'Joyful, Joyful, We Adore Thee' by Henry Van Dyke

† *Restore us again, O God our Savior, and put away your displeasure toward us. Will you not revive us again, that your people may rejoice in you?* (Psalm 85:4, 6, NLT)

Sing the joy of worship

'You will meet a procession of prophets coming down from the high place with lyres, tambourines, flutes and harps being played before them, and they will be prophesying.'

(part of verse 5)

The prophets had just returned from worshipping God in the high places, elevated holy sites used before the temple was built. Their worship did not stop with the Benediction or when they left the front door. They continued singing, playing musical instruments and prophesying.

The Russian composer Igor Stravinsky had a genuine humility before God. He began his day with prayer. He recognised music as a means of communication with God.

The church knew what the prophets had known. Music praises God. Many people consider music the church's greatest ornament, more than the building and all its decoration. Music and the proclamation of God's word are intrinsically intertwined. Every spiritual awakening in church history has been accompanied by a revival of song, for singing is to worship as breathing is to life.

- Listen to: 'Symphony of Psalms' by Igor Stravinsky

- Sing:
  'When in our Music God is Glorified' by Fred Pratt Green
  'O Worship the King' by Robert Grant

| Sing to the Lord with thanksgiving; make music to our God on the harp. He covers the sky with clouds; he supplies the earth with rain and makes grass grow on the hills. (Psalm 147:7-9, NLT)

November

Sing the glory and wisdom of the Lord

Discouraged? Don't feel like singing? When music is made, something happens.

> **While the harpist was playing, the hand of the Lord came upon Elisha.**
>
> *(part of verse 15)*

Music has power to bring hope, encouragement and direction. Music is a gift of God, not a gift of men. Johann Sebastian Bach, perhaps the greatest composer of church music, believed that the primary reason for music should be the glory of God and the recreation of the mind. For over twenty years he composed instrumental and choral music for services at St Thomas' Church in Leipzig, Germany. He was dedicated to composing for the glory of God. His legacy, a wealth of glorious music, continues to enrich, inspire and uplift. He made no attempt to get his works published or win recognition. It was enough that he was able to express his faith and praise God in his music.

- Listen to: 'O Lord, my Darkened Heart Enlightened', from *The Christmas Oratorio* by J S Bach

- Sing:
  'All People that on Earth do Dwell', attributed to William Kethe
  'How Great Thou art' by Stuart K Hine

† *Then, I will praise you with music on the harp, because you are faithful to your promises, O my God. I will sing praises to you with a lyre, O Holy One of Israel. I will shout for joy and sing your praises, for you have ransomed me. (Psalm 71:22-23, NLT)*

2 Praise the Lord!

Notes by Peter Ibison
based on the New International Version

Married, with two children, Peter is a member
of the Anglican Church in Buckinghamshire
where he serves on the PCC and leads on the Alpha course. He
is studying with the Open Theological College and works in the
telecommunications industry.

Introduction

Worship through music is God's gift to us all. It is not just for
instrumentalists, nor is it just for singers, nor is it to be just
observed or listened to. No, worship is for us all, to be enjoyed
and entered into – and for God's glory.

Text for the week: Psalm 92:1-2
*It is good to praise the LORD and make music to your name,
O Most High, to proclaim your love in the morning and your
faithfulness at night.*

For group discussion and personal thought

• What hinders us most in our worship of God?

• If worship is concerned with the giving of our whole lives to
God, what *particular* part can music play?

Music – a tool in God's hand

Of all the characteristics of David mentioned in today's passage – his courage, his skill in warfare, his eloquence and his good looks – it was David's musical ability that was first put to use in the king's service. David's technical ability in music qualifies him for service, but it was his relationship with Yahweh that makes the difference:

> **'I have seen a son of Jesse . . . who knows how to play the harp . . . and the LORD is with him.'**
>
> *(part of verse 18)*

Whenever David played, relief came to King Saul; music soothed his troubled state of mind. Perhaps David sang the music of the psalms, but what is certain is that his music came from a heart that loved God and lived to worship.

When we select musicians to lead worship in our churches, let us not just look to technical ability, but also for hearts of worship. When a search was made for the king's musician there was one objective in mind: to bring comfort. Music can touch our emotions and stir our hearts, but in the case of Saul, music's influence went deeper. Music brought physical and emotional relief and drove evil from Saul's life. Music can influence the spiritual realm and place us in a position where we can better hear the voice of God.

† Lord, through music speak to my soul, through music speak to my spirit – and draw me closer to you. Amen.

Music – brought wholeheartedly before the Lord

King David had just won a great victory against the Philistine army and now he was determined to ensure that the ark of the Lord, representing the very presence of God, should reside at his seat of government in Jerusalem. As the ark was brought in,

David and the whole house of Israel were celebrating with all their might before the LORD, with songs.

(part of verse 5)

Music and song were the means of expressing their joy, and all Israel joined in.

Let us note two things about David's worship. Firstly, he worshipped with all his might. David's worship was not half-hearted or timorous – it was exuberant praise and involved his whole being. This is not the first time David was recorded as worshipping in this way. God delights when we involve our whole being in worship, music and song. Secondly, David worshipped *before the Lord*. Worship with music and song is meaningless if it is before men – with one eye on what others think or on the impression given. There is something about worship which involves abandonment to God's purpose, with little regard for the opinion of men. David's worship was before the Lord. There is a connection between these two: if we worship with all our might, we will be free from concerns about the opinion of others. In this way, our offering becomes an acceptable sacrifice of worship.

† *May my worship in music and song be wholehearted and acceptable to you, O Lord.*

Preparing ourselves for worship

King David had in his mind to build a temple for the Lord, but it was in fact Solomon, his son, who commissioned the work. The temple was completed, the Levites brought the ark to rest in the Holy Place, and music was played. Notice that of the worshippers,

> **all the priests who were there had consecrated themselves.**
>
> *(part of verse 11)*

Before worship in song took place, the worshippers prepared their hearts before God. This can be likened to the time when Moses was asked to take off his sandals before approaching God: he was asked to prepare himself. In today's world, perhaps we emphasise our privilege in boldly approaching God's throne of grace, but neglect the important matter of preparing our hearts. Both are needed: to understand the love of God in welcoming us, and to appreciate the holiness of God which moves us to be cleansed before entering into his presence.

The worshippers played in unison, as with one voice, and sang of the goodness of God:

> **'He is good;**
> **his love endures for ever.'**
> *(part of verse 13)*

Oh for a church that worships with one voice! When our focus is on God's character in our worship, then unity in our churches will more reliably be the result.

† *Lord, help me to be aware of both your love and your holiness as I come to worship, so that I may have confidence to approach and remember to take off my shoes before doing so...*

Many forms

Under King Ahaz, Solomon's temple fell into disuse and disrepair. King Hezekiah sought its restoration and purification. Animal sacrifices were made and

> **As the offering began, singing to the Lord began also . . . all this continued until the sacrifice . . . was completed.**
> *(part of verses 27 and 28)*

Two points stand out from this passage. First, worship involved not only singing and the playing of instruments but also sacrifices (presumably at financial cost), prostrations, kneeling and bowing. Music is a wonderful means of expressing our worship of a loving Father; but it is not the only means. When a circus acrobat found new life in Christ, he wanted to express his appreciation and worship to God. He knew no prayers, no liturgy, and no churchmanship that would help him. What did he do? He performed a somersault before God. God is certainly not asking such expressions from us all, but the story reminds us that worship can take many forms.

Second, no one was exempt from worship. The king organised the worship, provided instruments, arranged for the sacrifices and the music. But then he stood alongside the people – one among equals. Leaders need to be able to worship alongside us, as part of a fallen humanity loved by God.

† *Lord, I want to be a worshipper, to worship you in spirit and truth. I praise you today for your love and kindness, your grace, your mercy and your tenderness.*

November

Making time for worship with music

The apostle Paul gave specific instructions to the Ephesians about living holy lives. For Paul, time was short and he urged the first-century Christians to 'snatch back' time from the world; not to squander it but to use it wisely. It is interesting, therefore, that Paul goes on to talk about music – something we see today more as a leisure pursuit. For Paul, however, it was an elemental part of the Christian walk. He wrote:

> **Speak to one another with psalms, hymns and spiritual songs. Sing and make music in your heart to the Lord, always giving thanks to God the Father for everything, in the name of our Lord Jesus Christ.**

(verses 19-20)

Paul gives worship in song a twofold purpose. First, our songs, hymns and spiritual songs inspire others, providing instruction whilst exhorting us to faithful service. After the Last Supper, when Jesus had warned the disciples of impending dangers – what did they do? They sang a hymn together. Second, our worship in song blesses our heavenly Father. God delights in our worship when it is expressed from the heart. When Paul and Silas were beaten and imprisoned in Philippi, what did they do? They prayed and sang hymns to God. Let us not see worship in song as peripheral to life but instead allow music its expression in all circumstances and seasons of life.

† May we speak with psalms, hymns and spiritual songs in our worship, inspiring and encouraging others and blessing God our Father.

Music in heaven and on earth

Within this weekend's readings we catch a glimpse of heaven. Let us observe the similarities and differences between heaven's worship and that on the earth. Heaven's worship is centred on Jesus, the Lamb of God; so too is that of the earth. Heaven's worship is multi-ethnic; so too is that of the earth – though heaven's worship will be on a greater scale then ever before: 24 elders playing harps, hundreds of thousands of angels worshipping, and every creature in heaven and on earth singing God's praises! Heaven's worship is continuous – by night and day, and this is our aspiration on the earth:

> It is good to praise the LORD
> and make music to your name, O Most High,
> to proclaim your love in the morning
> and your faithfulness at night.
>
> *(Psalm 92, verses 1-2)*

Our worship on earth is a foretaste of heaven.

† *Lord, help me more and more to express my love and devotion to you in worship and song. May we recognise that our worship here is but a foretaste of heaven.*

1　Ready to hear

Notes by Meeli Tankler
based on the New International Version

Meeli Tankler lives in Pärnu, Estonia. She is
a psychologist, and teaches part-time in the
Theological Seminaries of the Methodist and Lutheran Churches
of Estonia. She is active in women's work nationally and
internationally, and in 2001–06 she was the President of the
Europe Continental Area of the World Federation of Methodist
and Uniting Church Women. Married to a Methodist pastor, she
is a local preacher, Sunday School teacher, leader of the choir,
Bible study leader, mother of three grown-up children, and a
grandmother.

Introduction

Our Advent theme brings together two kinds of readiness: our
willingness to hear the word of God and build lives of faithful
service on his promises; and our willingness to receive and
reflect the light of God revealed in the world. There are many
obstacles to our hearing, and to our willingness to listen to
the word of God. God can sometimes seem distant, hidden
or angry. The people of God may be scattered, fearful and
badly led. But if we are willing to hear, God gives signs of his
presence with us, and promises on which we can build.

Text for the week: Psalm 85:8
*I will listen to what God the LORD will say; he promises peace
to his people, his saints – but let them not return to folly.*

For group discussion and personal thought

• Have you ever felt that God is speaking directly to you?
  Was it a pleasant and encouraging experience or rather
  frightening?

• How can you prepare yourself/your church to listen God's
  voice this Advent?

Is God coming down?

Isaiah feels strongly the need for God's intervention in human history. 'Oh, that you would rend the heavens and come down,' he cries out in verse 1. People have gone astray, far away from God, and for many God is not very much a topic to speak, or even think, about. And at the same time, even those who are waiting for God feel as if God has hidden his face. Do they still have the courage to call his name, and ask for his presence? Isaiah certainly has this courage. He admits that people have sinned – but courageously adds:

> Yet, O LORD, you are our Father.
> We are the clay, you are the potter;
> we are all the work of your hand.
> Do not be angry beyond measure, O LORD;
> do not remember our sins for ever.
> Oh, look upon us, we pray,
> for we are all your people.
>
> *(verses 8-9)*

Stepping into the Advent time, we are reminded that God did come down to his people but not quite as people expected it to happen. For this reason, there were many who did not notice his coming. Are we aware today that God is actually coming down to us?

† *God, give us courage to cry for your intervention when we feel desperate. And help us to see your presence and your mighty deeds in our life. We are all your people, and willing to trust you. Amen.*

God who hides himself

Even when we have acknowledged God as our Creator, and the Creator of the whole world, it sometimes seems that he is a hidden God, a far-away God who has done his job once and then gone away, no longer available to hear our pleas. We feel this way mostly when we are in crisis or very lonely, and feeling as if we have been abandoned both by people and by God. Isn't it great that God has given us his assuring words just for these crucial moments:

> 'Surely God is with you, and there is no other; there is no other god.'
>
> *(verse14)*

So in moments of despair and loneliness we should let God speak to us and remind us how closely he is related to our lives – despite circumstances. And maybe we should not only *allow* him to speak to us, but rather *ask* him to speak. We can tell him honestly how much we need his reassurance and presence. He does not want to remain hidden from our eyes – he has deliberately revealed himself to humankind in order to make us aware of how much he loves us.

† *Dear God, we are longing to step into your holy presence right here and now. Even when it is difficult to feel your presence among our struggles and problems, help us to see you not as a hidden God any more but as our loving God remaining always close to us. Amen.*

Restore us, O God

There is expectation in the air – something new is going to happen; God is going to do something he has not done before. It is hard to wait, though, and people's longings have grown quite desperate: when will you finally act, Lord? When will you awaken your might and restore your people? People are seeking God, praying for a change in their lives, willing to be restored to new life – with God's mighty help.

> **Restore us, O LORD God Almighty,**
> **make your face shine upon us,**
> **that we may be saved.**
>
> *(verse 19)*

The psalmist praises God's mightiness, and tells God honestly how helpless his people are feeling. There have been tears 'by the bowlful', and contention and mocking from godless neighbours. They clearly understand that they have sinned before God and do not deserve any better. But they are asking for salvation, for God's grace, for a new beginning. Is God going to answer this plea? There is certainly expectation in the air – the psalmist reminds God about 'the man at your right hand, the son of man you have raised up for yourself' (*verse 17*), speaking of the Messiah who will one day come into this world to restore the relationship between God and humankind. The strong hope is already there but the prayer that has sounded like a refrain throughout the psalm (*verses 3, 7, 19*) continues:

† *Restore us, O Lord God Almighty, make your face shine upon us, that we may be saved. Amen.*

The righteous branch

Here God himself is speaking to his people. But his voice is full of reproach: there is something wrong going on in people's lives that needs immediate change. Those responsible for the spiritual health and welfare of others have seriously failed and God's people are scattered and untended.

Perhaps we do not think often enough about the huge responsibility attached to a shepherd's daily duties. When the shepherd goes astray the whole flock follows. Or the shepherd may just be totally careless, and all the sheep are left on their own. Yet God intends that care should always be available. Hear the good news: God promises that he himself will take care of his people in a reliable way:

> **'I myself will gather the remnant of my flock . . . I will place shepherds over them who will tend them . . .**
>
> **I will raise up to David a righteous Branch,**
> **a King who will reign wisely**
> **and do what is just and right in the land.'**
> *(part of verses 3-5)*

God himself is promising that the Messiah will certainly come. A righteous Branch will shepherd God's people in the very best way and will never abandon them. God's promise goes even further: the Messiah will bring salvation and safety. Listen to God's voice – it is giving us glorious hope.

† *We pray for those who are called by God to tend his flock. Give them your guidance, O Lord, and remind them about their responsibilities. Amen.*

Promises of peace

God's promises of peace are closely connected with the promise of salvation. For real peace begins from inside out, and there is no inner peace without a sincere relationship with God. God is willing to give us peace, and it is because of God's unfailing love that the salvation is made available to people. Only through salvation will real peace finally happen on earth, and in our hearts. This is an important part of the Advent message. The psalmist makes it very clear:

**[God] promises peace to his people, his saints –
but let them not return to folly.
Surely his salvation is near those who fear him,
that his glory may dwell in our land.**

(part of verse 8, and verse 9)

Standing before God in today's troubled world we have nothing to offer but our hope and trust that he still keeps his promises. He has shown favour to the land before, and he has forgiven the iniquity of his people before – and we are told that God is always the same because he does not change. The promises he gave long ago are still valid for us today – also the promises of peace. Are we ready to hear them?

† Lord, remind us of your promises of peace. Teach us to cherish the peace you have given us, and help us to bring your peace into troubled situations and relationships. We want to be messengers of your peace. Amen.

I will restore you to health

There are many rehabilitation centres in our world today. We are offered services that restore our lost abilities to a certain level. With professional help we can exercise, and train, and get back our mobility or our intellectual ability so that we can function almost as well as we did before the illness or accident.

This is not the restoration Jeremiah is speaking about. God's restoration plan does not help us back just to a 'certain level'. God is powerful enough to restore us to full health even when we are in a hopeless situation and no rehabilitation centre in this world would dare to take us in any more. In the presence of God there is always hope. Even when we are declared incurable, beyond healing and with no remedy, God wants us to hear the promise:

> **I am with you and will save you,**
> **declares the LORD . . .**
> **I will restore you to health and heal your wounds.**
> *(part of verses 11 and 17)*

Listen to God's voice. In the midst of our misery and brokenness, our faults and transgressions, there is still hope available. There is the promise of wholeness and health and restoration for us when we keep ourselves near to God.

† *Thank you for your glorious promises. Thank you for not leaving us in despair and brokenness. Help us to believe and come close to you, so that you can restore us to both physical and spiritual health. Amen.*

2 Promises for the people

Notes by Meeli Tankler
based on the New International Version

Introduction

God keeps faith with his people, whether or not they keep faith with him, and all his promises stem from this attitude of grace, compassion, mercy and forgiveness. He gives us his promises as a sign of his love, and as a reminder that he notices and understands our needs, and is willing to respond. We can always feel safe in his care.

Text for the week: Jeremiah 31:33
'I will put my law in their minds and write it on their hearts. I will be their God, and they will be my people.'

For group discussion and personal thought

• How real are God's promises for you personally? For you as a church?

• Have there been moments in your life/in your church's life when you have really stood on his promises in full trust?

• Are there promises in the Bible that are difficult for you to claim?

A highway for our God

Prepare the way for the Lord in the desert – this is the message of the prophet Isaiah. Preparing a way in the wilderness is a difficult task, and requires a lot of hard work. Preparing a highway is even harder. And still it needs to be done, for God is willing to reveal his glory. This is something unique, and needs our full attention. The message has been given to all people:

> **And the glory of the Lord will be revealed,**
> **and all mankind together will see it.**
>   *(part of verse 5)*

So we are called to prepare the way, and all of us together are called to observe the magnificent moment when the glory of the Lord will be revealed to all humankind.

And yet there is this other dimension to this magnificence: the Sovereign Lord coming into this world quietly as a simple shepherd carrying the lambs close to his heart (*verse 11*). Shepherds do not usually use highways, and that makes it sometimes difficult to notice and celebrate their coming. It is what happened with the Lord Jesus, the Messiah, at his birth. People were observing a wrong road.

† *Lord, help us to worship you in all situations. Help us to celebrate and build highways for your glory to be revealed – and help us to notice you when you come to us in a shepherd's simple garment. Amen.*

The palace will stand on its proper place

The prophetic voice brings to our attention the plans that God has for his people: the city that has been in ruins will be rebuilt, and the palace will stand on its proper place again. People who have experienced misery and defeat will be restored to their proper standing, and God will reveal his compassion to them.

It is always difficult to be dishonoured, defeated, and humiliated, especially when this is accompanied by the feeling that God has abandoned you and there is no more hope. Surely God does not want anyone to feel this way. His promises of restoring our honour are also available today:

> 'I will bring them honour,
> and they will not be disdained.
> Their children will be as in days of old,
> and their community will be established before me . . .
> So you will be my people,
> and I will be your God.'
>
> *(part of verses 19-20, and verse 22)*

How is your palace today? Is it on its proper place or is your city still in ruins? God encourages us to claim his promises even when we feel ourselves and our communities abandoned both by people and by God. This is the day to receive God's help, and to rely on his mercy and grace.

† Our merciful God, thank you for your promises for us and our communities. Sometimes it is difficult to wait for their fulfilment. Help us to trust you even while we are still waiting. Amen.

Favour in the desert

Isn't this the very best description of God's grace? People will find favour in the desert, and God is willing to provide rest for them, says the prophet (*verse 2*). God will do it simply because he has loved his people with an everlasting love and drawn them with loving-kindness (*verse 3*). God is equally willing to provide rest for you in your daily struggles. You will never finish your duties and be able to rest in peace – there will always be something new to bother you. So you need this promise because you need God's grace – favour in your desert, and rest given by God himself. What is really amazing here is God's promise to give his grace again and again, many times, and not just once:

> **I will build you up again . . .**
> **Again you will take up your tambourines . . .**
> **Again you will plant vineyards.**
> *(part of verses 4-5)*

God's promises of grace are abundant. His grace enables us to feel strengthened in our duties, to rejoice, and to work. It builds us up as God's people, and guides us on his path. Favour in the desert is perhaps one of God's most beautiful gifts – and sometimes the most difficult to embrace wholeheartedly.

† Thank you, Lord, for your amazing grace. Thank you for making it available to everyone. Teach us to be open before you and to receive your grace in our daily desert as your wonderful gift. Amen.

Hope for your future

It is wonderful to trust God, who knows not only our past
and present but also our future. Sometimes we refuse to be
comforted because our thoughts and feelings are trapped in
the troubles and problems of the past, and it is difficult to look
forward – and especially to look into the future with hope! In
situations like this we desperately need a message from God.
And God has something to say about it. Listen to his voice:

> 'Restrain your voice from weeping
> and your eyes from tears,
> for your work will be rewarded,' declares the LORD.
> 'They will return from the land of the enemy.
> So there is hope for your future,' declares the LORD.
> *(part of verses 16-17)*

Isn't this a wonderful declaration of hope? God himself, who
is able to see our past, present and future, encourages us to
face our future with hope. For there is hope for our future, he
declares. Things will change for the good. We cannot see it yet
but God already knows what will happen. We can celebrate this
privilege that God himself promises us: we can have realistic
hope for our future.

† *Our Father in Heaven, your will be done on earth as it is in
heaven. Thank you for the assurance that you have our future
in your hand, and that you will lead us towards hope. Amen.*

The promise of new strength

In difficult times, it is hard to believe that things will ever change for the better. People grow weary and begin to interpret everything pessimistically. God knows us well, and he understands that it may take several promises before we are able to listen, believe and receive new strength and hope again. So in today's passage he first describes the future when the people are back in their homeland and blessed. Only after this hopeful description does God make his first promise: to refresh the weary, and satisfy the faint (*verse 25*). But God seems to be aware of our tendency not to believe his promises too easily; so he adds another encouraging promise.

> **'I will plant the house of Israel and the house of Judah with the offspring of men and of animals. Just as I watched over them to uproot and tear down . . . so I will watch over them to build and to plant.'**
>
> *(part of verses 27-28)*

Notice this twofold promise: God himself will plant, and he will also watch over the people as they build and plant. There is something God does himself, and there is something he encourages people to do with the new strength that is given.

† *Dear God, so often we grow weary and stop believing that we could do something to change our surroundings. Help us to hear your promises, and to use the strength you give us for building and planting. Amen.*

Promises written on human hearts

Many of the promises in the Bible are given to God's people as a whole, but there are also promises given to individuals which sound very personal. In the first of this weekend's readings, God comes very close to each one of us. He speaks about his covenant with his people – but he wants a covenant not just with the nation as a whole but with every single person in that nation, a covenant that is written on people's hearts.

> **'I will put my law in their minds**
> **And write it on their hearts.**
> **I will be their God,**
> **And they will be my people . . .**
> **They will all know me,**
> **from the least of them to the greatest.'**
> *(part of verses 33-34)*

This is the only way that the nation once chosen by God can really continue to be his people – through their personal relationship with him. This is the only way that we can become part of God's people – through our personal relationship with him. The covenant written on everyone's heart will keep God's people in a mutual relationship with him – and also guarantee God's continual presence. People who are carrying God's covenant in their hearts will never cease to be his people.

† *Almighty God, thank you for coming so near to us through your promises. Thank you for being so powerful through your promises. Guide us into faith and trust so that we can claim your promises and be strengthened by them. Amen.*

3   Ready to respond

Notes by Meeli Tankler
based on the New International Version

Introduction

Faithful discipleship and good leadership are both necessary if we are to hear God's word, respond readily and claim the promises God has made to us as his people. John the Baptist is an example of a faithful disciple. The flock may not always be fortunate in its leaders. But God is our Shepherd. He values those who guard, guide and serve the people, and he seeks faithfulness in all of us.

Text for the week: Ezekiel 34:27-28
'They will know that I am the Lord, when I break the bars of their yoke and rescue them . . . They will live in safety, and no one will make them afraid.'

For group discussion and personal thought

* Do you think that people around you are ready to respond to God? What would prevent their readiness? What about your own readiness and willingness?

* Have you dedicated some time and effort during this Advent time to prepare yourself for responding to God at a deeper level? What are the practical ways in which you can do this?

A witness sent from God

God uses messengers, divine and human, to introduce significant moments that change human history. Christ's birth was announced by angels, both in advance and when it had already taken place. But just before Christ began his earthly ministry, God sent John the Baptist to prepare the way. In John's Gospel we are told that John was

a man who was sent by God . . . He came as a witness to testify concerning the light.

(part of verses 6-7)

In John's own words, he was 'the voice of one calling in the desert, "Make straight the way for the Lord"' (*verse 23*).

A witness to the light must first of all know the light. No witness can testify about things (s)he does not know or has never seen. We are all called by God to be witnesses to his light – and by doing so, to spread this light further. In Advent we remember this very special moment in human history when God became one of us, and a divine light entered this world in the person of Jesus Christ. But this was not the end of God's redemptive plan, only the beginning. The light is still here, and we are all called to be witnesses to it until Christ comes again.

† *Dear Lord Jesus, thank you for becoming a light for this world. Thank you for inviting us to live in your light, and help us to be the witnesses of light wherever we go. Amen.*

God looks after us

This is the uniqueness of the Christian faith: we do not have to rely on our own strength to search for God, he is looking for us! From the very first days of creation God asks 'Where are you?' and makes himself accessible to us. The incarnation is just another proof of God's willingness to be always there for us. Whenever we go astray he reminds us that he is patiently waiting for our return. But he is not just waiting, he is also actively looking for us.

> **'I myself will search for my sheep and look after them . . . I will bring them out from the nations and gather them from the countries . . . I will search for the lost and bring back the strays. I will bind up the injured and strengthen the weak, but the sleek and the strong I will destroy. I will shepherd the flock with justice.'**
>
> *(part of verses 11 and 13, and verse 16)*

We belong to his flock. And it is encouraging to know that God's shepherding is based on justice. He deals with us as individuals and always knows our needs, our weaknesses – and our arrogance. We can become 'strays' even in the midst of our cosy church setting, and then we need the reminder that God will first try to bring us back – but he may also need to discipline us because of his justice.

† Almighty God, help us stay close to you. Amen.

God who knows us

As we learnt from yesterday's reading, our God knows each of us well because we are sheep of his flock. Sometimes we are not too happy about this. We would like to keep some things to ourselves and only show him our good side. We may be ashamed of things we have done – or failed to do. And the message from God is very clear here: there will be a judgement day. The Good Shepherd in his justice 'will judge between one sheep and another' (*verses 17, 22*). However, we do not have to be too frightened. In God's knowledge of us, his love and mercy will always be available to us. He is still willing to give us 'a second chance', to provide us with the strength and goodwill to turn away from the mistakes of the past and live according to his will. And he never leaves us. He takes care of us – God's people – as he promises:

I will place over them one shepherd, my servant David, and he will tend them; he will tend them and be their shepherd. I the LORD will be their God.

(verse 23 and part of verse 24)

† *Our Good Shepherd, thank you for knowing us and still loving us with your unfailing love. Thank you for the encouragement of knowing that we shall never be left behind but that you will take care of us. Amen.*

A covenant of peace

Isn't it good news that God, knowing all our human weaknesses and struggles, is still willing to make a covenant with us? His love must really be abundant. And his willingness to take care of his people is amazing. Look at these great promises:

> 'There will be showers of blessing . . . when I break the bars of their yoke and rescue them . . . They will live in safety, and no one will make them afraid . . . I will provide for them . . . Then they will know that I, the LORD their God, am with them, and that they, the house of Israel, are my people.'

(part of verses 26-30)

God's covenant of peace reminds us, however, that he expects us to notice and glorify the giver of this abundant gift, not just enjoy a good life. He gives to us so abundantly because of his love. And we cannot really value God's gifts unless we appreciate his presence with us and respond with thankfulness to his love and grace.

As we come closer to Christmas, and prepare gifts for our loved ones, may this understanding guide us: the value of each gift depends on the value we attribute to its giver.

† *Thank you, God, that your love is so abundant. Thank you for giving us security and peace. Help us to remember you as the Creator and giver of everything good and valuable in this world. Amen.*

God who is looking for loyalty

The story of the disrespectful tenants is a serious warning. People may easily forget the real meaning of their task and begin to act as if there was no need for accountability. Caretakers may begin to act as sole owners – selfish and careless owners. Doesn't it sometimes happen also in our churches?

God in his sovereignty is tolerant to a certain extent. As the story shows, there is no immediate punishment for treating the landowner's servants badly for the first time, or even for the second time. There is still some hope for repentance and changed behaviour. But when it becomes clear that things are only getting worse, the landowner acts vigorously, and begins to look for

> 'other tenants who will give him his share of the crop at harvest time.'
>
> *(part of verse 41)*

God never forces us into loyalty. But he expects us to remember who is the real 'landowner', and to whom everything we have and use in this world belongs. He may now and then remind us about himself in different ways, and we should be attentive to notice these reminders. For without the loyalty derived from our free will we gradually become apathetic slaves and lose the possibility of meaningful relationship with God that he offers us.

† *Lord, teach us to be faithful in our everyday life, thankful for everything you have given into our hands, and your respectful tenants. Amen.*

God who is looking for fruit

Matthew tells us a story about Jesus, who looks for fruit but does not find it. He is looking in the right place – a fig tree should definitely bear fruit. How about our life – would Jesus find any fruit there? Paul gives some good advice in his letter to Thessalonians on how to increase our fruitfulness. He suggests persisting in good things – in being joyful, praying, giving thanks, holding on to the good, and avoiding evil. Being persistent in all this will make the greatest difference. In this way the fruits of our life will ripen continuously, one after another, and there will always be some good fruit available.

There is also a powerful promise added to Paul's advice. He affirms that God himself will help us to bear fruit because he is a faithful God. He has created us to be fruitful for his kingdom. So let us receive Paul's blessing:

> **May God himself, the God of peace, sanctify you through and through. May your whole spirit, soul and body be kept blameless at the coming of our Lord Jesus Christ. The one who calls you is faithful and he will do it.**
>
> *(1 Thessalonians, verses 23-24)*

† *Lord, help us to be fruitful in your ministry. Teach us to be persistent in holding fast to what is good. Thank you for your faithfulness. Amen.*

4   Ready to receive the light

Notes by Meeli Tankler
based on the New International Version

Introduction

The theme for the last ten days of the year is taken from Psalm 36. God is the fountain of life. In his light, we see light. God's life is abundant, steadfast, renewing. It is ours because of God's faithfulness, grace and compassion towards us. It brings about transformation, and so gives us hope for the future. The presence of this life in our midst, and the hope of yet more life to come, is the light of God in the world. Having seen it, we celebrate it, live in it, glory in it, share it. With this light, we recognise Christ wherever he appears, because he brings God's life to us, magnifies it, and makes it specific, personal and real for us.

Text for the week: Psalm 36:7, 9
Your love, O LORD, reaches to the heavens, your faithfulness to the skies . . . For with you is the fountain of life; in your light we see light.

For group discussion and personal thought

• In your community, what are the reasons people hesitate to accept God into their life?

• Are people more open to good news at Christmas time? How could you make use of this openness in your personal encounters, and in your church?

God is faithful

This is the bottom line of all God's promises in the Bible: God does not change his mind about his promises, for he is for ever faithful in his love to us. He never forgets his promises. In his promise to establish a house for King David, and to raise offspring to succeed him, God is speaking about Jesus' coming into this world. For God so loved the world that he wanted to save it from darkness.

When the prophet Nathan hears God's promise he cannot fully grasp its meaning. When we listen to God's promises we cannot fully grasp their meaning either. God is always bigger than our understanding of him and his promises. In our eager expectation we sometimes grow impatient, and time seems to go too slowly. We become like little children who have been promised something good tomorrow, and after fifteen minutes they ask: 'Is it tomorrow now?' When we really believe that God is faithful in all circumstances, it gives us patience to wait for his promises.

There are still some days before Christmas. There are still some days before we get our long-expected answers from God. But his promises are here for us:

The LORD declares to you that the LORD himself will establish a house for you.

(verse 11)

† Dear Lord, it is difficult to wait sometimes. Help us to keep in mind your faithfulness, and to be patient before you. Amen.

The life appeared

In his letter John helps us to understand the real reason for celebrating Christmas: God has revealed his abundant life to us in the person of Jesus Christ. Sending his Son into our world, the Word became flesh, it became the Word of life for the whole of humankind. And there were people who witnessed this miracle with their own eyes, and wanted to share it. As John so powerfully describes:

The life appeared; we have seen it and testify to it, and we proclaim to you the eternal life, which was with the Father and has appeared to us.

(verse 2)

Christmastime is the right time to celebrate the life that God offers to each of us again and again right up to the present. He offers us abundant life in this world, and eternal life beyond this world. When we embrace this as our Christmas gift from God, our joy will be complete. But let us not then forget about those around us whose Christmas celebration is still lifeless and empty. Let us proclaim to everyone a Christmas message that brings real life!

† *Life-giving God, we praise you for sending your Son into this world as your gift to humankind. Teach us to tell others about this gift in a way that attracts more and more people to accept it and rejoice in your abundant life. Amen.*

1 John 1:5-10

God is light

God is life; God is also the light we so desperately need in our life. Our experiences tell us that darkness can hide all kinds of dangerous things, and we do not like darkness. But John tells us that

God is light; in him there is no darkness at all.
(part of verse 5)

And we can all step into his light by accepting him into our life.

Lighting the candles on the Christmas tree on Christmas Eve was always an exciting moment that I remember from my childhood. We used to have real candles on the tree, usually white and red ones. Every candle had to be lit separately and, as this was done, the light around the tree grew and grew. It felt warm and inviting, and finally the whole room seemed to be very special and different from usual. The magical Christmas light was there.

God is a light for our life. The closer we get to him, and the longer we stay there, the more light we have on our path. It grows and grows, and it feels so warm and inviting to step into this light, and stay there close to God. John also reminds us that when we are really walking daily in this godly light, our fellowship with one another will grow and strengthen.

† God, we want to walk in your light. Help us to look for you in all our paths. Help us to stay close to you. Amen.

The true light for all people

With God, there is never any short supply. His riches are endless and eternal. His supplies of light never run out – there is enough for all the people in this world, and much more.

In him was life, and that life was the light of men.
(verse 4)

The only problem we may encounter is an unwillingness from our side to accept God's light. As John says, the darkness does not understand – and sometimes may not want to understand – the light. God often reveals himself to people in light. Shepherds in the field saw the glory of the Lord shining, and were terrified (*Luke 2:9*). Paul on the Damascus road saw a light from heaven flashing around him and fell to the ground (*Acts 9:3*). But God never intends to frighten us with his light, but to show us a way, as the shepherds and Paul were shown their way to Jesus.

Once more it is Christmas Day, and the message of the true light coming into the world for all people is proclaimed again in our churches. Has the darkness around us understood the message better this Christmas? How can we help people understand the joyful message from God that should reach each and every one? How can we show them the true light?

† *Lord, come into our midst with your light this Christmas Day. May your light show us the way that you have intended for us, and shine in our life. Amen.*

God among us, unrecognised

Today's reading begins very pessimistically, with a complaint that we may well recognise as our own: too many people around us have not recognised God. They may have encountered God's grace and mercy, they may have experienced answers to their prayers – but they still do not fully recognise God. People lay down their own terms for God, and refuse to acknowledge God on his terms. God comes to his people, and they are not ready to receive him. But John ends on a much more positive note:

> **Yet to all who received him, to those who believed in his name, he gave the right to become children of God.**
>
> *(verse 12)*

We belong to God's family. This family is continually growing, and there is still enough space for all the people on earth who have not yet recognised God. And at Christmas, all together in this big growing family we can sing this wonderful Christmas carol:

> **We have seen his glory, the glory of the one and only, who came from the Father, full of grace and truth.**
>
> *(verse 14)*

† *Our Lord Jesus, thank you for this great gift – to belong to God's family. Help us to help others to recognise you and believe in your name. Let this Christmas be a celebration time in your family as new people find their way to you. Amen.*

The fullness of his grace

Christ came into this world to make God known to us. The world had not really known God before – although God had revealed himself now and then. When God sent his Son, his intention was to reveal his grace in person. As John tells us, we can see God's grace in its fullness in Christ.

> **From the fullness of his grace we have all received one blessing after another.**
>
> *(verse 16)*

We have all received one blessing after another. John really means it.

There is a saying in English about 'counting your blessings' that I have never fully understood. But in the light of today's reading I feel that I am beginning to understand it. Our problem may be that we have not really counted all our blessings as blessings. We often speak about having good luck or being fortune's favourite. More often we complain about things that 'almost' happened to us – without seeing the hand that saved us at the very last minute. At the end of this year, take a look back and count the blessings you have had. There are definitely more and more, one after another, when you look carefully and prayerfully.

† How priceless is your unfailing love! Both high and low among men find refuge in the shadow of your wings. They feast on the abundance of your house; you give them drink from your river of delights. For with you is the fountain of life; in your light we see light. Amen.

December

Arise, shine, for your light has come

The prophet Isaiah becomes very personal in today's reading. He is speaking about God's presence revealed gloriously in light – but then he adds that the light is not impersonal, it is meant personally for you! The glory of God rises upon *you*, and it appears over *you*. It is sometimes easier to point out God's light to others – those neighbours certainly need it, this friend of mine would benefit from it, so many people in my community are still in darkness . . . But how about you? Have you risen, and accepted the light for your life?

> **Arise, shine, for your light has come, and the glory of the LORD rises upon you.**
>
> *(verse 1)*

The promise here is given to God's people, and the prophet describes the great moment when all people are drawn to God's light and praise God's glory. We are still waiting for this to happen. There are still many people whose eyes have not seen this light, and whose ears have not heard the message about God. And yet it all begins with you and me. Sometimes a group of people in the dark are waiting for someone to make the first move and lead the way for others. Think about it when you complain about the darkness.

† *God, help me to follow your light in my life. Help me to be a light for those who need it. Help me to be active and willing to be used by you. Amen.*

Living in the light

John reminds us today of 'an old command', as he puts it. As we come closer to the end of the year, and prepare to step into the New Year, we are usually more interested in new things. We make new promises to each other and to ourselves, we look for new beginnings and new ideas to enrich our life. And yet there are these old things that are worth remembering – old commands and old promises that should stay in place. Today's 'old command' tells us to love our neighbour. But John approaches this command from a new angle: he shows us very clearly the close connection between our relationship with God and our relationships with other human beings.

Anyone who claims to be in the light but hates his brother is still in the darkness. Whoever loves his brother lives in the light, and there is nothing in him to make him stumble.

(verses 9-10)

Perhaps this is a good time to look around, and think about our relationships. Am I 'still in the darkness'? Are there conflicts and unsolved problems between, for example, me and my brother or sister? Can I let more light from God into our tense relations? When we claim that we live in the light, this light should help us to connect with each other in a peaceful and graceful way.

† Dear Lord Jesus, I am willing to live in your light. Show me where I fall short, and enlighten my way. Amen.

Galatians 4:4-7*

God has made you an heir

On the last day of the year, we can celebrate the fact that God has sent his Son into our world to create a new relationship with us. Whenever we are willing to step into this new relationship it is now open for us. Through the redemption that began with Christ's birth into our world we may become God's children with the full rights of heirs.

> **God sent the Spirit of his Son into our hearts, the Spirit who calls out, '*Abba*, Father'. So you are no longer a slave, but a son; and . . . God has made you also an heir.**
> *(part of verses 6-7)*

What a wonderful and encouraging message to step into New Year with! It is a new quality of life given by God. It is a promise that gives strength and hope. But we need to remember that, much as it is a great privilege, it also includes a great responsibility. A child usually has some likeness to its parents. An heir usually represents the one who handed down the inheritance. We are supposed to pass on the legacy. God's children and heirs should represent God in this world in the best way possible.

† God, let us enter the New Year as your children and heirs. Teach us to behave with proper dignity, and help us to live as your family members should live in order to give you glory. Amen.

INTERNATIONAL BIBLE READING ASSOCIATION
A worldwide service of Christian Education
at work in five continents

HEADQUARTERS
1020 Bristol Road
Selly Oak
Birmingham
B29 6LB
Great Britain

www.christianeducation.org.uk
ibra@christianeducation.org.uk

and the following agencies:

AUSTRALIA
UniChurch Books
130 Little Collins Street
Melbourne
VIC 3001

GHANA
IBRA Secretary
Box GP 919
Accra

asempa@ghana.com

INDIA
All India Sunday School Association
Plot No 83, 3rd Cross,
Threemurthy Colony
Mahendra Hills
Secunderabad – 500 026
Andhra Pradesh

sundayschoolindia@yahoo.co.in

Fellowship of Professional Workers
SAMANVAY
Deepthi Chambers
Vijayapuri
Hyderabad – 500 017
Andhra Pradesh

hyd1_cipiardi@sancharnet.in

NEW ZEALAND
Epworth Bookshop
PO Box 6133
75 Taranaki Street
Wellington 6035

NIGERIA
IBRA Representative
PMB 5298
Hinderer House
Cathedral Church of St David
Kudeti
Ibadan
Oyo State

SOUTH AND CENTRAL AFRICA
IBRA South Africa
2 Crest View
Goedemoed Road
Durbanville 7550

biblereading@evmot.com

Scheme of readings for 2009

Who is Jesus?
Epiphanies of Jesus – A window to God

Widows, orphans and aliens
The sacred duty to care for the
alien, the orphan and the widow
– Sojourners and aliens – Widows and
orphans

Nehemiah
Rebuilding the walls of Jerusalem – The
religious life of the city

Johannine images
Source of light, life and love – The
Good Shepherd – The Way – Life that
is stronger than death – The beloved

Holy fools

Readings in Mark
To the cross and beyond – The good
news of Jesus Christ

Politics of God
Justice, power and the state – Marks of
God's kingdom

Oneness of humanity
One human family – All one in God:
barriers are taken away

Eucharistic themes
Thanksgiving and thankful living – The
shape of our life together – Living
eucharistically

Readings in Mark
Parables and healings – Stirrings of
conflict

Burden bearers
Friends and supporters – Mentors
and teachers – Colleagues and peers
– Challengers and critics

Ezekiel
The call of Ezekiel – Words of warning
– Words against foreign nations
– Words of hope

Readings in Mark
Training the disciples – Going up to
Jerusalem

Idols
The many guises of idolatry – Making
the appropriate choice – Countering
idols and idolatry

Readings in Mark
Jesus in the temple – The days are
coming

**Visions of abundance: for ourselves
and others**
Creating abundant life – The vision
of abundance: for ourselves and for
others – Abundant life for all

Hebrews
Jesus our great high priest – Faith, hope
and love

Christian Love
The greatest commandment – What
Love means – What Love does

Readings in Revelation
Letters to the churches – Seals,
trumpets and woes – The triumph of
the Lamb – God's wrath and God's
salvation – The new heaven and the
new earth